Speedwriting
A B C SHORTHAND ®

COLLEGE
EDITION

DICTIONARY

Speedwriting
SHORTHAND

COLLEGE EDITION

Speedwriting shorthand is presently taught in 28 countries and is available in 8 languages:

ENGLISH	PORTUGUESE
FRENCH	GERMAN
SPANISH	FLEMISH
ITALIAN	AFRIKAANS

Shorthand Plates Written by Verleigh Ernest

PREFACE

This *SPEEDWRITING Shorthand Dictionary, College Edition,* will serve you throughout your secretarial career as a practical, helpful, modern, and comprehensive aid. Your training in the theory of SPEEDWRITING shorthand has covered specifically the 3,000 words of greatest frequency and has given you principles that cover *all* possible words in the English language. In business you will occasionally be faced with a new word and will need to check the outline. You will also occasionally want to check on the outline of a word that you have already studied to make sure you have "automatized" it correctly. This is where the *Dictionary* comes to your assistance.

In the *Dictionary* you will find the 20,000 most commonly used words in business. In addition, this *College Edition Dictionary* is as modern as the atomic and rocket age. In it, you will find all of the more commonly used words relating to the latest advances in science and technology including the "new vocabulary" that has been created for the world of automation and data processing.

Here are some of the specific features that you should note concerning this *College Edition Dictionary:*

... The phonics for each word are based upon *Webster's Seventh New Collegiate Dictionary* published by the G. & C. Merriam Co.

... Word division by syllable is indicated for each word. This is offered as an additional aid to the secretary, but should not be relied upon to replace her necessary knowledge of the rules of word division.

... The suffixes -*ed*, -*ing*, and indications of plurals have been omitted when such word endings follow the regular SPEED-WRITING shorthand rules.

... Only samples of derivatives, prefixes, and suffixes are given to guide the student in writing similar words.

... Included in this *Dictionary* are the outlines for all 50 United States and 12 Canadian Provinces and Territories as well as the leading cities in the United States and Canada.

This *SPEEDWRITING Shorthand Dictionary, College Edition,* is designed to be one of your most helpful guides to shorthand success. Keep it with you throughout your entire secretarial career. It will prove to be an invaluable aid.

—The SPEEDWRITING Publishing Company

a	*a*	ab·er·rance	*aβl*
a·back	*abc*	ab·er·rant	*aβ-*
ab·a·cus	*abcr*	ab·er·ra·tion	*aβj*
a·baft	*abf*	a·bet	*abl*
ab·a·lo·ne	*ablne*	a·bey·ance	*aba/*
✓ a·ban·don	*ab——n*	ab·hor	*abho*
a·ban·don·ment	*ab——n-*	ab·hor·rence	*abho/*
a·base	*abs*	ab·hor·rent	*abho-*
a·base·ment	*abs-*	a·bide	*abd*
a·bash	*abℓ*	a·bil·i·ty	*ab)*
a·bat·a·ble	*abab*	ab·ject	*abjc*
a·bate	*aba*	ab·jec·tion	*abjcj*
a·bate·ment	*aba-*	ab·ju·ra·tion	*abℓj*
ab·at·toir	*ablvr*	ab·jure	*abju*
ab·bé	*aba*	ab·late	*aba*
ab·bess	*ab?*	ab·la·tion	*abj*
ab·bey	*abe*	ab·la·tive	*abv*
ab·bot	*abl*	a·blaze	*abℨ*
✓ ab·bre·vi·ate	*aβva*	a·ble	*ab?*
ab·bre·vi·a·tion	*aβvj*	✓ a·ble-bod·ied	*abbdē*
ab·di·cate	*abdca*	a·bloom	*abu*
ab·di·ca·tion	*abdcj*	ab·lu·tion	*abj*
ab·do·men	*abdm*	a·bly	*ab'*
ab·dom·i·nal	*abdml*	ab·ne·gate	*abnga*
ab·duct	*abdc*	ab·ne·ga·tion	*abngj*
ab·duc·tion	*abdcj*	✓ ab·nor·mal	*abNℓ*
ab·duc·tor	*abdc/*	ab·nor·mal·i·ty	*abNℓ)*

ab·nor·mal·ly	✓ ab·sen·tee·ism
✓ a·board	ab·sinthe
a·bode	✓ ab·so·lute
a·bol·ish	ab·so·lute·ly
ab·o·li·tion	ab·so·lu·tion
ab·o·li·tion·ism	ab·so·lut·ism
ab·o·li·tion·ist	ab·solve
a·bom·i·na·ble	ab·sorb
a·bom·i·nate	ab·sorb·ent
a·bom·i·na·tion	ab·sorp·tion
ab·o·rig·i·nal	ab·sorp·tive
ab·o·rig·i·nes	ab·stain
a·bort	ab·stain·er
a·bor·tion	ab·ste·mi·ous
a·bor·tive	ab·sten·tion
a·bound	ab·sti·nence
a·bout	ab·sti·nent
✓ a·bove	ab·stract
a·bove·board	ab·strac·tion
ab·ra·ca·dab·ra	ab·struse
ab·rade	ab·struse·ness
✓ ab·ra·sion	ab·surd
ab·ra·sive	ab·surd·i·ty
✓ a·breast	a·bun·dance
✓ a·bridge	✓ a·bun·dant
a·bridg·ment	✓ a·buse
a·broad	a·bu·sive
ab·ro·gate	a·bu·sive·ly
ab·ro·ga·tion	a·bu·sive·ness
✓ ab·rupt	a·but
ab·rupt·ly	a·but·ment
✓ ab·rupt·ness	a·but·tal
ab·scess	a·bysm
ab·scond	a·bys·mal
✓ ab·sence	a·byss
ab·sent	ac·a·dem·ic
ab·sen·tee	a·cad·e·mi·cian

a·cad·e·my	*acdre*	ac·com·plish	*akps*
ac·cede	*xd*	ac·com·plish·ment	*akps–*
ac·cel·er·ant	*xL–*	ac·cord	*aCd*
ac·cel·er·ate	*xLa*	ac·cord·ance	*aCd /*
ac·cel·er·a·tion	*xLy*	ac·cord·ant	*aCd–*
✓ac·cel·er·a·tor	*xLa /*	ac·cord·er	*aCd*
ac·cent	*x–*	✓ac·cord·ing·ly	*aCdl*
ac·cen·tu·ate	*xCa*	ac·cor·di·on	*aCden*
ac·cen·tu·a·tion	*xCy*	ac·cost	*ac,*
✓ac·cept	*xp*	✓ac·count	*akl*
ac·cept·a·bil·i·ty	*xpb)*	ac·count·a·bil·i·ty	*aklb)*
ac·cept·a·ble	*xpb*	ac·count·a·ble	*aklb*
ac·cept·ance	*xp /*	ac·count·an·cy	*akl /*
ac·cep·ta·tion	*xpy*	ac·count·ant	*akl–*
✓ac·cess	*x'*	ac·cou·ter	*acu /*
ac·ces·si·bil·i·ty	*xsb)*	ac·cred·it	*acr*
ac·ces·si·ble	*xsb*	ac·cre·tion	*aCy*
ac·ces·sion	*xsy*	ac·cru·al	*aCul*
ac·ces·so·ry	*xsy*	ac·crue	*aCu*
ac·ci·dence	*xd /*	✓ac·cu·mu·late	*acrla*
✓ac·ci·dent	*xd–*	ac·cu·mu·la·tion	*acrly*
ac·ci·den·tal	*xd–l*	ac·cu·mu·la·tive	*acrlv*
ac·ci·den·tal·ly	*xd–l*	ac·cu·mu·la·tor	*acrla /*
ac·claim	*aca*	ac·cu·rate·ly	*aCll*
ac·cla·ma·tion	*acy*	✓ac·cu·ra·cy	*aCse*
ac·cli·mate	*acl*	ac·cu·rate	*aCl*
ac·cli·ma·tize	*aclz*	ac·curs·ed	*aC,*
ac·cliv·i·ty	*acv)*	ac·cu·sa·tion	*aczy*
ac·co·lade	*acld*	ac·cu·sa·tive	*acsv*
✓ac·com·mo·date	*akda*	ac·cuse	*acz*
ac·com·mo·da·tion	*akdy*	ac·cus·er	*acz /*
ac·com·mo·da·tive	*akdav*	ac·cus·tom	*acs)*
ac·com·mo·da·tor	*akda /*	ace	*as*
ac·com·pa·ni·ment	*aco–*	a·cer·bi·ty	*asb)*
ac·com·pa·nist	*aco,*	ac·e·tate	*asla*
ac·com·pa·ny	*aco*	a·ce·tic	*aslc*
ac·com·plice	*akps*	ac·e·tone	*asln*

a·cet·y·lene		ac·ro·bat·ic	
ache		ac·ro·nym	
a·chieve		a·crop·o·lis	
a·chieve·ment		✓ a·cross	
ach·ro·mat·ic		a·cros·tic	
ac·id		a·cryl·ic	
a·cid·i·fy		act	
a·cid·i·ty		ac·tin·ic	
ac·id·proof		✓ ac·tion	
a·cid·u·late		ac·tion·a·ble	
a·cid·u·lous		ac·ti·vate	
✓ ac·knowl·edge		ac·tive	
ac·knowl·edg·ment		ac·tive·ly	
ac·me		ac·tiv·i·ty	
ac·ne		ac·tor	
ac·o·lyte		ac·tress	
ac·o·nite		✓ ac·tu·al	
a·corn		✓ ac·tu·al·i·ty	
a·cous·tic		✓ ac·tu·al·ly	
a·cous·ti·cal		ac·tu·ar·i·al	
ac·quaint		ac·tu·ar·y	
ac·quaint·ance		ac·tu·ate	
ac·qui·esce		a·cu·i·ty	
ac·qui·es·cence		a·cu·men	
ac·qui·es·cent		✓ a·cute	
ac·quire		a·cute·ly	
ac·qui·si·tion		a·cute·ness	
ac·quis·i·tive		ad	
ac·quit		ad·age	
ac·quit·tal		a·da·gio	
a·cre		ad·a·mant	
a·cre·age		✓ a·dapt	
ac·rid		a·dapt·a·bil·i·ty	
a·crid·i·ty		a·dapt·a·ble	
ac·ri·mo·ni·ous		ad·ap·ta·tion	
ac·ri·mo·ny		a·dapt·er	
ac·ro·bat		add	

Word	Shorthand
ad·den·da	
ad·den·dum	
ad·dict	
ad·dic·tion	
ad·di·tion	
ad·di·tion·al	
ad·di·tive	
ad·dle	
ad·dress	
ad·dressed	
ad·dress·ee	
ad·duce	
ad·e·noid	
ad·ept	
ad·e·qua·cy	
ad·e·quate	
ad·e·quate·ly	
ad·here	
ad·her·ence	
ad·her·ent	
ad·he·sion	
ad·he·sive	
a·dieu	
ad in·fi·ni·tum	
ad·i·pose	
ad·ja·cent	
ad·jec·tive	
ad·join	
ad·journ	
ad·journ·ment	
ad·judge	
ad·ju·di·cate	
ad·ju·di·ca·tion	
ad·junct	
ad·ju·ra·tion	
ad·jure	
ad·just	
ad·just·a·ble	
ad·just·er	
ad·just·ment	
ad·ju·tant	
ad·lib	
ad·man	
ad·min·is·ter	
ad·min·is·trate	
ad·min·is·tra·tion	
ad·min·is·tra·tive	
ad·min·is·tra·tor	
ad·mi·ra·ble	
ad·mi·ral	
ad·mi·ral·ty	
ad·mi·ra·tion	
ad·mire	
ad·mir·er	
ad·mis·si·bil·i·ty	
ad·mis·si·ble	
ad·mis·sion	
ad·mit	
ad·mit·tance	
ad·mix·ture	
ad·mon·ish	
ad·mo·ni·tion	
ad·mon·i·to·ry	
ad nau·se·am	
a·do	
a·do·be	
ad·o·les·cence	
ad·o·les·cent	
a·dopt	
a·dop·tion	
a·dop·tive	
a·dor·a·ble	
ad·o·ra·tion	
a·dore	

a·dorn		ad·ver·si·ty	
a·dorn·ment		ad·vert	
ad·re·nal		ad·ver·tise	
ad·ren·al·ine		ad·ver·tise·ment	
a·drift		ad·ver·tis·er	
a·droit		ad·vice	
a·droit·ly		ad·vis·a·bil·i·ty	
ad·sorb		ad·vis·a·ble	
ad·sorp·tion		ad·vise	
ad·u·late		ad·vis·er	
ad·u·la·tion		ad·vise·ment	
ad·u·la·to·ry		ad·vi·so·ry	
a·dult		ad·vo·ca·cy	
a·dul·ter·ant		ad·vo·cate	
a·dul·ter·ate		adz	
a·dul·ter·a·tion		ae·gis	
a·dul·ter·a·tor		ae·on	
a·dul·ter·er		aer·ate	
a·dul·ter·ous		aer·a·tion	
a·dul·ter·y		aer·a·tor	
a·dult·hood		ae·ri·al	
ad·um·brate		aer·o·dy·nam·ics	
ad·vance		aer·o·naut	
ad·vanced		aer·o·nau·tic	
ad·vance·ment		aer·o·sol	
ad·van·tage		aes·thete	
ad·van·ta·geous		aes·thet·ic	
ad·vent		aes·thet·i·cal·ly	
ad·ven·ti·tious		a·far	
ad·ven·ture		af·fa·bil·i·ty	
ad·ven·tur·er		af·fa·ble	
ad·ven·ture·some		af·fair	
ad·ven·tur·ous		af·fect	
ad·verb		af·fec·ta·tion	
ad·ver·bi·al		af·fect·ed·ly	
ad·ver·sar·y		af·fec·tion	
ad·verse		af·fec·tion·ate	

Word	Shorthand	Word	Shorthand
af·fi·ance		aft·er·most	
af·fi·ant		aft·er·noon	
af·fi·da·vit		aft·er·taste	
af·fil·i·ate		aft·er·thought	
af·fil·i·a·tion		aft·er·ward	
af·fin·i·ty		a·gain	
af·firm		a·gainst	
af·fir·ma·tion		a·gape	
af·firm·a·tive		ag·ate	
af·fix		age	
af·flict		age·less	
af·flic·tion		a·gen·cy	
af·flu·ence		a·gen·da	
af·flu·ent		a·gent	
af·ford		ag·glom·er·ate	
af·fray		ag·glom·er·a·tion	
af·front		ag·glu·ti·nate	
af·ghan		ag·gran·dize	
a·field		ag·gran·dize·ment	
a·fire		ag·gra·vate	
a·flame		ag·gra·va·tion	
a·float		ag·gre·gate	
a·foot		ag·gre·ga·tion	
a·fore·men·tioned		ag·gres·sion	
a·fore·said		ag·gres·sive	
a·fore·thought		ag·gres·sive·ness	
a·fore·time		ag·gres·sor	
a·foul		ag·grieve	
a·fraid		a·ghast	
a·fresh		ag·ile	
aft		ag·ile·ly	
aft·er		a·gil·i·ty	
aft·er·burn·er		ag·i·tate	
aft·er·care		ag·i·ta·tion	
aft·er·ef·fect		ag·i·ta·tor	
aft·er·glow		a·glow	
aft·er·math		ag·nos·tic	

a·go	*aq*	air·lift	*alf*
a·gog	*agg*	air·line	*ali*
ag·o·nize	*agnz*	air·lin·er	*ali*
ag·o·ny	*agne*	air·mail	*arl*
a·grar·i·an	*agyn*	air·mind·ed	*aru —*
a·gree	*age*	air·plane	*apn*
a·gree·a·bil·i·ty	*ageb)*	air·port	*asl*
a·gree·a·ble	*ageb*	air·proof	*asl*
a·gree·ment	*age—*	air·ship	*as*
ag·ri·cul·tur·al	*agclcrl*	air·space	*ass*
ag·ri·cul·ture	*agclc*	air·speed	*asd*
a·ground	*agr—*	air·strip	*asp*
a·gue	*agu*	air·tight	*ali*
a·head	*ahd*	air·wave	*ara*
a·hoy	*ahy*	air·way	*ara*
aid	*ad*	air·y	*ae*
aide	*ad*	aisle	*z*
ai·grette	*agl*	a·jar	*ajr*
ail	*a*	a·kim·bo	*ac-bo*
ai·ler·on	*An*	a·kin	*acn*
ail·ment	*a—*	al·a·bas·ter	*abS*
aim	*ar*	a la carte	*acl*
aim·less	*arl'*	a·lac·ri·ty	*alC)*
air	*a*	a la mode	*ard*
air base	*a bas*	a·larm	*al*
air·borne	*aBn*	a·larm·ist	*al,*
air brake	*a bc*	a·las	*als*
air·brush	*aBS*	al·ba·tross	*abt'*
air·con·di·tion	*akdf*	al·be·it	*abl*
air·craft	*acf*	al·bi·no	*abino*
air·drome	*aD°*	al·bum	*ab*
air·drop	*aDP*	al·bu·min	*abm*
air ex·press	*a xP'*	al·co·hol	*achal*
air·field	*afld*	al·co·hol·ic	*achlc*
air·foil	*afyl*	al·cove	*aco*
air force	*a fo*	al·der·man	*alD'—*
air·freight	*afa*	ale	*a*

✓ a·lert	al·li·ance
al·fal·fa	al·li·ga·tor
al·ge·bra	al·lit·er·a·tion
al·ge·bra·ic	al·lo·cate
al·ge·bra·i·cal	al·lo·ca·tion
a·li·as	al·lot
al·i·bi	al·lot·ment
al·ien	al·low
al·ien·a·ble	al·low·ance
al·ien·ate	✓ al·loy
al·ien·a·tion	✓ all right
al·ien·ist	al·lude
a·light	al·lure
a·lign	al·lu·sion
a·lign·ment	al·lu·sive
a·like	al·lu·vi·al
al·i·ment	al·lu·vi·um
al·i·men·ta·ry	al·ly
al·i·men·ta·tion	al·ma ma·ter
al·i·mo·ny	al·ma·nac
a·live	al·might·y
al·ka·li	al·mond
al·ka·line	✗ ✓ al·most
al·ka·loid	alms
al·kyd	a·loft
all	✓ a·lone
al·lay	a·long
al·le·ga·tion	a·long·side
al·lege	a·loof
al·le·giance	a·loud
al·le·gor·i·cal	alp
al·le·go·ry	al·pac·a
al·ler·gy	al·pha·bet
al·ler·gic	al·pha·bet·ize
al·le·vi·ate	al·pine
al·le·vi·a·tion	✗ ✓ al·read·y
al·ley	✓ al·so

al·tar		am·bi·gu·i·ty	
al·ter		am·big·u·ous	
al·ter·a·tion		am·bi·tion	
al·ter·cate		am·bi·tious	
al·ter·ca·tion		am·biv·a·lent	
al·ter e·go		am·biv·a·lence	
al·ter·nate		am·ble	
✓ al·ter·na·tive		am·bro·si·a	
al·though		am·bu·lance	
al·tim·e·ter		am·bu·la·to·ry	
al·ti·tude		am·bus·cade	
al·to		am·bush	
✓ al·to·geth·er		a·mel·io·rate	
al·tru·ism		a·mel·io·ra·tion	
al·tru·ist		a·men	
al·tru·is·tic		a·me·na·ble	
al·um		a·mend	
✓ a·lu·mi·num		a·mend·ment	
a·lum·na		a·men·i·ty	
a·lum·nae		A·mer·i·ca	
a·lum·ni		A·mer·i·can	
a·lum·nus		A·mer·i·can·i·za·tion	
✓ al·ways		am·e·thyst	
am		a·mi·a·bil·i·ty	
a·mal·gam		a·mi·a·ble	
a·mal·gam·ate		am·i·ca·bil·i·ty	
a·mal·gam·a·tion		am·i·ca·ble	
a·man·u·en·sis		a·mid	
a·mass		a·mid·ships	
am·a·teur		a·midst	
am·a·to·ry		a·miss	
a·maze		am·i·ty	
am·bas·sa·dor		am·me·ter	
am·ber		am·mo·ni·a	
am·ber·gris		am·mu·ni·tion	
am·bi·dex·trous		am·ne·si·a	
am·bi·ence		am·nes·ty	

a·moe·ba		an·a·lyt·i·cal	
a·moe·bic		an·a·lyze	
a·mong		an·arch·ism	
a·mongst		an·arch·ist	
am·o·rous		an·arch·y	
a·mor·phous		a·nath·e·ma	
a·mor·ti·za·tion		an·a·tom·i·cal	
a·mor·tize		a·nat·o·my	
a·mount		an·ces·tor	
am·per·age		an·ces·try	
am·pere		an·chor	
am·phib·i·an		an·chor·age	
am·phib·i·ous		an·chor·ite	
am·phi·the·a·ter		an·cho·vy	
am·ple		an·cient	
am·pli·fi·ca·tion		an·cil·lar·y	
am·pli·fy		and	
am·pli·fi·er		an·dan·te	
am·pli·tude		and·i·ron	
am·ply		an·ec·dote	
am·pu·tate		a·ne·mi·a	
am·pu·ta·tion		a·ne·mic	
am·poule		an·e·mom·e·ter	
am·u·let		an·er·oid	
a·muse		an·es·the·si·a	
an		an·es·thet·ic	
a·nach·ro·nism		an·es·the·tist	
a·nach·ro·nis·tic		an·es·the·tize	
an·a·gram		a·new	
a·nal		an·gel	
an·al·ge·sia		an·ger	
an·a·log		an·gle	
an·a·log·i·cal		an·gler	
a·nal·o·gous		an·gli·cize	
a·nal·o·gy		an·gri·ly	
a·nal·y·sis		an·gry	
an·a·lyst		an·guish	

an·gu·lar		an·nun·ci·a·tor	
an·gu·lar·i·ty		an·ode	
an·i·line		an·o·dyne	
an·i·mad·ver·sion		a·noint	
an·i·mad·vert		a·nom·a·lous	
an·i·mal		a·nom·a·ly	
an·i·mate		a·non	
an·i·ma·tion		an·o·nym·i·ty	
an·i·mos·ity		a·non·y·mous	
an·i·mus		an·oth·er	
an·ise		an·swer	
an·kle		an·swer·a·ble	
an·klet		ant	
an·nals		ant·ac·id	
an·neal		an·tag·o·nism	
an·nex		an·tag·o·nist	
an·nex·a·tion		an·tag·o·nis·tic	
an·ni·hi·late		an·tag·o·nize	
an·ni·hi·la·tion		ant·arc·tic	
an·ni·hi·la·tor		an·te·ced·ent	
an·ni·ver·sa·ry		an·te·cham·ber	
an·no Dom·i·ni	(A.D.)	an·te·date	
an·no·tate		an·te·lope	
an·no·ta·tion		an·te·me·rid·i·an	(A.M.)
an·no·ta·tor		an·ten·na	
an·nounce		an·te·pe·nul·ti·mate	
an·nounce·ment		an·te·ri·or	
an·nounc·er		an·te·room	
an·noy		an·them	
an·noy·ance		an·thol·o·gy	
an·nu·al		an·thra·cite	
an·nu·i·ty		an·thrax	
an·nul		an·thro·poid	
an·nul·ment		an·thro·pol·o·gy	
an·num		an·ti	
an·nun·ci·ate		an·ti·bi·ot·ic	
an·nun·ci·a·tion		an·ti·bod·y	

Word	Shorthand	Word	Shorthand
an·tic		a·part·ment	
an·tic·i·pate		ap·a·thet·ic	
an·tic·i·pa·tion		ap·a·thy	
an·tic·i·pa·tor		ape	
an·ti·cli·max		ap·er·ture	
an·ti·dote		a·pex	
an·ti·his·ta·mine		a·pha·si·a	
an·ti·mo·ny		ap·i·ces	
an·tip·a·thy		aph·o·rism	
an·tip·o·des		a·pi·ar·y	
an·ti·quar·i·an		ap·i·cal	
an·ti·quate		a·piece	
an·tique		a·plomb	
an·tiq·ui·ty		a·poc·a·lypse	
an·ti·sep·sis		a·poc·ry·phal	
an·ti·sep·tic		ap·o·gee	
an·ti·so·cial		a·pol·o·get·ic	
an·tith·e·sis		a·pol·o·gi·a	
an·ti·thet·i·cal		a·pol·o·gist	
an·ti·tox·in		a·pol·o·gize	
ant·ler		a·pol·o·gy	
an·to·nym		ap·o·plec·tic	
an·trum		ap·o·plex·y	
an·vil		a·pos·ta·sy	
anx·i·ety		a·pos·tate	
anx·ious		a pos·te·ri·o·ri	
an·y		a·pos·tle	
an·y·bod·y		a·pos·to·late	
an·y·how		ap·os·tol·ic	
an·y·more		a·pos·tro·phe	
an·y·one		a·pos·tro·phize	
an·y·thing		a·poth·e·car·y	
an·y·way		a·poth·e·o·sis	
an·y·where		Ap·pa·lach·i·an	
a·or·ta		ap·pall	
a·part		ap·pa·ra·tus	
a·part·heid		ap·par·el	

✓ ap·par·ent		ap·po·si·tion	
✓ ap·par·ent·ly		ap·prais·al	
ap·pa·ri·tion		ap·praise	
✓ ap·peal		ap·prais·er	
✓ ap·pear		ap·pre·ci·a·ble	
✓ ap·pear·ance		ap·pre·ci·ate	
ap·pease		ap·pre·ci·a·tion	
ap·pel·lant		ap·pre·ci·a·tive	
ap·pel·late		ap·pre·hend	
ap·pel·la·tion		ap·pre·hen·si·ble	
ap·pel·lee		ap·pre·hen·sion	
✓ ap·pend		ap·pre·hen·sive	
ap·pend·age		ap·pren·tice	
ap·pen·dec·to·my		ap·pren·tice·ship	
ap·pen·di·ci·tis		ap·prise	
ap·pen·dix		ap·proach	
ap·per·tain		ap·proach·a·ble	
ap·pe·tite		ap·pro·ba·tion	
ap.pe·tiz·er		ap·pro·ba·tive	
ap·pe·tiz·ing		ap·pro·ba·to·ry	
ap·plaud		ap·pro·pri·ate	
ap·plause		ap·pro·pri·ate·ness	
ap·ple		ap·pro·pri·a·tion	
ap·ple·jack		ap·prov·al	
ap·pli·ance		ap·prove	
ap·pli·ca·bil·i·ty		ap·prox·i·mate	
ap·pli·cant		ap·prox·i·mate·ly	
✓ ap·pli·ca·tion		ap·prox·i·ma·tion	
ap·pli·ca·tor		ap·pur·te·nance	
ap·pli·qué		ap·pur·te·nant	
✓ ap·ply		a·pri·cot	
ap·point		A·pril	
ap·point·ee		apri·o·ri	
ap·point·ment		a·pron	
ap·por·tion		ap·ro·pos	
ap·por·tion·ment		apse	
ap·po·site		apt	

ap·ti·tude	*apld*	arch·er·y	
aq·ua·cade		ar·che·type	
aq·ua·lung		ar·chi·pel·a·go	
aq·ua·ma·rine		ar·chi·tect	
aq·ua·plane		ar·chi·tec·tur·al	
a·quar·i·um		ar·chi·tec·ture	
a·quat·ic		ar·chi·trave	
aq·ue·duct		ar·chives	
a·que·ous		arch·ness	
aq·ui·line		arch·way	
ar·a·besque		arc·tic	
Ar·a·bic		ar·dent	
ar·a·ble		ar·dor	
ar·bi·ter		ar·du·ous	
ar·bi·tra·ble		are	
✓ar·bi·trar·y		ar·e·a	
ar·bi·trate		a·re·na	
ar·bi·tra·tion		✓aren't	
ar·bi·tra·tor		ar·gent	
ar·bor		ar·gon	
ar·bo·re·al		ar·go·sy	
ar·bo·re·tum		ar·got	
arc		ar·gu·a·ble	
ar·cade		ar·gue	
ar·cane		ar·gu·ment	
arch		ar·gu·men·ta·tive	
ar·chae·o·log·i·cal		ar·gyle	
ar·chae·ol·o·gist		a·ri·a	
ar·chae·ol·o·gy		ar·id	
ar·cha·ic		a·rise	
arch·an·gel		ar·is·toc·ra·cy	
arch·bish·op		a·ris·to·crat	
arch·dea·con		a·ris·to·crat·ic	
arch·duch·ess		a·rith·me·tic	
arch·duke		ar·ith·met·i·cal	
arch·en·e·my		a·rith·me·ti·cian	
arch·er		ark	

arm		ar·se·nal	
ar·ma·da		ar·se·nate	
ar·ma·dil·lo		ar·se·nic	
ar·ma·ment		ar·son	
ar·ma·ture		art	
arm·chair		ar·te·ri·al	
arm·ful		ar·te·ri·o·scle·ro·sis	
ar·mi·stice		ar·ter·y	
ar·mor		ar·te·sian	
ar·mor·y		art·ful	
arm·pit		ar·thri·tis	
arm·rest		ar·ti·choke	
ar·my		ar·ti·cle	
a·ro·ma		ar·tic·u·late	
ar·o·mat·ic		ar·tic·u·la·tion	
a·rose		ar·ti·fact	
a·round		ar·ti·fice	
a·rouse		ar·ti·fi·cial	
ar·peg·gio		ar·ti·fi·ci·al·i·ty	
ar·raign		ar·til·ler·y	
ar·raign·ment		ar·ti·san	
✓ ar·range		art·ist	
ar·range·ment		ar·tis·tic	
ar·rant		art·ist·ry	
ar·ras		art·less	
ar·ray		Ar·y·an	
ar·rears		as	
ar·rear·age		as·bes·tos	
ar·rest		as·cend	
ar·riv·al		as·cend·an·cy	
ar·rive		as·cend·ant	
ar·ro·gance		as·cen·sion	
ar·ro·gant		as·cent	
ar·ro·gate		as·cer·tain	
ar·row		as·cet·ic	
ar·row·head		a·scor·bic	
ar·roy·o		as·cribe	

as·crip·tion	*asCpΓ*	as·sas·si·na·tion	*assnΓ*
a·sep·sis	*aspss*	as·sault	*asll*
a·sep·tic	*aspc*	as·say	*asa*
✓ash	*aß*	as·sem·blage	*asrbΓ*
a·shamed	*aßā*	as·sem·ble	*asrb*
ash·en	*aßn*	as·sem·bly	*asrb*
a·shore	*aßo*	as·sent	*as—*
A·sian	*aΓ*	as·sert	*asll*
A·si·at·ic	*azelc*	as·ser·tion	*adΓ*
a·side	*asd*	as·ser·tive	*asv*
as·i·nine	*asnn*	as·sess	*as'*
as·i·nin·i·ty	*asnn)*	as·sess·a·ble	*assb*
ask	*sc*	as·sess·ment	*ass—*
a·skance	*asc/*	as·ses·sor	*ass/*
a·skew	*ascu*	as·set	*asl*
a·slant	*as—*	as·sev·er·ate	*asva*
a·sleep	*asp*	as·sev·er·a·tion	*asvΓ*
as·par·a·gus	*aSgΓ*	as·si·du·i·ty	*asdu)*
✓as·pect	*asc*	as·sid·u·ous	*asdx*
as·pen	*asn*	as·sign	*asn*
as·per·i·ty	*aS)*	as·sign·a·ble	*asnb*
as·per·sion	*asΓ*	as·sig·nate	*asgna*
as·phalt	*asfll*	as·sig·na·tion	*asgnΓ*
as·phyx·i·a	*asfva*	as·sign·ee	*asine*
as·phyx·i·ate	*asfva*	as·sign·er	*asn/*
as·phyx·i·a·tion	*asfΓ*	as·sign·ment	*asn—*
as·pic	*asc*	as·sim·i·late	*asrla*
as·pir·ant	*aS—*	as·sim·i·la·tion	*asrΓ*
as·pi·rate	*aSa*	as·sim·i·la·tive	*asrv*
as·pi·ra·tion	*aSΓ*	as·sim·i·la·to·ry	*asrlly*
as·pi·ra·tor	*aSa/*	✓as·sist	*as,*
as·pire	*asc*	as·sist·ance	*aso/*
as·pi·rin	*aSn*	as·sist·ant	*ass—*
as·sail	*asl*	as·size	*asz*
as·sail·ant	*asl—*	✓as·so·ci·ate	*asso*
as·sas·sin	*assn*	as·so·ci·a·tion	*assoΓ*
as·sas·si·nate	*assna*	as·so·ci·a·tive	*assov*

as·so·nance		at·a·vism
as·so·nant		ate
✓ as·sort		at·el·ier
as·sort·ment		a·the·ism
as·suage		a·the·ist
✓ as·sume		a·the·is·tic
✓ as·sump·tion		ath·e·nae·um
as·sur·ance		ath·lete
as·sure		ath·let·ic
as·sur·ed·ly		a·thwart
as·ter		At·lan·tic
as·ter·isk		at·las
a·stern		at·mo·sphere
as·ter·oid		at·mos·pher·ic
asth·ma		a·toll
asth·mat·ic		at·om
as·tig·mat·ic		a·tom·ic
a·stig·ma·tism		at·om·ize
as·ton·ish		at·om·iz·er
as·tound		a·tone
as·tral		a·tri·um
a·stray		a·tro·cious
a·stride		a·troc·i·ty
as·trin·gent		at·ro·phy
as·tro·labe		at·ro·pine
as·trol·o·ger		at·tach
as·trol·o·gy		at·ta·ché
as·tro·naut		at·tach·ment
as·tron·o·mer		at·tack
as·tro·nom·i·cal		at·tain
as·tron·o·my		at·tain·a·ble
as·tro·phys·ics		at·tain·der
as·tute		at·tain·ment
a·sun·der		at·taint
a·sy·lum		at·tar
a·sym·met·ri·cal		✓ at·tempt
at		✓ at·tend

Word	Shorthand	Word	Shorthand
at·tend·ance		aunt	
at·tend·ant		au·ra	
at·ten·tion		au·ral	
at·ten·tive		au·re·ole	
at·ten·u·ate		au·re·o·my·cin	
at·test		au·ric	
at·tes·ta·tion		au·ri·cle	
at·tic		au·ric·u·lar	
at·tire		au·rif·er·ous	
at·ti·tude		au·ro·ra	
at·tor·ney		aus·pice	
at·tract		aus·pi·cious	
at·trac·tion		aus·tere	
at·trac·tive		aus·ter·i·ty	
at·trib·ute		Aus·tra·lian	
at·trib·u·tive		Aus·tri·an	
at·tri·tion		au·then·tic	
at·tune		au·then·ti·cate	
au·burn		au·then·tic·i·ty	
auc·tion		au·thor	
auc·tion·eer		au·thor·ess	
au·da·cious		au·thor·i·tar·i·an	
au·dac·i·ty		au·thor·i·ta·tive	
au·di·ble		au·thor·i·ty	
au·di·ence		au·thor·i·za·tion	
au·di·o		au·thor·ize	
au·di·o·phile		au·thor·ship	
au·dit		au·to	
au·di·tion		au·to·bi·og·ra·phy	
au·di·tor		au·toc·ra·cy	
au·di·to·ri·um		au·to·crat	
au·di·to·ry		au·to·crat·ic	
aug·ment		au·to·graph	
au gra·tin		au·to·mate	
au·gur		au·to·mat·ic	
au·gu·ry		au·tom·a·tize	
Au·gust		au·tom·a·ton	

✓ au·to·mo·bile		a·void·ance	
au·to·mo·tive		av·oir·du·pois	
au·ton·o·mous		a·vow	
au·ton·o·my		a·vow·ed·ly	
au·top·sy		a·vun·cu·lar	
au·to·sug·ges·tion		a·wait	
au·tumn		a·wake	
au·tum·nal		a·wak·en	
aux·il·ia·ry		a·ward	
a·vail		a·ware	
a·vail·a·bil·i·ty		a·ware·ness	
a·vail·a·ble		a·wash	
av·a·lanche		a·way	
a·vant-garde		awe	
av·a·rice		awe·some	
av·a·ri·cious		awe·strick·en	
a·venge		✓ aw·ful	
✓ av·e·nue		a·while	
a·ver		awk·ward	
av·er·age		awl	
a·verse		awn·ing	
a·ver·sion		a·woke	
a·vert		a·wry	
a·vi·an		ax	
a·vi·ar·y		ax·i·om	
a·vi·a·tion		ax·i·o·mat·ic	
a·vi·a·tor		ax·is	
av·id		ax·le	
a·vid·i·ty		aye	
a·vi·on·ics		a·zal·e·a	
av·o·ca·do		az·i·muth	
av·o·ca·tion		Az·tec	
a·void		az·ure	
a·void·a·ble			

bab·bitt	*bbl*	badge	*by*
bab·ble	*bb*	badg·er	*by*
babe	*bab*	bad·i·nage	*bdnz*
ba·by	*bbe*	bad·ly	*bdl*
bac·ca·lau·re·ate	*bclyl*	bad·min·ton	*bd⌐m*
bac·ca·rat	*bCa*	bad·ness	*bd'*
bac·cha·na·lia	*bcnla*	baf·fle	*bfl*
bach·e·lor	*bCl*	baf·fle·ment	*bfl-*
ba·cil·li	*bsli*	bag	*bg*
ba·cil·lus	*bslx*	bag·a·telle	*bgel*
back	*bc*	bag·gage	*bgg*
back·bone	*bcbn*	bag·pipe	*bgpp*
back·er	*bc'*	bail	*bal*
back·fire	*bcfr*	bail·ee	*ble*
back·gam·mon	*bcgm*	bail·iff	*blf*
back·ground	*bcg—*	bail·i·wick	*blvc*
back·lash	*bcls*	bail·or	*bl*
back·slide	*bcsd*	bait	*ba*
back·ward	*bcvd*	bake	*bc*
back·ward·ness	*bcvd'*	bak·er·y	*bcy*
ba·con	*bcn*	Ba·ke·lite	*bcli*
bac·te·ri·a	*bcya*	bal·ance	*(bal) bl/*
bac·te·ri·cide	*bcysd*	bal·co·ny	*blke*
bac·te·ri·ol·o·gist	*bcyly*	bald	*bld*
bac·te·ri·ol·o·gy	*bcylge*	bal·der·dash	*blDds*
bad	*bd*	bale·ful	*blf*
bade	*bd*	balk	*bc*

21

balk·y		bang	
ball		ban·gle	
bal·lad		ban·ish	
bal·lad·ry		ban·ish·ment	
bal·last		ban·is·ter	
bal·le·ri·na		ban·jo	
bal·let		✓bank	
bal·lis·tic		✓bank·book	
bal·loon		bank·er	
bal·lot		bank·rupt	
ball·room		bank·rupt·cy	
bal·ly·hoo		ban·ner	
balm		ban·nock	
balm·y		ban·quet	
balm·i·ness		ban·shee	
bal·sa		ban·tam	
bal·sam		ban·ter	
bal·us·ter		Ban·tu	
bal·us·trade		ban·yan	
bam·boo		bap·tism	
bam·boo·zle		bap·tis·ter·y	
ban		bap·tize	
ba·nal		bar	
ba·nal·i·ty		barb	
ba·nan·a		bar·bar·i·an	
band		bar·bar·ic	
band·age		bar·ba·rism	
ban·dan·na		bar·bar·i·ty	
band·box		bar·ba·rous	
ban·deau		bar·be·cue	
ban·dit		bar·ber	
band·mas·ter		bar·ber·shop	
ban·do·lier		bar·bi·tu·rate	
band·stand		bar·ca·role	
ban·dy		bard	
bane		bare	
bane·ful		bare·back	

bare·ness		bar·ter	
bar·gain		ba·sal	
barge		ba·salt	
barge·man		base	
bar·i·tone		base·ball	
bar·i·um		base·board	
bark		based	
bar·keep·er		base·less	
bark·en·tine		base·ment	
bark·er		base·ness	
bar·ley		bash·ful	
bar·maid		bas·ic	
barn		bas·i·cal·ly	
bar·na·cle		ba·sil·i·ca	
barn·storm·er		ba·sin	
barn·yard		ba·sis	
bar·o·graph		bask	
ba·rom·e·ter		bas·ket	
bar·o·met·ric		bas·ket·ball	
bar·on		bas·ket·ful	
bar·on·ess		bas·ket·ry	
bar·on·et		Basque	
ba·ro·ni·al		bas-re·lief	
ba·roque		bass	
bar·o·scope		bas·si·net	
bar·racks		bas·soon	
bar·ra·cu·da		baste	
bar·rage		bas·tion	
bar·ra·try		bat	
✓ bar·rel		batch	
bar·ren		bate	
bar·ri·cade		ba·teau	
bar·ri·er		bath	
bar·ris·ter		bathe	
bar·room		ba·ther	
bar·row		ba·thet·ic	
bar·tend·er		ba·thos	

bath·room		be·at·i·tude	
ba·tiste		beau	
ba·ton		beau·te·ous	
bat·tal·ion		beau·ti·cian	
bat·ten		beau·ti·ful	
bat·ter		beau·ty	
bat·ter·y		bea·ver	
bat·tle		be·calm	
bat·tle·field		be·came	
bat·tle·ship		be·cause	
bau·ble		beck	
bawl		beck·on	
bay		be·cloud	
bay·o·net		be·come	
bay·ou		bed	
ba·zaar		bed·cham·ber	
ba·zoo·ka		be·dev·il	
be		bed·lam	
beach		bed·ou·in	
beach·comb·er		be·drag·gle	
bea·con		bed·room	
bead		bed·time	
bea·dle		bee	
bea·gle		beech	
beak		beech·nut	
beak·er		beef	
beam		beef·steak	
bean		bee·hive	
bear		been	
bear·a·ble		beer	
beast		beet	
beast·li·ness		bee·tle	
beast·ly		be·fall	
beat		be·fore	
beat·er		be·fore·hand	
be·a·tif·ic		be·fore·time	
be·at·i·fi·ca·tion		be·friend	

be·fud·dle		bel·la·don·na	
beg		bel·li·cose	
✓be·gan		bel·lig·er·ence	
be·get		bel·lig·er·ent	
beg·gar		bel·low	
beg·gar·ly		bel·ly	
beg·gar·y		✓be·long	
✓be·gin		be·lov·ed	
be·got		✓be·low	
be·grime		belt	
be·grudge		bel·ve·dere	
be·guile		be·moan	
✓be·gun		bench	
be·half		bend	
be·have		✓be·neath	
be·hav·ior		ben·e·dict	
be·held		ben·e·dic·tion	
be·he·moth		ben·e·fac·tor	
be·hest		ben·e·fact·ress	
✓be·hind		ben·e·fice	
be·hold		be·nef·i·cence	
be·hoove		be·nef·i·cent	
beige		ben·e·fi·cial	
be·la·bor		ben·e·fi·ci·ar·y	
be·lat·ed		ben·e·fit	
be·lay		be·nev·o·lence	
belch		be·nev·o·lent	
be·lea·guer		be·night·ed	
bel·fry		be·nign	
Bel·gian		be·nig·nan·cy	
be·lie		be·nig·nant	
be·lief		be·nig·ni·ty	
be·liev·a·ble		ben·i·son	
be·lieve		bent	
be·liev·er		ben·zine	
be·lit·tle		ben·zo·ate	
bell		ben·zo·in	

be·queath	*bql*	bey	*ba*
be·quest	*bq,*	✓be·yond	*by —*
be·reave	*bre*	bez·el	*bzl*
be·reft	*brf*	bi·an·nu·al	*baul*
ber·i·ber·i	*byby*	bi·as	*bis*
ber·ry	*by*	bi·be·lot	*bblo*
ber·serk	*bSc*	Bi·ble	*bb*
berth	*Bl*	bib·li·cal	*bbcl*
ber·yl	*Bl*	bib·li·og·ra·pher	*bbegf*
✓be·ryl·li·um	*(Bl) Ble*	bib·li·og·ra·phy	*bbegfe*
be·seech	*bsC*	bib·li·o·phile	*bbefl*
be·side	*bsd*	bib·u·lous	*bblx*
be·siege	*bsy*	bi·cam·er·al	*bcrl*
be·sought	*bsl*	bi·car·bon·ate	*bCbnl*
✓best	*b,*	bi·cen·ten·ni·al	*bs—nel*
bes·tial	*bscl*	bi·ceps	*bsps*
bes·ti·al·i·ty	*bscl)*	bi·chlo·ride	*bCd*
be·stir	*bS*	bi·chro·mate	*bCra*
be·stow	*bso*	bick·er	*bc*
bet	*bl*	bi·cus·pid	*bcsd*
be·took	*blc*	bi·cy·cle	*bscl*
be·tray	*bTa*	bi·cy·clist	*bscl,*
be·tray·al	*bTal*	bid	*bd*
be·troth	*bTl*	bide	*bd*
be·troth·al	*bTll*	bi·en·ni·al	*bnel*
✓bet·ter	*b*	bier	*be*
bet·ter·ment	*bT—*	bi·fo·cal	*bfcl*
✓be·tween	*bl*	bi·fur·cate	*bTca*
be·twixt	*blx+*	big	*bq*
bev·el	*bvl*	big·a·mist	*bq,*
bev·er·age	*bV1*	big·a·mous	*bqx*
bev·y	*bve*	big·a·my	*bqe*
be·wail	*bⁿl*	big·ger	*bq*
be·ware	*bⁿa*	big·gest	*bq,*
be·wil·der	*bⁿld*	big·ness	*bq?*
be·wil·der·ment	*bⁿlD—*	big·ot	*bql*
be·witch	*bⁿC*	big·ot·ry	*bqⁿe*

big·wig		bi·par·tite	
bi·ki·ni		bi·ped	
bi·lat·er·al		bi·plane	
bile		bi·ra·cial	
bilge		birch	
bi·lin·gual		bird	
bil·ious		bird·ie	
bilk		bird's-eye	
bill		birth	
bill·board		birth·day	
bil·let		birth·mark	
bil·liards		birth·place	
bil·lion		birth·right	
bil·lion·aire		birth·stone	
bil·lionth		bis·cuit	
bil·low		bi·sect	
bill·y		bish·op	
bill·post·er		bish·op·ric	
bi·me·tal·ic		bis·muth	
bi·month·ly		bi·son	
bin		bisque	
bi·na·ry		bis·tro	
bin·au·ral		bit	
bind		bite	
bind·er		✓ bit·ter	
bind·er·y		bit·tern	
bin·na·cle		bit·ter·sweet	
bin·oc·u·lar		bi·tu·men	
bi·no·mi·al		bi·tu·mi·nous	
bi·o·chem·is·try		bi·valve	
bi·og·ra·pher		biv·ou·ac	
bi·o·graph·ic		bi·zarre	
bi·og·ra·phy		✓ black	
bi·o·log·i·cal		black·board	
bi·ol·o·gy		black·en	
bi·op·sy		black·guard	
bi·par·ti·san		black·mail	

black·out		blest	
blad·der		blew	
blade		blight	
blam·a·ble		blind	
✓ blame		blind·er	
blame·less		blind·fold	
blame·wor·thy		blind·ly	
blanch		blink	
bland		blink·er	
blan·dish		bliss	
blan·dish·ment		bliss·ful	
✓ blank		blis·ter	
blan·ket		blithe	
blank·ness		blitz	
blare		bliz·zard	
blar·ney		bloat	
bla·sé		block	
blas·pheme		block·ade	
blas·phe·mous		block·bust·er	
blas·phe·my		block·head	
✓ blast		block·house	
bla·tan·cy		blond	
bla·tant		blood	
blath·er		blood·hound	
blaze		blood·i·est	
bla·zon		blood·i·ly	
bleach		blood·i·ness	
bleak		blood·less	
blear·y		blood·shed	
bleat		blood·shot	
bled		blood·stain	
bleed		bloom	
blem·ish		bloop·er	
blench		blos·som	
blend		blot	
bless		blotch	
bless·ed·ness		blot·ter	

blouse		bod·ice	
blow		bod·i·less	
blow·out		bod·i·ly	
blow·torch		bod·kin	
blowz·y		bod·y	
blub·ber		bod·y·guard	
blub·ber·y		Boer	
blu·cher		bog	
bludg·eon		bo·gey	
blue		bog·gle	
blue·jack·et		bo·gus	
blue·print		boil	
bluff		boil·er	
blun·der		bois·ter·ous	
blun·der·buss		bold	
blunt		bold·er	
blunt·ly		bold·face	
blunt·ness		bold·ly	
blur		bold·ness	
blurb		bo·le·ro	
blurt		boll	
blush		Bol·she·vik	
blus·ter		bol·ster	
blus·ter·ous		bolt	
bo·a		bo·lus	
boar		bomb	
board		bom·bard	
board·ing·house		bom·bard·ier	
board·walk		bom·bard·ment	
boast		bom·bast	
boast·ful		bom·bas·tic	
boat		bom·ba·zine	
boat·build·er		bomb·sight	
bob		bo·na fi·de	
bob·bin		bo·nan·za	
bob·sled		√ bond	
bode		bond·age	

bond·hold·er	*b— hol*	born	*Bn*
bone	*bn*	bo·ron	*(B) Bn*
bon·fire	*bnfr*	bor·ough	*Bo*
bon·net	*bnt*	bor·row	*Bo*
bon·ny	*bne*	bosh	*bS*
bo·nus	*bnx*	bos·om	*bz*
boo·by	*bbe*	boss	*b'*
boo·dle	*bdl*	bo·tan·i·cal	*blncl*
book	*bc*	bot·a·nist	*bln,*
book·bind·er	*bcbi*	bot·a·ny	*blne*
book·case	*bccs*	botch	*bC*
book·keep·er	*bccp*	both	*bo*
book·keep·ing	*bccp*	both·er	*bT*
book·let	*bell*	both·er·some	*bT s*
book·mo·bile	*bcrbl*	bot·tle	*bll*
boom	*bu*	bot·tom	*bl*
boom·er·ang	*b lg*	bot·tom·less	*bll'*
boon	*bn*	bou·doir	*bdr*
boon·dog·gle	*bndgl*	bouf·fant	*bf–*
boor	*bu*	bough	*br*
boor·ish	*buS*	bought	*bl*
boost	*bu,*	bouil·lon	*bln*
boost·er	*bS*	boul·der	*bol*
boot·black	*bubc*	bou·le·vard	*blvd*
booth	*bul*	bounce	*br /*
boot·leg	*bulg*	bound	*br —*
boot·less	*bul'*	bound·a·ry	*br—y*
boo·ty	*bu)*	bound·er	*br—/*
booze	*bz*	bound·less	*br—l'*
bo·rac·ic	*Bsc*	boun·te·ous	*br—x*
bo·rate	*Ba*	boun·ti·ful	*br—f*
bo·rax	*Bx*	boun·ty	*br—e*
bor·der	*Bd*	bou·quet	*bca*
bore	*bo*	bour·geois	*Bzra*
bo·re·al	*Bel*	bour·geoi·sie	*Bzrze*
bore·dom	*bod*	bourse	*Bs*
bor·ic	*Bc*	bout	*bul*

Word	Shorthand	Word	Shorthand
bou·tique		bran·dy	
bou·ton·niere		brass	
bo·vine		bras·sard	
bow	*(bo)*	bras·siere	
bowd·ler·ize		brat	
bow·el		bra·va·do	
bow·er		brave	
bow·knot		brav·er·y	
bowl		brav·est	
bow·string		bra·vo	
box		bra·vu·ra	
box·car		brawl	
box·er		brawn	
boy		brawn·i·est	
boy·cott		brawn·y	
boy·hood		bray	
boy·ish		bra·zen	
brace		bra·zier	
brace·let		Bra·zil·ian	
brack·et		breach	
brack·ish		bread	
brad		breadth	
brag		bread·win·ner	
brag·ga·do·ci·o		break	
brag·gart		break·a·ble	
braid		break·age	
braille		break·down	
brain		break·er	
brain·less		break·fast	
brain·wash		break·neck	
braise		break·wa·ter	
brake		breast	
bram·ble		breast·bone	
bran		breath	
branch		breath·a·ble	
brand		breathe	
bran·dish		breath·er	

breath·less	*bll'*	bright	*bc*
bred	*bd*	bright·en	*bcn*
breech	*bec*	bright·ly	*bcl*
breed	*bd*	bright·ness	*bc'*
breeze	*bz*	bril·liance	*bl/*
breeze·way	*bzea*	bril·lian·cy	*bl/*
breez·y	*bze*	bril·liant	*bl-*
breth·ren	*bbn*	bril·lian·tine	*bl-n*
breve	*be*	brim	*bn*
bre·vet	*bvl*	brim·ful	*bf*
bre·vi·ar·y	*bvry*	brim·stone	*bsn*
brev·i·ty	*bv)*	brin·dle	*b—l*
brew	*bu*	brine	*bn*
brew·er·y	*bury*	bring	*bq*
briar	*be'*	brink	*bg*
bribe	*blb*	brin·y	*bne*
brib·er·y	*bby*	bri·quette	*bcl*
bric-a-brac	*bcbc*	brisk	*bsc*
brick	*bc*	bris·ket	*bscl*
brick·bat	*bcbl*	bris·tle	*bsl*
brick·lay·er	*bcla'*	Brit·ish	*bls*
brick·yard	*bcfd*	brit·tle	*bll*
brid·al	*bdl*	broach	*boc*
bride	*bd*	broad	*bd*
bride·groom	*bdgu*	broad·cast	*bdc,*
brides·maid	*bdsnd*	broad·cloth	*bdcl*
bridge	*by*	broad·en	*bdn*
bridge·head	*byhd*	broad·ly	*bdl*
bridge·work	*byrc*	broad-mind·ed	*bdu—*
bri·dle	*bdl*	broad·side	*bdsd*
brief	*bef*	broad·sword	*bdsd*
brief·ly	*bfl*	broad·tail	*bdll*
brig	*bq*	bro·cade	*bcd*
bri·gade	*bgd*	broc·co·li	*bcl*
brig·a·dier	*bgde*	bro·chette	*bsl*
brig·and	*bq—*	bro·chure	*blu*
brig·an·tine	*bq-n*	brogue	*boq*

broil		bru·nette	
broke		brunt	
bro·ken		brush	
bro·ker		brush·work	
bro·ker·age		brusque	
bro·mate		bru·tal	
bro·mide		bru·tal·i·ty	
bro·mid·ic		bru·tal·ize	
bro·mine		brute	
bron·chi·al		bub·ble	
bron·chi·tis		bu·bon·ic	
bron·cho		buc·ca·neer	
bronze		buck	
brooch		buck·et	
brood		buck·le	
brook		buck·ler	
brook·let		buck·ram	
broom		bu·col·ic	
broom·stick		bud	
broth		Bud·dhism	
broth·er		Bud·dhist	
broth·er·hood		budge	
broth·er·in·law		budg·et	
broth·er·ly		buff	
brougham		buf·fa·lo	
brought		buf·fer	
brou·ha·ha		buf·fet	
brow		buf·foon	
brow·beat		buf·foon·er·y	
brown		bug	
brown·ie		bug·a·boo	
brown·stone		bug·bear	
browse		bu·gle	
bru·in		build	
bruise		build·er	
bruit		built	
brunch		bulb	

bulb·ous	*blbx*	bun·ting	*b=*
bulge	*blg*	buoy	*bue*
bulk	*blc*	buoy·an·cy	*by/*
bulk·head	*blchd*	buoy·ant	*by—*
bulk·y	*blce*	bur·den	*Bdn*
bull	*bl*	bur·den·some	*Bdns*
bull·dog	*bldg*	bur·dock	*Bdc*
bull·doze	*bldz*	bu·reau	*Bu*
bull·doz·er	*bldz/*	bu·reauc·ra·cy	*BCse*
bul·let	*bll*	bu·reau·crat	*BCl*
bul·le·tin	*blln*	bu·rette	*Bl*
bull·fight	*blfe*	bur·geon	*Bjn*
bull·frog	*blfg*	burgh·er	*Bg/*
bul·lion	*bln*	bur·glar	*Bg*
bull·ock	*blc*	bur·glar·ize	*Bgz*
bull's-eye	*blse*	bur·gla·ry	*Bgy*
bul·ly	*bl*	bur·i·al	*byl*
bul·rush	*blrS*	burl	*Bl*
bul·wark	*bll rc*	bur·lap	*Blp*
bum	*b*	bur·lesque	*Blsc*
bum·ble	*brb*	bur·ly	*Bl*
bum·ble·bee	*brbbe*	Bur·mese	*Brz*
bump	*brp*	burn	*Bn*
bump·kin	*brcn*	bur·nish	*BnS*
bump·tious	*brx*	bur·noose	*Bns*
bump·y	*rpe*	burn·out	*Bnou*
bun	*bn*	burnt	*B—*
bunch	*bC*	burp	*Bp*
bun·combe	*bnco*	burr	*b*
bun·dle	*b — l*	bur·row	*Bo*
bung	*bg*	bur·sar	*Bs/*
bun·ga·low	*bglo*	bur·si·tis	*Bsls*
bun·gle	*bgl*	burst	*B,*
bun·ion	*bhn*	bur·y	*by*
bunk	*bg*	bus	*bo*
bunk·er	*bg/*	bush	*bS*
bun·ny	*bne*	bush·el	*bSl*

bush·wack·er		but·ter·milk	
bus·i·er		but·ter·nut	
bus·i·est		but·ter·y	
bus·i·ly		but·tocks	
busi·ness		but·ton	
busi·ness·man		but·ton·hole	
busi·ness·men		but·tress	
bust		bux·om	
bus·tle		buy	
bus·y		buy·er	
but		buzz	
butch·er		buz·zard	
butch·er·y		by	
but·ler		by·gone	
butte		by·law	
but·ter		by·pass	
but·ter·cup		by·road	
but·ter·fat		by·stand·er	
but·ter·fly			

cab	*cb*	√ ca·den·za	*cdnza*
ca·bal	*cbl*	ca·det	*cdt*
cab·a·lis·tic	*cblsc*	cadge	*cj*
ca·ba·na	*cbna*	cad·mi·um	*(cd)cdrez*
cab·a·ret	*cBa*	cad·re	*cDe*
cab·bage	*cbj*	ca·du·ce·us	*cdsx*
cab·in	*cbn*	ca·fé	*cfa*
cab·i·net	*cbnt*	ca·fe·te·ri·a	*cftya*
cab·i·net·mak·er	*cbntrc*	caf·fe·ine	*cfn*
√ ca·ble	*cb*	cage	*caj*
√ ca·ble·gram	*cbg*	ca·hoots	*chus*
ca·boose	*cbs*	cais·son	*csn*
cab·ri·o·let	*cBla*	ca·jole	*cjl*
cab·stand	*cbs—*	Ca·jun	*cjn*
ca·ca·o	*ccv*	cake	*cc*
cache	*cS*	cal·a·bash	*clbS*
ca·chet	*cSa*	cal·a·boose	*clbs*
cack·le	*ccl*	ca·lam·i·tous	*clrlx*
ca·coph·o·nous	*ccfnx*	cal·lam·i·ty	*cl)*
ca·coph·o·ny	*ccfne*	cal·car·e·ous	*clCx*
cac·ti	*cci*	cal·ci·fi·ca·tion	*clsfcj*
cac·tus	*ccx*	cal·ci·fy	*clsf*
cad	*cd*	cal·ci·mine	*clsrun*
ca·dav·er	*cdv*	cal·ci·na·tion	*clsnj*
ca·dav·er·ous	*cdvr*	cal·cine	*clsun*
cad·die	*cde*	cal·ci·um	*(ca)clse*
ca·dence	*cd/*	cal·cu·late	*clcla*

36

✓cal·cu·la·tion		ca·mel·li·a	
✓cal·cu·la·tor		cam·e·o	
cal·cu·lus		cam·er·a	
cal·dron		cam·er·a·man	
✓cal·en·dar		cam·i·sole	
calf		cam·o·mile	
calf·skin		cam·ou·flage	
cal·i·ber		camp	
cal·i·brate		cam·paign	
cal·i·bra·tor		cam·pa·ni·le	
cal·i·co		camp·ground	
cal·i·per		cam·phor	
ca·liph		cam·pus	
cal·is·then·ics		can	
calk		Ca·na·di·an	
call		ca·nal	
cal·lig·ra·phy		ca·nal·boat	
cal·los·i·ty		ca·nal·i·za·tion	
cal·lous		ca·na·pé	
cal·low		ca·nard	
cal·lus		ca·nar·y	
✓calm		can·cel	
calm·ness		can·cel·la·tion	
cal·o·mel		can·cer	
ca·lor·ic		can·cer·ous	
cal·o·rie		can·de·la·bra	
ca·lum·ni·ate		can·de·la·brum	
ca·lum·ni·a·tor		can·did	
ca·lum·ni·ous		can·di·da·cy	
cal·um·ny		can·di·date	
calves		can·did·ly	
ca·lyx		can·did·ness	
ca·ma·ra·de·rie		can·dle	
cam·ber		can·dle·light	
cam·bric		can·dle·stick	
came		can·dor	
cam·el		can·dy	

cane		✓ ca·pa·ble	
ca·nine		ca·pa·bly	
can·is·ter		ca·pa·cious	
can·ker		ca·pa·cious·ness	
can·ker·ous		ca·pac·i·tor	
can·ner		ca·pac·i·ty	
can·ner·y		cape	
can·ni·bal		ca·per	
can·ni·bal·is·tic		cap·il·lar·y	
can·ni·ly		cap·i·tal	
can·ni·ness		cap·i·tal·ism	
can·non		cap·i·tal·ist	
can·non·eer		cap·i·tal·ize	
can·not		cap·i·tol	
can·ny		ca·pit·u·late	
ca·noe		ca·pit·u·la·tion	
can·on		ca·pon	
ca·non·i·cal		ca·price	
can·on·ize		ca·pri·cious	
can·o·py		ca·pri·cious·ness	
can't		cap·size	
can·ta·loupe		cap·stan	
can·tan·ker·ous		cap·sule	
can·ta·ta		cap·tain	
can·teen		cap·tion	
cant·er		cap·tious	
can·ti·cle		cap·ti·vate	
can·ti·le·ver		cap·ti·va·tion	
can·to		cap·tive	
can·ton		cap·tiv·i·ty	
can·ton·ment		cap·tor	
can·tor		cap·ture	
can·vas		car	
can·vass		ca·rafe	
can·yon		car·a·mel	
cap		car·a·pace	
ca·pa·bil·i·ty		car·at	

car·a·van		car·et	
car·a·van·sa·ry		care·worn	
car·a·vel		car·go	
car·a·way		car·i·bou	
car·bide		car·i·ca·ture	
car·bine		car·ies	
car·bo·hy·drate		car·il·lon	
car·bol·ic		car·mine	
car·bon		car·nage	
car·bo·na·ceous		car·nal	
car·bon·ate		car·na·tion	
car·bon·ic		car·nau·ba	
car·bon·if·er·ous		car·nel·ian	
car·bon·ize		car·ni·val	
car·bo·run·dum		car·niv·o·rous	
car·boy		car·ol	
car·bun·cle		car·om	
car·bu·ret·or		ca·rot·id	
car·cass		ca·rouse	
car·cin·o·gen		car·pen·ter	
car·ci·no·ma		car·pen·try	
card		car·pet	
card·board		car·riage	
card·case		car·ri·er	
car·di·ac		car·ri·on	
car·di·gan		car·rot	
car·di·nal		car·rou·sel	
car·di·o·graph		car·ry	
care		car·ry·all	
ca·reen		cart	
ca·reer		cart·age	
care·ful		carte blanch	
care·ful·ly		car·tel	
care·ful·ness		Car·te·sian	
care·less		car·ti·lage	
care·less·ness		car·ti·lag·i·nous	
ca·ress		car·tog·ra·phy	

car·ton	*Cln*	cat·a·clysm	*clcz*
car·toon	*Cln*	cat·a·comb	*clco*
car·toon·ist	*Cln,*	cat·a·lep·sy	*cllpse*
car·tridge	*CM*	cat·a·lep·tic	*cllpc*
carve	*Cv*	cat·a·log	*Cal*
cas·cade	*cscd*	ca·tal·y·sis	*cllss*
case	*cas*	cat·a·lyt·ic	*clllc*
case·hard·en	*csHdn*	cat·a·ma·ran	*cl m*
ca·se·in	*csn*	cat·a·pult	*clpll*
case·ment	*Cs—*	cat·a·ract	*cJc*
cash	*c8*	ca·tas·tro·phe	*clSfe*
cash·book	*cSbc*	cat·a·stroph·ic	*clSfc*
ca·shew	*clu*	catch	*cC*
cash·ier	*cle*	catch·all	*cCal*
cash·mere	*czre*	catch·er	*cC*
ca·si·no	*clno*	catch·word	*cCl rd*
cask	*csc*	cat·e·chism	*clcz*
cas·ket	*cscl*	cat·e·chize	*clcz*
casque	*csc*	cat·e·chu·men	*clc m*
cas·se·role	*cll*	cat·e·gor·i·cal	*clGcl*
cas·si·a	*cla*	cat·e·go·ry	*clgy*
cas·sock	*csc*	cat·e·go·rize	*clGz*
cast	*c,*	ca·ter	*ca*
cas·ta·net	*csnl*	ca·ter·er	*c*
cast·a·way	*csava*	cat·er·pil·lar	*clpl al*
caste	*c,*	cat·er·waul	*c as*
cas·tel·lat·ed	*cslā*	ca·thar·sis	*c ss*
cas·ti·gate	*csga*	ca·thar·tic	*cJc*
cas·ti·ga·tion	*csgl*	ca·the·dral	*clDl*
cas·tle	*csl*	cath·e·ter	*cl*
cast·off	*csof*	cath·ode	*cld*
cas·trate	*cSa*	cath·o·lic	*cllc*
✓ cas·u·al	*czul*	ca·thol·i·cism	*cllsz*
cas·u·al·ty	*czul)*	ca·thol·i·cize	*cllsz*
cas·u·ist	*cz ,*	cat·nip	*clnp*
cas·u·ist·ry	*cz Se*	cat·tle	*cll*
cat	*cl*	cat·ty-cor·ner	*clCn*

cat·walk		cel·e·brate	
Cau·ca·sian		cel·e·bra·tion	
cau·cus		cel·e·bra·tor	
cau·dal		ce·leb·ri·ty	
✓caught		ce·ler·i·ty	
caul·dron		cel·er·y	
cau·li·flow·er		ce·les·tial	
caulk		cel·i·ba·cy	
caus·al		cel·i·bate	
cau·sa·tion		cell	
caus·a·tive		cel·lar	
cause		cel·lar·et	
cau·se·rie		cel·list	
cause·way		cel·lo	
caus·tic		cel·lo·phane	
cau·ter·i·za·tion		cel·lu·lar	
cau·ter·ize		cel·lu·loid	
cau·ter·y		cel·lu·lose	
✓cau·tion		Celt	
cau·tion·ar·y		ce·ment	
✓cau·tious		ce·men·ta·tion	
cav·al·cade		cem·e·ter·y	
cav·a·lier		cen·o·taph	
cav·al·ry		cen·sor	
cav·il		cen·so·ri·ous	
cave		cen·sor·ship	
cav·ern		cen·sur·a·ble	
cav·ern·ous		cen·sure	
cav·i·ar		cen·sus	
cav·i·ty		✓cent	
ca·vort		cen·taur	
cease		cen·ta·vo	
cease·less		cen·te·nar·y	
ce·dar		cen·ten·ni·al	
cede		✓cen·ter	
ceiling		cen·ter·piece	
cel·e·brant		cen·ti·grade	

Word	Shorthand	Word	Shorthand
cen·ti·gram		chafe	
cen·ti·li·ter		chaff	
cen·time		cha·grin	
cen·ti·me·ter		chain	
cen·ti·pede		chair	
cen·tral		chair·man	
cen·tral·i·za·tion		cha·let	
cen·tral·ize		chal·ice	
cen·trif·u·gal		chalk	
cen·trip·e·tal		chal·lenge	
cen·tu·ri·on		chal·lis	
cen·tu·ry		cham·ber	
ce·phal·ic		cham·ber·lain	
ce·ram·ic		cha·me·leon	
ce·re·al		cham·ois	
cer·e·bral		champ	
cer·e·brate		cham·pagne	
cer·e·mo·ni·al		cham·pi·on	
cer·e·mo·ni·ous		cham·pi·on·ship	
cer·e·mo·ny		chance	
ce·rise		chan·cel	
cer·tain		chan·cel·lor	
cer·tain·ly		chan·cer·y	
cer·tain·ty		chan·de·lier	
cer·tif·i·cate		chan·dler	
cer·ti·fi·ca·tion		chan·dler·y	
cer·ti·fy		change	
cer·ti·tude		change·a·bil·i·ty	
ce·ru·le·an		change·a·ble	
cer·vi·cal		change·less	
cer·vix		change·ling	
ce·si·um		chan·nel	
cess		chan·son	
ces·sa·tion		chant	
ces·sion		chan·teuse	
cess·pit		cha·os	
cess·pool		cha·ot·ic	

chap		chas·tise·ment	
cha·peau		chas·ti·ty	
chap·el		chas·u·ble	
chap·er·on		chat	
chap·lain		châ·teau	
chap·let		chat·e·laine	
chap·ter		chat·tel	
char		chat·ter	
char·ac·ter		chat·ter·box	
char·ac·ter·is·tic		chat·ter·er	
char·ac·ter·i·za·tion		chauf·feur	
char·ac·ter·ize		chau·vin·ist	
cha·rade		cheap	
char·coal		cheap·en	
charge		cheap·er	
charge·a·ble		cheap·ly	
char·gé d'af·faires		cheat	
char·i·ot		cheat·er	
char·i·ot·eer		check	
char·is·mat·ic		check·book	
char·i·ta·ble		check·er	
char·i·ty		check·mate	
char·la·tan		check·point	
charm		check·rein	
char·nel		check·room	
✓ chart		cheek	
char·ter		cheer	
char·treuse		cheer·ful	
chart·room		cheer·ful·ness	
char·wom·an		cheer·less	
char·y		cheer·y	
chase		cheese	
chasm		cheese·cake	
chas·sis		chef	
chaste		chem·i·cal	
chas·ten		che·mise	
chas·tise		chem·ist	

chem·is·try		chi·me·ra	
chem·ur·gy		chi·mer·i·cal	
che·nille		chim·ney	
cher·ish		chim·pan·zee	
che·root		chin	
cher·ry		chi·na	
cher·ub		chin·chil·la	
chess		Chi·nese	
chess·man		chink	
chest		chi·no	
chest·nut		chintz	
chev·a·lier		chip	
chev·i·ot		chip·munk	
chev·ron		chi·rop·odist	
chew		chi·ro·prac·tor	
chic		chirp	
chi·can·er·y		chis·el	
chick		chis·el·er	
chick·en		chit·chat	
chi·cle		chiv·al·rous	
chic·o·ry		chiv·al·ry	
chide		chlo·ral	
chief		chlo·rate	
chief·ly		chlo·ride	
chief·tain		chlo·rin·ate	
chif·fon		chlo·rine	(cl)
chif·fo·nier		chlo·ro·form	
chig·ger		chlo·ro·phyll	
chi·gnon		chock·a·block	
chil·blain		choc·o·late	
child		choice	
child·hood		choir	
child·ish		choke	
chil·dren		chok·er	
chill		chol·er	
chill·y		chol·er·a	
chime		chol·er·ic	

cho·les·ter·ol	*clSe*	chrys·o·lite	*csle*
choose	*Cz*	chub·by	*Cbe*
chop	*Cp*	chuck	*Cc*
chop·per	*Cp*	chuck·le	*Ccl*
cho·ral	*Cl*	chuk·ker	*Cc*
chord	*Cd*	chum	*Cs*
chore	*Co*	chump	*Crp*
cho·re·a	*Ca*	chunk	*Cg*
cho·re·og·ra·pher	*Cegf*	church	*CrC*
chor·is·ter	*CS*	church·go·er	*CrCg*
chor·tle	*Crll*	church·war·den	*CrCdn*
cho·rus	*Cr*	churl	*Crl*
chose	*Cz*	churl·ish	*CrlS*
cho·sen	*Czn*	churn	*Crn*
chow·der	*Crd*	chute	*Su*
Christ	*cl,*	chut·ney	*Clne*
chris·ten	*csn*	ci·ca·da	*scda*
Chris·ten·dom	*csnd*	cic·a·trix	*sc*
Chris·tian	*csCn*	ci·der	*sd*
Chris·ti·an·i·ty	*csCn)*	ci·gar	*sgr*
Christ·ly	*csl*	cig·a·rette	*sgl*
Christ·mas	*Krs*	cinch	*sc*
Christ·mas·tide	*Krsld*	cin·cho·na	*sgna*
chro·mat·ic	*crlc*	cinc·ture	*sgC*
chrome	*co*	cin·der	*s*
chro·mi·um	*(Cr)cre*	cin·e·ma	*snra*
chro·mo	*cro*	cin·na·bar	*snbr*
chro·mo·some	*crso*	cin·na·mon	*snm*
chron·ic	*cnc*	ci·pher	*sf*
chron·i·cle	*cncl*	cir·cle	*Scl*
chron·o·graph	*cngf*	cir·cuit	*Scl*
chron·o·log·i·cal	*cnljcl*	cir·cu·i·tous	*Sculx*
chro·nol·o·gy	*cnlje*	cir·cu·lar	*Scl*
chro·nom·e·ter	*cn*	cir·cu·lar·ize	*ScLz*
chron·o·met·ric	*cnrc*	cir·cu·late	*Scla*
chrys·a·lis	*csls*	cir·cu·la·tion	*Scly*
chrys·an·the·mum	*csnln*	cir·cu·la·tive	*Sclv*

cir·cu·la·tor	*Scla*	civ·i·lize	*svlz*
cir·cu·la·to·ry	*Sclly*	civ·il·ly	*svl*
cir·cum·cise	*Sksz*	clack	*cc*
cir·cum·ci·sion	*Sksj*	clad	*cd*
cir·cum·fer·ence	*Skf/*	claim	*ca*
cir·cum·flex	*Skfx*	claim·ant	*ca-*
cir·cum·lo·cu·tion	*Sklcj*	clair·voy·ance	*Cvy/*
cir·cum·nav·i·gate	*Sknvga*	clair·voy·ant	*Cvy-*
cir·cum·nav·i·ga·tor	*Sknvga*	clam	*cr*
cir·cum·scribe	*SksCb*	clam·ber	*cr*
cir·cum·spect	*Sksc*	clam·mi·ness	*cre'*
cir·cum·stance	*c/*	clam·my	*cre*
cir·cum·stan·tial	*c/x*	clam·or	*cr*
cir·cum·stan·ti·ate	*c/a*	clam·or·ous	*c 2x*
cir·cum·vent	*Skv-*	clamp	*crp*
cir·cum·ven·tion	*Skvj*	clan	*cn*
cir·cus	*Scx*	clan·des·tine	*c — sn*
cir·rho·sis	*Sss*	clang	*cq*
cir·rus	*Sx*	clan·gor	*cg*
cis·tern	*sSn*	clank	*cq*
cit·a·del	*sldl*	clan·nish	*cns*
ci·ta·tion	*slj*	clap	*cp*
cite	*su*	clap·per	*cp*
cit·i·zen	*slzn*	claque	*cc*
cit·i·zen·ship	*slznS*	clar·et	*Cl*
cit·rate	*sra*	clar·i·fi·ca·tion	*Cfcj*
cit·ric	*src*	clar·i·fy	*Cf*
cit·ron	*srn*	clar·i·net	*Cnl*
cit·ron·el·la	*srnla*	clar·i·on	*cyn*
cit·rus	*sr*	clar·i·ty	*C)*
cit·y	*s)*	clash	*cS*
civ·et	*svl*	clasp	*cs,*
civ·ic	*svc*	class	*c'*
civ·il	*svl*	clas·sic	*csc*
ci·vil·ian	*svln*	clas·si·cal	*cecl*
ci·vil·i·ty	*svl)*	clas·si·fi·a·ble	*csfb*
civ·i·li·za·tion	*svlzj*	clas·si·fi·ca·tion	*csfcj*

clas·si·fy		click	
class·mate		cli·ent	
class·room		cli·en·tele	
clat·ter		cliff	
clause		cli·mate	
claus·tro·pho·bia		cli·max	
clav·i·cle		climb	
cla·vi·er		clime	
claw		clinch	
clay		cling	
clean		clin·ic	
clean·ly		clin·i·cal	
clean·li·ness		cli·ni·cian	
cleanse		clink	
clear		clip	
clear·ance		clip·per	
clear·er		clique	
clear·est		clo·a·ca	
clear·ing·house		cloak	
clear·ly		cloche	
clear·ness		clock	
cleat		clock·wise	
cleave		clod	
cleav·er		clod·hop·per	
clef		clog	
cleft		cloi·son·né	
clem·en·cy		clois·ter	
clem·ent		clop	
clench		close	
clere·sto·ry		close	
cler·gy		close·ly	
cler·gy·man		close·ness	
cler·ic		clos·er	
cler·i·cal		clos·et	
clerk		clo·sure	
clev·er		clot	
cli·ché		cloth	

clothe	*col*	co·a·les·cent	*cols–*
clothes·pin	*czpn*	coal·bin	*clbn*
cloth·ier	*cle*	coal·box	*clbx*
cloth·ing	*col*	coal·field	*clfld*
clo·ture	*cC*	co·a·li·tion	*colj*
cloud	*curd*	coarse	*Cs*
cloud·burst	*curdB*	coars·en	*Csn*
cloud·less	*curdl'*	coarse·ness	*Cs'*
clout	*curl*	coast	*co,*
clove	*co*	coast·al	*csl*
clo·ven	*con*	coast·er	*cS*
clo·ver	*cv*	coast·line	*csli*
clown	*cun*	coat	*co*
clown·ish	*cuns*	co·au·thor	*caT*
cloy	*cy*	coax	*cox*
club	*cb*	co·ax·i·al	*ckel*
club·foot	*cbfl*	cob	*cb*
club·room	*cbr*	co·balt	*(co) cbll*
cluck	*cc*	cob·ble	*cb*
clue	*cu*	co·bra	*cBa*
clump	*crp*	cob·web	*cb-b*
clum·si·er	*crze*	co·caine	*ccn*
clum·si·ly	*crzl*	coc·cyx	*ccsx*
clum·si·ness	*crze'*	coch·i·neal	*cCnel*
clum·sy	*crze*	cock	*cc*
clung	*cq*	cock·a·too	*cclu*
clus·ter	*cS*	cock·a·trice	*ccT s*
clutch	*cC*	cock·le	*ccl*
clut·ter	*c*	cock·ney	*ccne*
coach	*coC*	cock·pit	*ccpl*
coach·man	*cC–*	cock·sure	*ccsu*
co·ad·ju·tant	*cajt–*	cock·tail	*ccl*
co·ad·ju·tor	*coj*	co·coa	*cco*
co·ag·u·late	*cogla*	co·co·nut	*ccnl*
co·ag·u·la·tion	*cogly*	co·coon	*ccn*
coal	*col*	cod	*cd*
co·a·lesce	*cols*	cod·dle	*cdl*

code	*cd*	co·hort	
co·de·fend·ant	*cdf— —*	coif	
co·deine	*cdn*	coif·feur	
co·dex	*cdx*	coif·fure	
cod·ger		coil	
cod·i·cil	*cdsl*	coin	
cod·i·fi·ca·tion	*cdfc*	co·in·cide	
cod·i·fy	*cdf*	co·in·ci·dence	
co-ed	*cod*	co·in·ci·den·tal	
co·ef·fi·cient	*cefs–*	co·in·sure	
co·erce	*cos*	co·i·tion	
co·er·cion		coke	
co·e·val	*covl*	col·an·der	
co·ex·ist	*cx,*	cold	*col*
cof·fee	*cfe*	cold·er	*col*
cof·fee·pot	*cfepl*	cold·ness	*col'*
cof·fer	*cf*	col·ic	*clc*
cof·fin	*cfn*	col·i·se·um	*clse*
cog	*cq*	co·li·tis	*clls*
co·gen·cy	*cy/*	col·lab·o·rate	*clBa*
co·gent	*cy–*	col·lab·o·ra·tor	*clBa*
cog·i·tate	*cyla*	col·lage	*clz*
cog·i·ta·tion	*cyly*	col·lapse	*clps*
co·gnac	*cnyc*	col·laps·i·ble	*clpsb*
cog·nate	*cgna*	col·lar	*cl*
cog·ni·tion	*cgny*	col·lar·band	*clb —*
cog·ni·zance	*cgnz/*	col·lar·bone	*clbn*
cog·ni·zant	*cgnz–*	col·late	*cla*
cog·no·men	*cgn m*	col·lat·er·al	*cl l*
cog·wheel	*cgrl*	col·la·tion	*cly*
co·hab·it	*chbl*	col·league	*clg*
co·heir	*cd*	col·lect	*cc*
co·here	*che*	col·lect·i·ble	*ccb*
co·her·ence	*che/*	col·lec·tion	*ccy*
co·her·ent	*che–*	col·lec·tive·ly	*ccvl*
co·he·sion	*chy*	col·lec·tor	*cc*
co·he·sive	*chsv*	col·leen	*cln*

col·lege	*cly*	comb	*Co*
col·le·gi·ate	*clgl*	com·bat	*kbl*
col·lide	*cld*	com·bat·ant	*kbl–*
col·lie	*cl*	com·ba·tive	*kbv*
col·lier	*cl*	com·bi·na·tion	*kbny*
col·lier·y	*cly*	com·bine	*kbn*
col·li·sion	*cly*	com·bus·ti·ble	*kbsb*
col·lo·di·on	*clden*	com·bus·tion	*kbsCn*
col·loid	*clyd*	come	*k*
col·lo·qui·al	*clgel*	co·me·di·an	*kden*
col·lo·qui·al·ism	*clglz*	com·e·dy	*kde*
col·lo·quy	*clge*	come·li·ness	*kl'*
col·lu·sion	*cly*	come·ly	*kl*
co·logne	*cln*	co·mes·ti·ble	*ksb*
co·lon	*cln*	com·et	*kl*
colo·nel	(Col.) *Cnl*	come·up·pance	*kp/*
colo·nel·cy	*Cnlse*	com·fit	*kfl*
co·lo·ni·al	*clnl*	com·fort	*kfl*
col·o·nist	*cln,*	com·fort·a·ble	*kflb*
col·o·ni·za·tion	*clnzy*	com·fort·a·bly	*kflb*
col·on·nade	*clnd*	com·fort·er	*kf*
col·o·ny	*clne*	com·fort·less	*kfll'*
col·o·phon	*clfn*	com·ic	*kc*
col·or	*cl*	com·i·cal	*kcl*
col·or·a·tion	*cly*	com·ma	*ka*
col·o·ra·tu·ra	*clra*	com·mand	*k—*
col·or·blind	*clbl—*	com·man·dant	*k——*
col·or·ful	*clf*	com·man·deer	*k—e*
col·or·less	*cll'*	com·mand·er	*k—/*
co·los·sal	*clsl*	com·mand·ment	*k——*
co·los·sus	*clsx*	com·man·do	*k—o*
colt	*coll*	com·mem·o·rate	*k⌐a*
col·umn	*cl*	com·mem·o·ra·tion	*k⌐y*
co·lum·nar	*clm*	com·mem·o·ra·tive	*k⌐v*
col·um·nist	*cl,*	com·mence	*k/*
co·ma	*cra*	com·mence·ment	*k/—*
com·a·tose	*crls*	com·mend	*k—*

Word	Outline	Word	Outline
com·mend·a·ble	k —— b	com·mu·ni·ca·tor	knca
com·men·da·tion	k —— $_1$	com·mun·ion	knn
com·mend·a·to·ry	k —— ly	com·mu·ni·que	knca
com·men·su·ra·ble	k/rb	com·mu·nism	knz
com·men·su·rate	k/ra	com·mu·nist	kn,
com·ment	$k-$	com·mu·ni·ty	kn)
com·men·tar·y	$k-y$	com·mu·ta·tion	kly
com·men·ta·tor	$k-a$	com·mute	ku
com·merce	Ks	com·mut·er	ku
com·mer·cial	Kr	✓ com·pact	kpc
com·mer·cial·ly	Kr	com·pan·ion	kpnn
com·min·gle	kgl	com·pan·ion·a·ble	kpnnb
com·mis·er·ate	kSa	com·pan·ion·ship	kpnnS
com·mis·er·a·tion	kSy	com·pa·ny	co
com·mis·sar·i·at	ksyl	com·pa·ra·ble	kSb
com·mis·sar	ksr	com·par·a·tive	kSv
com·mis·sar·y	ksy	com·pare	kpa
com·mis·sion	k₁	com·par·i·son	kSsn
com·mis·sion·aire	kja	com·part·ment	kSt-
com·mis·sion·er	kj	com·part·men·tal·ize	kSt-lz
com·mit	kl	com·pass	kp'
com·mit·ment	kl-	com·pas·sion	kpj
com·mit·tee	k	com·pas·sion·ate	kpjl
com·mode	kd	com·pat·i·bil·i·ty	kpllb)
com·mo·di·ous	kdx	com·pat·i·ble	kpllb
com·mod·i·ty	kd)	com·pa·tri·ot	kp
com·mo·dore	kdo	com·pel	kpl
com·mon	kn	com·pen·di·um	kp—en
com·mon·er	kn	com·pen·sate	kp/a
com·mon·place	knpl	com·pen·sa·tion	kp/₁
com·mo·tion	kj	com·pen·sa·to·ry	kp/ly
com·mu·nal	knl	com·pete	kpe
com·mune	kn	com·pe·tence	kpl/
com·mu·ni·ca·ble	kncb	com·pe·ten·cy	kpl/
com·mu·ni·cant	knc-	com·pe·tent	kpl-
com·mu·ni·cate	knca	com·pe·ti·tion	kplj
com·mu·ni·ca·tion	kncj	com·pet·i·tive	kplv

com·pet·i·tor		com·pound	
com·pi·la·tion		com·pre·hend	
com·pile		com·pre·hen·si·ble	
com·pil·er		com·pre·hen·sion	
com·pla·cence		com·press	
com·pla·cen·cy		com·press·i·ble	
com·pla·cent		com·pres·sion	
com·plain		com·pres·sor	
com·plain·ant		com·prise	
com·plaint		com·pro·mise	
com·plai·sance		comp·tom·e·ter	
com·ple·ment		comp·trol·ler	
com·ple·men·tal		com·pul·sion	
com·plete		com·pul·so·ry	
com·plete·ly		com·punc·tion	
com·plete·ness		com·put·a·ble	
com·ple·tion		com·pu·ta·tion	
com·plex		com·pute	
com·plex·ion		com·rade	
com·plex·ity		con	
com·pli·ance		con·cat·e·na·tion	
com·pli·ant		con·cave	
com·pli·cate		con·cav·i·ty	
com·pli·ca·tion		con·ceal	
com·plic·i·ty		con·cede	
com·pli·ment		con·ceit	
com·pli·men·ta·ry		con·ceiv·a·ble	
com·ply		con·ceive	
com·po·nent		con·cen·trate	
com·port		con·cen·tra·tion	
com·port·ment		con·cen·tra·tor	
com·pose		con·cen·tric	
com·pos·ite		con·cept	
com·po·si·tion		con·cep·tion	
com·pos·i·tor		con·cern	
com·post		con·cert	
com·po·sure		con·cer·ti·na	

con·cer·to	*kCrlo*	con·di·ment	*kd –*
con·ces·sion	*ksy*	con·di·tion	*kdy*
con·ces·sion·aire	*ksja*	con·dole	*kdl*
conch	*kC*	✓con·do·lence	*kdl /*
con·ci·erge	*c/rz*	con·do·min·i·um	*kd men*
con·cil·i·ate	*ksla*	con·done	*kdn*
con·cil·i·a·tion	*kslf*	con·dor	*kd*
con·cil·i·a·to·ry	*kslly*	con·duce	*kds*
con·cise	*kss*	con·du·cive	*kdsv*
con·clave	*kca*	con·duct	*kdc*
✓con·clude	*kcd*	con·duc·tion	*kdcy*
con·clu·sion	*kcly*	con·duc·tor	*kdc*
con·clu·sive	*kcsv*	con·duit	*kdrl*
con·coct	*kcc*	cone	*cn*
con·coc·tion	*kccy*	con·fab·u·la·tion	*kfbly*
con·com·i·tant	*kkl –*	con·fec·tion	*kfcy*
con·cord	*kCd*	con·fec·tion·er	*kfcy*
con·cord·ance	*kCd /*	con·fec·tion·er·y	*kfcyy*
con·cord·ant	*kCd –*	con·fed·er·a·cy	*kfDse*
con·cor·dat	*kCdl*	con·fed·er·ate	*kfDl*
con·course	*kCs*	con·fed·er·a·tion	*kfDy*
con·crete	*kCe*	con·fer	*kf*
con·crete·ly	*kCel*	con·fer·ee	*kfe*
con·cu·bine	*kcbin*	✓con·fer·ence	*kf /*
con·cur	*kc*	con·fess	*kf'*
con·cur·rent	*kC –*	con·fes·sion	*kfy*
con·cus·sion	*kcy*	con·fes·sor	*kfs*
con·demn	*kd*	con·fet·ti	*kf)*
con·dem·na·tion	*kdmy*	con·fide	*kfd*
con·dem·na·to·ry	*kdmly*	✓con·fi·dence	*kfd /*
con·den·sa·tion	*kd/y*	con·fi·dent	*kfd –*
con·dense	*kd /*	con·fi·den·tial	*kfdx*
con·dens·er	*kd V*	con·fig·u·ra·tion	*kfgy*
con·de·scend	*kds —*	con·fine	*kfi*
con·de·scend·ing·ly	*kds — l*	con·fine·ment	*kfi –*
con·de·scen·sion	*kdsy*	✓con·firm	*kf*
con·dign	*kdin*	con·fir·ma·tion	*kfy*

con·firm·a·tive		con·gru·ent	
con·fis·cate		con·gru·i·ty	
con·fis·ca·tion		con·gru·ous	
con·fla·gra·tion		con·ic	
✓con·flict		con·i·cal	
con·flic·tion		co·ni·fer	
con·flu·ence		co·nif·er·ous	
con·flu·ent		con·jec·tur·al	
con·form		✓con·jec·ture	
con·for·ma·tion		con·join	
con·form·ist		con·ju·gal	
con·form·i·ty		con·ju·gate	
con·found		con·ju·ga·tion	
con·frere		con·junc·tion	
con·front		con·junc·ti·va	
con·fuse		con·junc·ture	
con·fus·ed·ly		con·jure	
con·fu·sion		con·jur·er	
con·fu·ta·tion		✓con·nect	
con·fute		con·nec·tion	
con·geal		con·nec·tive	
✓con·gen·ial		con·nip·tion	
con·ge·ni·al·i·ty		con·niv·ance	
con·gen·i·tal		con·nive	
con·ge·ries		con·nois·seur	
con·gest		con·no·ta·tion	
con·ges·tion		con·not·a·tive	
con·glom·er·ate		con·note	
con·glom·er·a·tion		con·nu·bi·al	
con·grat·u·late		con·quer	
con·grat·u·la·tion		con·quer·or	
con·grat·u·la·to·ry		con·quest	
con·gre·gate		con·san·guin·e·ous	
con·gre·ga·tion		con·san·guin·i·ty	
con·gress		con·science	
con·gres·sion·al		con·sci·en·tious	
con·gress·man		con·scious	

Word	Outline		Word	Outline
con·scious·ness	_kx'_		con·sor·ti·um	_ksSe_
con·script	_ksCp_		con·spec·tus	_kscx_
con·scrip·tion	_ksCpy_		con·spic·u·ous	_kscx_
con·se·crate	_ksCa_		con·spir·a·cy	_kSse_
con·se·cra·tion	_ksCy_		con·spir·a·tor	_kS/_
con·sec·u·tive	_kscv_		con·spire	_ksu_
con·sen·sus	_ks/x_		con·sta·ble	_ksb_
✓con·sent	_ks—_		con·stab·u·lar·y	_ksbly_
con·se·quence	_ksg/_		con·stan·cy	_ks/_
con·se·quent	_ksg—_		con·stant	_ks—_
con·se·quen·tial	_ksgx_		con·stel·la·tion	_ksly_
✓con·se·quent·ly	_ksg—l_		con·ster·na·tion	_kSny_
con·ser·va·tion	_kSvy_		con·sti·pate	_kspa_
con·serv·a·tive	_kSvv_		con·sti·pa·tion	_kspy_
con·serv·a·to·ry	_kSvly_		con·stit·u·en·cy	_kslu/_
con·serve	_kSv_		con·stit·u·ent	_kslu—_
✓con·sid·er	_ks_		con·sti·tute	_kslu_
✓con·sid·er·a·ble	_ksb_		con·sti·tu·tion	_ksly_
✓con·sid·er·a·bly	_ksb_		con·sti·tu·tion·al·ly	_kslyl_
con·sid·er·ate	_ksl_		con·strain	_kSn_
con·sid·er·a·tion	_ksy_		con·straint	_kSa—_
✓con·sign	_ksun_		con·strict	_kSc_
✓con·sign·ee	_ksune_		con·stric·tion	_kScy_
✓con·sign·ment	_ksun—_		con·stric·tor	_kSc/_
con·sign·or	_ksun/_		con·struct	_kSc_
✓con·sist	_ks,_		✓con·struc·tion	_kScy_
con·sist·en·cy	_kss/_		con·struc·tive	_kScv_
con·sist·ent	_kss—_		con·strue	_kSu_
con·so·la·tion	_ksly_		con·sul	_ksl_
con·sol·a·to·ry	_kslly_		con·su·lar	_ksl._
con·sole	_ksl_		con·su·late	_ksll_
con·sol·i·date	_kslda_		con·sult	_ksll_
con·sol·i·da·tion	_ksldy_		con·sult·ant	_ksll—_
con·som·mé	_ksra_		con·sul·ta·tion	_kslly_
con·so·nance	_ksn/_		con·sume	_ksu_
con·so·nant	_ksn—_		✓con·sum·er	_ksu/_
con·sort	_ksl_		con·sum·mate	_ksra_

con·sum·ma·tion	*ksɯ*	con·tin·u·ance	*kʋ /*
con·sump·tion	*ksɯ*	con·tin·u·a·tion	*kʋ*
con·sump·tive	*ksɯv*	✓ con·tin·ue	*kʋ*
✓ con·tact	*klc*	con·ti·nu·i·ty	*kʋ)*
con·ta·gion	*klʝn*	con·tin·u·ous	*kʋx*
con·ta·gious	*klʝx*	con·tin·u·ous·ly	*kʋx*
✓ con·tain	*kln*	con·tin·u·um	*kʋ*
✓ con·tain·er	*kln/*	con·tort	*kʈ*
con·tam·i·nate	*klma*	con·tor·tion	*kʈ1*
con·tam·i·nant	*klm–*	con·tor·tion·ist	*kʈ1'*
con·tam·i·na·tion	*klmɥ*	con·tour	*klu*
con·temn	*kl⌒*	con·tra·band	*kʈb —*
con·tem·plate	*klpa*	con·tra·cep·tion	*kʈ ʸp1*
con·tem·pla·tion	*klpf*	✓ con·tract	*kc*
con·tem·po·ra·ne·ous	*klʈᵖⁿx*	con·trac·tile	*kcl*
con·tem·po·rar·y	*klʈᵖʸ*	con·trac·tion	*kc1*
con·tempt	*kl⌒*	con·trac·tor	*kc*
con·tempt·i·ble	*klrb*	con·tra·dict	*kʈdc*
con·temp·tu·ous	*klrx*	con·tra·dic·tion	*kʈdc1*
con·tend	*kl —*	con·tra·dic·to·ry	*kʈdcy*
con·tent	*kl –*	con·tral·to	*kʈelo*
con·ten·tion	*kly*	con·trap·tion	*kʈP1*
con·ten·tious	*klx*	con·tra·ri·e·ty	*kʈᵘ)*
con·tent·ment	*kl – –*	con·tra·ri·ness	*kʈy'*
con·ter·mi·nous	*kʈ mx*	con·tra·ri·wise	*kʈyɜ*
con·test	*kl,*	✓ con·tra·ry	*kʈy*
con·test·ant	*kls –*	✓ con·trast	*kʈ,*
con·text	*klx*	con·tra·vene	*kʈⁿn*
con·tex·ture	*klʋC*	con·tra·ven·tion	*kʈⁿy*
con·ti·gu·i·ty	*klgu)*	con·tre·temps	*kʈˡa*
con·tig·u·ous	*klgx*	✓ con·trib·ute	*kʈbu*
con·ti·nence	*kln /*	con·tri·bu·tion	*kʈby*
con·ti·nent	*kln –*	con·trib·u·tor	*kʈbu*
con·ti·nen·tal	*kln – l*	con·trib·u·to·ry	*kʈbly*
con·tin·gen·cy	*kly /*	con·trite	*kʈc*
con·tin·gent	*kly –*	con·tri·tion	*kʈ1*
✓ con·tin·u·al	*kul*	con·triv·ance	*kʈc /*

con·trive		con·vict	
✓con·trol		con·vic·tion	
con·trol·ler		✓con·vince	
con·tro·ver·sial		con·vinc·ing·ly	
con·tro·ver·sy		con·viv·i·al	
con·tro·vert		con·viv·i·al·i·ty	
con·tu·ma·cious		con·vo·ca·tion	
con·tum·e·ly		con·voke	
con·tuse		con·vo·lu·tion	
con·tu·sion		con·voy	
co·nun·drum		con·vulse	
con·va·lesce		con·vul·sion	
con·va·les·cence		con·vul·sive	
con·va·les·cent		cook	
con·vec·tion		cook·er·y	
con·vene		cook·y	
✓con·ven·ience		cool	
✓con·ven·ient		cool·ant	
con·vent		cool·ie	
con·ven·ti·cle		cool·ly	
con·ven·tion		cool·ness	
con·ven·tion·al		coop	
con·ven·tion·al·i·ty		co·op	
con·ven·tion·eer		coop·er	
con·verge		co·op·er·ate	
con·ver·gence		✓co·op·er·a·tion	
con·ver·sant		co·op·er·a·tive	
✓con·ver·sa·tion		co·opt	
con·ver·sa·tion·al		co·or·di·nate	
con·ver·sa·tion·al·ist		co·or·di·na·tion	
con·verse		cope	
con·ver·sion		co·pi·ous	
con·vert		✓cop·per	
con·vert·i·ble		cop·per·head	
con·vex		✓cop·per·plate	
con·vey		cop·pice	
con·vey·ance		cop·ra	

copse	*cps*	cor·o·ner	*Cn*
cop·u·la	*cpla*	cor·o·net	*Cnl*
cop·u·la·tive	*cplv*	cor·po·ral	*Cpl*
cop·y	*cpe*	cor·po·rate	*Cpt*
cop·y·book	*cpebc*	cor·po·ra·tion	*corp*
cop·y·hold·er	*cpehol*	cor·po·re·al	*Cpyl*
cop·y·ist	*cpe,*	corps	*co*
cop·y·right	*cperc*	corpse	*Cps*
co·quette	*ccl*	cor·pu·lence	*Cpl /*
co·quet·ry	*cc^e*	cor·pu·lent	*Cpl –*
cor·al	*Cl*	cor·pus	*Cpx*
cord	*Cd*	cor·pus·cle	*Cpsl*
cord·age	*Cdy*	cor·ral	*Cl*
cor·dial	*Cyl*	correct	*Kc*
cor·dial·i·ty	*Cyel)*	cor·rec·tion	*Kcy*
cor·don	*Cdn*	cor·rect·ly	*Kcl*
core	*co*	cor·rec·tive	*Kcv*
co·re·spond·ent	*crs — –*	cor·re·late	*Cla*
cork	*Cc*	cor·re·la·tion	*Cly*
cork·screw	*CcsCu*	cor·rel·a·tive	*Clv*
cor·mo·rant	*C^)–*	cor·re·spond	*Cs—*
corn	*Cn*	cor·re·spond·ence	*Cs — /*
corn·cob	*Cncb*	cor·re·spond·ent	*Cs — –*
cor·ne·a	*Cna*	cor·ri·dor	*Cd*
cor·ner	*Cn*	cor·rob·o·rate	*CBa*
cor·ner·stone	*CNsn*	cor·rob·o·ra·tion	*CBy*
cor·ner·wise	*CNi–z*	cor·rode	*Cd*
cor·net	*Cnl*	cor·ro·sion	*Cy*
corn·field	*Cnfld*	cor·ro·sive	*Csv*
cor·nice	*Cns*	cor·ru·gate	*Cga*
corn·stalk	*Cnsc*	cor·ru·ga·tion	*Cgy*
corn·starch	*CnSC*	cor·rupt	*Cp*
cor·nu·co·pi·a	*Cncpa*	cor·rupt·i·ble	*Cpb*
co·rol·la	*crla*	cor·rup·tion	*Cpy*
cor·ol·lar·y	*Cly*	cor·sage	*Csz*
co·ro·na	*crna*	cor·sair	*Csa*
cor·o·na·tion	*Cny*	cor·set	*Csl*

cor·tege		coun·ter·claim	
cor·tex		coun·ter·feit	
cor·ti·sone		coun·ter·feit·er	
cor·us·cate		coun·ter·ir·ri·tant	
cor·us·ca·tion		coun·ter·mand	
cor·vette		coun·ter·pane	
co·sine		coun·ter·point	
cos·met·ic		coun·ter·sign	
cos·me·tol·o·gist		count·ess	
cos·mic		count·less	
cos·mol·o·gy		coun·try	
cos·mo·pol·i·tan		coun·try·side	
cos·mop·o·lite		coun·ty	
cos·mos		coup	
√cost		coup d' e·tat	
√cost·ly		cou·pe	
cos·tume		cou·ple	
cos·tum·er		cou·pler	
cot		cou·plet	
co·te·rie		cou·pon	
cot·tage		cour·age	
cot·ton		cou·ra·geous	
couch		cour·i·er	
cou·gar		course	
cough		court	
could		court·e·ous	
couldn't		cour·te·ous·ly	
coun·cil		cour·te·san	
coun·cil·man		cour·te·sy	
coun·sel		cour·ti·er	
coun·se·lor		court·room	
count		court·ship	
count·down		cous·in	
coun·te·nance		cove	
count·er		cov·e·nant	
coun·ter·act		cov·er	
coun·ter·bal·ance		cov·er·age	

cov·er·all		crank·i·ness	
cov·er·let		crank·y	
cov·ert		cran·ny	
cov·et		crash	
cov·et·ous		crass	
cov·ey		crate	
cow		cra·ter	
cow·ard		cra·vat	
cow·ard·ice		crave	
cow·er		cra·ven	
cowl		crawl	
cowl·ing		cray·fish	
co-work·er		cray·on	
cox·comb		craze	
cox·swain		cra·zi·ly	
coy		cra·zi·ness	
coy·ote		cra·zy	
coz·en		creak	
co·zy		cream	
crab		cream·er·y	
crab ap·ple		cream·y	
crack		crease	
crack·er		cre·ate	
crack·le		cre·a·tion	
crack·pot		cre·a·tor	
cra·dle		crea·ture	
craft		cre·dence	
crafts·man		cre·den·tial	
craft·y		cred·i·bil·i·ty	
crag		cred·i·ble	
cram		cred·it	
cramp		cred·it·a·ble	
cran·ber·y		cred·i·tor	
crane		cre·do	
cra·ni·al		cre·du·li·ty	
cra·ni·um		cred·u·lous	
crank		creed	

creek	~cec~	criss·cross	~csC'~
creel	~cel~	cri·te·ri·on	~clyn~
creep	~cep~	crit·ic	~clc~
cre·mate	~cra~	crit·i·cal	~clcl~
cre·ma·to·ry	~crly~	crit·i·cise	~clsz~
Cre·ole	~cel~	crit·i·cism	~clsz~
cre·o·sote	~ceso~	cri·tique	~clc~
crepe	~cap~	croak	~coc~
crept	~cp~	cro·chet	~cSa~
cre·pus·cu·lar	~cpxcl~	crock	~cc~
cre·scen·do	~cS—o~	crock·er·y	~ccy~
cres·cent	~cs-~	croc·o·dile	~ccdl~
cress	~c'~	cro·cus	~ccx~
crest	~c,~	crone	~cn~
crest·fall·en	~csfln~	cro·ny	~cne~
cre·ta·ceous	~clx~	crook	~cc~
cre·tonne	~cln~	croon	~cn~
cre·vasse	~cvs~	croon·er	~cn'~
crev·ice	~cvs~	crop	~cp~
crew	~cu~	crop·per	~cp'~
crew·el	~cul~	cro·quet	~cca~
crib	~cb~	cro·quette	~ccl~
crib·bage	~cby~	cross	~c'~
crick·et	~ccl~	cross·o·ver	~csO~
crime	~cu~	cross·ques·tion	~csg~
crim·i·nal	~cml~	cross·road	~csrd~
crim·i·nal·ly	~cml~	cross·walk	~csrc~
crim·i·nol·o·gy	~cmlje~	crotch	~cC~
crimp	~crp~	crotch·et·y	~cC)~
crim·son	~czn~	crouch	~cuC~
cringe	~cy~	croup	~cup~
crin·kle	~cgl~	crou·pi·er	~cpe~
crin·o·line	~cnln~	crou·ton	~cln~
crip·ple	~cp~	crow	~co~
cri·ses	~csz~	crow·bar	~cobr~
cri·sis	~css~	crowd	~urd~
crisp	~cs~	crown	~cnn~

cru·cial		cu·bi·cle	
cru·ci·ble		cub·ist	
cru·ci·fix		cu·bit	
cru·ci·fix·ion		cuck·old	
cru·ci·fy		cuck·oo	
crude		cu·cum·ber	
cru·di·ty		cud	
cru·el		cud·dle	
cru·el·ly		cud·gel	
cru·el·ty		cue	
cru·et		cuff	
cruise		cui·sine	
cruis·er		cul-de-sac	
crul·ler		cu·li·nar·y	
crumb		cull	
crum·ble		cul·mi·nate	
crum·pet		cul·mi·na·tion	
crum·ple		cul·pa·bil·ity	
crunch		cul·pa·ble	
cru·sade		cul·prit	
crush		cult	
crust		cul·ti·vate	
crus·ta·cean		cul·ti·va·tion	
crutch		cul·ti·va·tor	
crux		cul·tur·al	
cry		cul·ture	
crypt		cul·vert	
cryp·tic		cum·ber·some	
cryp·to·gram		cum·brous	
cryp·tog·ra·phy		cum·mer·bund	
crys·tal		cu·mu·la·tion	
crys·tal·line		cu·mu·la·tive	
crys·tal·lize		cu·mu·lus	
cub		cu·ne·i·form	
cub·by·hole		cun·ning·ly	
cube		cup	
cu·bic		cup·bear·er	

cup·board	*cBd*	cur·vi·lin·e·ar	*Cvlne*
cup·ful	*cpl*	cush·ion	*cy*
cu·pid	*cpd*	cusp	*cs*
cu·pid·i·ty	*cpd)*	cus·pi·dor	*csdo*
cu·po·la	*cpla*	cus·tard	*cSd*
cur	*c*	cus·to·di·an	*csden*
cur·a·ble	*cub*	cus·to·dy	*csde*
cu·rate	*Ca*	cus·tom	*cs*
cu·ra·tor	*Ca*	cus·tom·ar·y	*csry*
curb	*Cb*	✓ cus·tom·er	*K*
curb·stone	*Cbsn*	✓ cut	*cl*
curd	*Cd*	cute	*cu*
cur·dle	*Cdl*	cu·ti·cle	*clcl*
cure	*cu*	cut·lass	*cll'*
cu·rette	*cul*	cut·ler·y	*clly*
cur·few	*Cfu*	cut·let	*cll'*
cu·ri·o	*cyo*	✓ cut·ter	*c*
cu·ri·os·i·ty	*cys)*	cut·off	*clof*
cu·ri·ous	*cyx*	/ cut·out	*clou*
curl	*Cl*	cut·throat	*clo*
cur·lew	*Clu*	cy·an·am·ide	*sun rd*
curl·i·cue	*Clcu*	cy·an·ic	*sinc*
curl·y	*Cl*	cy·an·ide	*sind*
cur·rent	*C–*	cy·an·o·gen	*sinjn*
cur·ren·cy	*C/*	cy·a·no·sis	*sinss*
cur·ric·u·lum	*Ccl*	✓ cy·cle	*scl*
cur·ry	*cy*	cy·clom·e·ter	*sc*
cur·ry·comb	*cyco*	cy·clone	*scn*
curse	*Cs*	cy·clo·ra·ma	*sCra*
cur·sive	*Csv*	cy·clo·tron	*scTn*
cur·so·ry	*Csy*	cyl·in·der	*sl*
curt	*Cl*	cyl·in·dri·cal	*sl — rcl*
cur·tail	*Cll*	cym·bal	*srb*
cur·tain	*Cln*	cyn·ic	*snc*
curt·sy	*Clse*	cyn·i·cal	*sncl*
cur·va·ture	*CvC*	cyn·i·cism	*snsz*
curve	*Cv*	cy·no·sure	*snSu*

cy·press	*sP'*	czar	*zr*
cyst	*s,*	czar·e·vitch	*zvC*
cys·tic	*ssc*	cza·ri·na	*zna*
cyst·oid	*ssyd*	Czech	*Cc*

dab	*db*	dain·ti·ly	*da-l,*
dab·ble	*db*	dain·ti·ness	*da-e'*
dachs·hund	*deh-*	dain·ty	*da-e*
da·coit	*dcyl*	dair·y	*dy*
Da·cron	*dCn*	da·is	*das*
dac·tyl	*dcl*	dai·sy	*dze*
dad	*dd*	dale	*dal*
dad·dy	*dde*	dal·li·ance	*dle /*
da·do	*ddo*	dal·ly	*dl*
daf·fo·dil	*dfdl*	dam	*d*
daft	*df*	dam·age	*dy*
dag·ger	*dg*	dam·age·a·ble	*dryb*
da·guerre·o·type	*dGlp*	dam·a·scene	*drsn*
dahl·ia	*dlya*	dam·ask	*drsc*
dai·ly	*dl*	dame	*da*

damn		da·tum	
dam·na·ble		daub	
dam·na·tion		daugh·ter	
damp		daugh·ter-in-law	
damp·er		daunt	
dam·sel		daunt·less	
dance		dau·phin	
danc·er		dav·en·port	
dan·de·li·on		dav·it	
dan·der		daw·dle	
dan·dle		dawn	
dan·druff		day	
dan·dy		day·break	
Dane		day·dream	
dan·ger		day·light	
dan·ger·ous		day·time	
dan·gle		daze	
dank		daz·zle	
dan·seuse		dea·con	
dap·per		de·ac·ti·vate	
dap·ple		dead	
dare		dead·beat	
✓ dark		dead·en	
dark·en		dead·line	
dark·er		dead·li·ness	
dark·ness		dead·lock	
dark·room		dead·ly	
dar·ling		dead·weight	
darn		dead·wood	
dart		deaf	
dash		deaf·en	
dash·board		deaf·ness	
das·tard		deal	
das·tard·ly		deal·er	
da·ta		dean	
date		dear	
date·line		dear·er	

dear·ly		de·cap·i·tate	
dearth		de·cath·lon	
death		de·cay	
death·bed		de·cease	
death·blow		de·ce·dent	
death·less		de·ceit	
death·like		de·ceit·ful	
death·ly		de·ceiv·a·ble	
death·watch		de·ceive	
de·ba·cle		de·ceiv·er	
de·bar		de·cel·er·ate	
de·bark		De·cem·ber	
de·base		de·cen·cy	
de·bat·a·ble		de·cent	
de·bate		de·cen·tral·ize	
de·bauch		de·cep·tion	
de·bauch·er·y		de·cep·tive	
de·ben·ture		de·ci·bel	
de·bil·i·tate		de·cide	
de·bil·i·ty		de·cid·ed·ly	
deb·it		de·cid·u·ous	
deb·o·nair		dec·i·mal	
√ de·bris		dec·i·mate	
debt		de·ci·pher	
debt·or		√ de·ci·sion	
de·bug		de·ci·sive	
de·bunk		deck	
de·but		de·claim	
deb·u·tante		de·claim·er	
dec·ade		de·clar·a·ble	
de·ca·dence		dec·la·ra·tion	
de·ca·dent		de·clar·a·tive	
de·cal·co·ma·ni·a		de·clar·a·to·ry	
dec·a·logue		√ de·clare	
de·camp		de·clen·sion	
de·cant		de·clin·a·ble	
de·cant·er		√ de·cline	

de·cliv·i·ty		de·fea·si·ble	
de·code		de·feat	
de·col·le·té		de·fect	
de·com·pose		de·fec·tive	
de·com·po·si·tion		de·fec·tor	
de·com·pres·sion		de·fend	
de·con·tam·i·nate		de·fend·er	
de·cor		de·fense	
dec·o·rate		de·fen·sive	
dec·o·ra·tion		de·fer	
dec·o·ra·tor		def·er·ence	
dec·o·rous		def·er·en·tial	
de·co·rum		de·fer·ment	
de·coy		de·fi·ance	
de·crease		de·fi·ant	
de·cree		de·fi·cien·cy	
de·crep·it		de·fi·cient	
de·cry		def·i·cit	
de·cum·bent		de·file	
ded·i·cate		de·file·ment	
ded·i·ca·tion		de·fin·a·ble	
de·duce		de·fine	
de·duc·i·ble		def·i·nite	
de·duct		def·i·nite·ly	
de·duc·tion		def·i·ni·tion	
deed		de·flate	
deem		de·flect	
deep		de·flec·tion	
deep·er		de·form	
deer		de·form·i·ty	
de·face		de·fraud	
de fac·to		de·fray	
de·fal·cate		de·funct	
de·fal·ca·tion		de·fy	
def·a·ma·tion		de·gen·er·a·cy	
de·fame		de·gen·er·ate	
de·fault		de·gen·er·a·tion	

deg·ra·da·tion		del·ta	
de·grade		de·lude	
de·gree		del·uge	
de·hy·drate		de·lu·sion	
de·ice		✓ de·luxe	
de·ic·er		delve	
de·i·fy		de·mag·ne·tize	
deign		dem·a·gogue	
de·i·ty		✓ de·mand	
de·jec·tion		de·mar·cate	
de·ju·re		de·mar·ca·tion	
de·lay		de·mean	
de·lec·ta·ble		de·mean·or	
del·e·gate		de·ment	
del·e·ga·tion		de·men·ti·a	
✓ de·lete		de·mer·it	
del·e·te·ri·ous		dem·i·god	
de·le·tion		de·mi·john	
delft		de·mise	
de·lib·er·ate		dem·i·tasse	
de·lib·er·a·tion		de·mo·bi·lize	
del·i·ca·cy		de·moc·ra·cy	
del·i·cate		dem·o·crat	
del·i·ca·tes·sen		de·mog·ra·pher	
de·li·cious		de·mol·ish	
de·light		dem·o·li·tion	
de·lin·e·ate		de·mon	
de·lin·e·a·tion		de·mon·e·tize	
de·lin·e·a·tor		de·mo·ni·ac	
de·lin·quen·cy		de·mon·ic	
de·lin·quent		✓ dem·on·strate	
de·lir·i·ous		✓ dem·on·stra·tion	
de·lir·i·um		de·mon·stra·tive	
✓ de·liv·er		de·mon·stra·tor	
de·liv·er·ance		de·mor·al·ize	
✓ de·liv·er·y		de·mote	
dell		de·mur	

Word	Shorthand
de·note	
de·noue·ment	
de·nounce	
dense	
den·si·ty	
dent	
den·tal	
den·ti·frice	
den·tist	
den·tist·ry	
den·ture	
de·nude	
de·nun·ci·ate	
de·nun·ci·a·tion	
de·nun·ci·a·to·ry	
de·ny	
de·o·dor·ant	
de·part	
de·part·ment	
de·par·ture	
de·pend	
de·pend·a·ble	
de·pend·ent	
de·pict	
de·pic·tion	
de·pil·a·to·ry	
de·plete	

Word	Shorthand
de·ple·tion	
de·plor·a·ble	
de·plore	
de·ploy	
de·po·nent	
de·pop·u·late	
de·pop·u·la·tion	
de·port	
de·por·ta·tion	
de·port·ment	
de·pose	
de·pos·it	
dep·o·si·tion	
de·pos·i·tor	
de·pos·i·to·ry	
de·pot	
de·prave	
de·prav·i·ty	
dep·re·cate	
dep·re·ca·to·ry	
de·pre·ci·ate	
de·pre·ci·a·tion	
dep·re·da·tion	
de·press	
de·press·ant	
de·pres·sion	
dep·ri·va·tion	
de·prive	
depth	
dep·u·ta·tion	
de·pute	
dep·u·tize	
dep·u·ty	
de·rail	
de·range	
der·by	
der·e·lict	

der·e·lic·tion	de·sir·ous
de·ride	de·sist
de·ri·sion	desk
de·ri·sive	des·o·late
de·riv·a·tive	des·o·la·tion
✓de·rive	de·spair
der·ma·tol·o·gy	des·per·a·do
der·o·gate	des·per·ate
de·rog·a·to·ry	des·per·a·tion
der·rick	de·spi·ca·ble
der·vish	de·spise
des·cant	✓de·spite
de·scend	de·spoil
de·scend·ant	de·spond
de·scent	de·spond·ent
de·scribe	des·pot
✓de·scrip·tion	des·pot·ic
✓de·scrip·tive	des·pot·ism
de·scry	des·sert
des·e·crate	des·ti·na·tion
des·e·cra·tion	des·tine
de·seg·re·gate	des·ti·ny
des·ert	des·ti·tute
de·sert·er	des·ti·tu·tion
de·ser·tion	de·stroy
de·serve	de·stroy·er
des·ic·cant	de·struct
des·ic·cate	de·struc·tion
des·ic·ca·tion	de·struc·tive
de·sid·er·a·ta	de·struc·tor
de·sid·er·a·tum	des·ul·to·ry
✓de·sign	de·tach
des·ig·nate	de·tach·ment
des·ig·na·tion	de·tail
de·sign·er	de·tain
de·sir·a·ble	de·tect
de·sire	de·tec·tion

de·tec·tive	*dlcv*	de·vise	*dvz*
de·tec·tor	*dlc*	de·vi·tal·ize	*dvilz*
de·ten·tion	*dly*	de·void	*dvyd*
de·ter	*de*	de·volve	*dvlv*
de·ter·gent	*dT-*	de·vote	*dvo*
de·te·ri·o·rate	*dtlfa*	dev·o·tee	*dv)*
de·te·ri·o·ra·tion	*dtlf*	de·vo·tion	*dvy*
de·ter·mi·na·ble	*d mb*	de·vour	*dvr*
de·ter·mi·na·tion	*d my*	de·vout	*dvvl*
✓ de·ter·mine	*d m*	dew	*du*
de·ter·rent	*dT-*	dew·y	*due*
de·test	*dl,*	✓ dex·ter·i·ty	*deT)*
de·test·a·ble	*dlsb*	dex·ter·ous	*deTx*
de·tes·ta·tion	*dlsy*	dex·trose	*deTs*
de·throne	*d n*	dhow	*d*
det·i·nue	*dlnu*	di·a·be·tes	*diblz*
det·o·nate	*dlna*	di·a·bet·ic	*diblc*
det·o·na·tion	*dlny*	di·a·ble·rie	*deBe*
det·o·na·tor	*dlna*	di·a·bol·ic	*diblc*
✓ de·tour	*dlu*	di·a·cri·ti·cal	*diClcl*
de·tract	*dTc*	di·a·dem	*dids*
de·trac·tion	*dTy*	di·ag·nose	*digns*
det·ri·ment	*dT-*	di·ag·no·sis	*dignss*
det·ri·men·tal	*dT-l*	di·ag·nos·tic	*dignsc*
deuce	*dus*	di·ag·nos·ti·cian	*dignsy*
✓ dev·as·tate	*dvsa*	✓ di·ag·o·nal	*dignl*
dev·as·ta·tion	*dvsy*	di·a·gram	*dig*
✓ de·vel·op	*dv*	di·a·gram·mat·ic	*diglc*
✓ de·vel·op·ment	*dv-*	di·al	*dil*
de·vi·ate	*dva*	di·a·lect	*dilc*
de·vi·a·tion	*dvy*	di·a·logue	*dilg*
de·vi·ant	*dve-*	✓ di·am·e·ter	*div*
de·vice	*dvs*	di·a·met·ric	*divTc*
dev·il	*dvl*	di·a·met·ri·cal·ly	*divTcl*
dev·il·ish	*dvlS*	✓ di·a·mond	*dis-*
dev·il·ment	*dvl-*	di·a·per	*dip*
de·vi·ous	*dvr*	di·aph·a·nous	*difnx*

di·a·phragm

di·ar·rhe·a

di·a·ry

di·a·ther·my

di·a·ton·ic

di·a·tribe

dice

di·chot·o·my

dick·er

dic·ta

Dic·ta·phone

dic·tate

dic·ta·tion

dic·ta·tor

dic·ta·to·ri·al

dic·tion

dic·tion·ar·y

dic·tum

did

didn't

di·dac·tic

die

di·e·lec·tric

die·mak·er

die·sel

di·et

di·e·tar·y

di·e·tet·ic

di·e·ti·tion

√dif·fer

√dif·fer·ence

√dif·fer·ent

dif·fer·en·ti·ate

dif·fer·ent·ly

√dif·fi·cult

√dif·fi·cul·ty

dif·fi·dence

dif·fi·dent

dif·frac·tion

dif·fuse

dif·fu·sion

dig

di·gest

di·gest·i·ble

di·ges·tion

dig·it

dig·i·tal

dig·i·ta·lis

dig·ni·fy

dig·ni·tar·y

dig·ni·ty

di·gress

di·gres·sion

di·gres·sive

dike

di·lap·i·date

di·lap·i·da·tion

di·late

di·la·tion

dil·a·tory

di·lem·ma

dil·et·tan·te

dil·i·gence

dil·i·gent

dil·ly·dal·ly

di·lute

di·lu·tion

dim

dime

√di·men·sion

√di·min·ish

dim·i·nu·tion

di·min·u·tive

dim·i·ty

dim·ly		dis·ad·van·tage	
dim·mer		dis·af·fect	
dim·ple		dis·a·gree	
din		dis·al·low	
dine		dis·ap·pear	
din·er		dis·ap·point	
din·gy		dis·ap·pro·ba·tion	
din·gus		dis·ap·prove	
din·ner		dis·arm	
di·no·saur		dis·ar·range	
dint		dis·ar·ray	
di·o·cese		dis·as·sem·ble	
di·ode		dis·as·so·ci·ate	
dip		dis·as·ter	
diph·the·ri·a		dis·as·trous	
diph·thong		dis·a·vow	
di·plex·er		dis·band	
di·plo·ma		dis·bar	
di·plo·ma·cy		dis·be·lief	
dip·lo·mat		dis·be·lieve	
dip·per		dis·burse	
dire		dis·burse·ment	
✓di·rect		disc	
✓di·rec·tion		dis·card	
✓di·rec·tive		dis·cern	
✓di·rec·tly		dis·cern·i·ble	
di·rec·tor		dis·charge	
di·rec·to·ry		dis·ci·ple	
dire·ful		dis·ci·plin·ar·y	
dirge		dis·ci·pline	
dir·i·gi·ble		dis·claim	
dirt		dis·claim·er	
dirt·i·ness		dis·close	
dirt·y		dis·clo·sure	
✓dis·a·bil·i·ty		dis·col·or	
dis·a·ble		dis·com·bob·u·late	
dis·a·buse		dis·com·fit	

dis·com·fi·ture		dis·fig·ure	
dis·com·fort		dis·fran·chise	
dis·com·mode		dis·gorge	
dis·com·pose		dis·grace	
dis·com·po·sure		dis·grun·tle	
dis·con·cert		dis·guise	
dis·con·nect		dis·gust	
dis·con·so·late		dish	
dis·con·tent		dis·ha·bille	
dis·con·tin·ue		dis·hear·ten	
dis·cord		di·shev·el	
dis·count		dis·hon·est	
dis·cour·age		dis·hon·or	
dis·course		dish·wash·er	
dis·cour·te·ous		dis·il·lu·sion	
dis·cov·er		dis·in·cli·na·tion	
dis·cov·er·er		dis·in·fect	
dis·cred·it		dis·in·gen·u·ous	
dis·creet		dis·in·her·it	
dis·crep·an·cy		dis·in·te·grate	
dis·cre·tion		dis·in·ter	
dis·crim·i·nate		dis·in·ter·est·ed	
dis·crim·i·na·tion		dis·join	
dis·cur·sive		dis·joint	
✓ dis·cuss		dis·junc·tion	
dis·cussed		disk	
✓ dis·cus·sion		dis·like	
dis·dain		dis·lo·cate	
dis·ease		dis·lodge	
dis·em·bark		dis·loy·al	
dis·em·bod·y		dis·mal	
dis·en·chant		dis·man·tle	
dis·en·cum·ber		dis·mast	
dis·en·gage		dis·may	
dis·en·tan·gle		dis·mem·ber	
dis·es·teem		dis·miss	
dis·fa·vor		dis·mount	

dis·o·be·di·ent	*dsobde–*	dis·sat·is·fac·tion	*dssal*
dis·o·bey	*dsoba*	dis·sect	*dsc*
dis·or·der	*dsO*	dis·sem·ble	*dsrb*
dis·or·gan·i·za·tion	*dsoq*	dis·sem·i·nate	*dsma*
dis·or·gan·ize	*dsoq*	dis·sen·sion	*dsj*
dis·own	*dson*	dis·sent	*ds–*
dis·par·age	*dSj*	dis·ser·ta·tion	*dSlj*
dis·pa·rate	*dSl*	dis·serv·ice	*dSvs*
dis·par·i·ty	*dS)*	dis·si·dent	*dsd–*
dis·pas·sion·ate	*dsjl*	dis·sim·i·lar	*dsrl*
✓ dis·patch	*dsC*	dis·sim·u·late	*dsrla*
dis·pel	*dsl*	dis·si·pate	*dspa*
dis·pen·sa·ry	*ds/y*	dis·si·pa·tion	*dspj*
dis·pense	*ds/*	dis·so·ci·ate	*dsSa*
dis·perse	*dSo*	dis·sol·u·ble	*dslb*
dis·pir·it	*dSl*	dis·so·lute	*dslu*
dis·place	*dspl*	✓ dis·solve	*dzlv*
dis·play	*dsa*	dis·so·nant	*dsn–*
dis·please	*dsp*	dis·suade	*dsvd*
dis·port	*dSl*	dis·sua·sion	*dsj*
dis·pose	*dsz*	dis·taff	*dsf*
dis·po·si·tion	*dszj*	✓ dis·tance	*ds/*
dis·pos·sess	*dsz'*	✓ dis·tant	*ds–*
dis·pro·por·tion	*dSPj*	dis·taste	*dsa,*
dis·prove	*dsv*	dis·taste·ful	*dssf*
dis·pu·ta·tious	*dSlx*	dis·tem·per	*dsrp*
✓ dis·pute	*dsu*	dis·tend	*ds——*
dis·qual·i·fy	*dsqlf*	dis·ten·tion	*dsj*
dis·qui·et	*dsqil*	dis·till	*dsl*
dis·qui·si·tion	*dsqzj*	dis·til·late	*dsla*
dis·re·gard	*dsrGd*	dis·till·er	*dsl*
dis·re·pair	*dsrpa*	dis·tinct	*dsq*
dis·rep·u·ta·ble	*dsrplb*	✓ dis·tinc·tion	*dsqj*
dis·re·pute	*dsrpu*	✓ dis·tinct·ly	*dsql*
✓ dis·re·spect	*dsrsc*	✓ dis·tin·guish	*dsqrS*
dis·robe	*dsrb*	dis·tort	*dSl*
dis·rupt	*dsrp*	dis·tract	*dSc*

dis·traint		diz·zi·ness	
dis·traught		diz·zy	
dis·tress		do	
dis·trib·ute		do·cile	
dis·tri·bu·tion		do·cil·i·ty	
dis·trib·u·tor		dock	
dis·trict		dock·et	
dis·trust		doc·tor	
dis·turb		doc·tor·ate	
dis·u·nite		doc·trine	
dis·un·i·ty		doc·u·ment	
dis·use		doc·u·men·ta·ry	
ditch		dod·der	
dith·er		dodge	
dit·to		doe	
di·ur·nal		does	
di·va		doesn't	
di·van		dog	
dive		doge	
di·verge		dog·ger·el	
di·ver·gence		dog·ma	
di·verse		dog·mat·ic	
di·ver·si·fy		doi·ly	
di·ver·sion		do·ing	
di·vert		dol·drums	
di·vest		dole·ful	
di·vide		dole	
div·i·dend		doll	
di·vid·er		dol·lar	
div·i·na·tion		dol·man	
di·vine		do·lor	
di·vis·i·bil·i·ty		dol·or·ous	
di·vis·i·ble		dol·phin	
di·vi·sion		dolt	
di·vorce		do·main	
div·ot		dome	
di·vulge		do·mes·tic	

do·mes·ti·cate	*dsca*	doubt·ful	*dul*
do·mes·tic·i·ty	*drss)	doubt·less	*dull*
dom·i·cile	*drsl*	dough	*do*
✓dom·i·nant	*dm–*	dough·boy	*doby*
dom·i·nate	*dma*	dough·nut	*donl*
dom·i·na·tion	*dmy*	dove	*dv (do)*
dom·i·neer	*dme*	dove·tail	*dvll*
do·min·ion	*dmn*	dow·a·ger	*dvg*
dom·i·no	*dmo*	dow·el	*dvl*
don	*dn*	dow·er	*dv*
✓do·nate	*dna*	down	*dvn*
✓do·na·tion	*dny*	down·cast	*dvnc,*
done	*dn*	down·fall	*dvnfal*
don·key	*dge*	down·hill	*dvnhl*
do·nor	*dn*	down·pour	*dvnpo*
don't	*do–*	down·range	*dvnry*
doom	*du*	down·right	*dvnri*
dooms·day	*dusd*	down·stairs	*dvnsas*
✓door	*do*	down·town	*dvnln*
door·way	*dowa*	down·ward	*dvnld*
Dopp·ler	*dp*	dow·ry	*dvre*
dor·mant	*D–*	dox·ol·o·gy	*dolje*
dor·mer	*Dv*	doze	*dz*
dor·mi·to·ry	*Drly*	doz·en	*dzn (dz)*
dor·sal	*Dsl*	drab	*db*
dor·y	*dy*	drach·ma	*dcra*
dos·age	*dsy*	draft	*df*
dose	*dos*	drafts·man	*dfs–*
dos·sier	*dsa*	drag	*dg*
dot	*dl*	drag·net	*dgnl*
dot·age	*dly*	drag·o·man	*dg–*
dote	*do*	drag·on	*dgn*
✓dou·ble	*db*	drag·on·fly	*dgnfi*
dou·blet	*dbl*	dra·goon	*dgn*
dou·bloon	*dbn*	drain	*dn*
dou·bly	*db*	drain·age	*dny*
doubt	*dvl*	drain·pipe	*dnpp*

dram		drink·a·ble	
dra·ma		drink·er	
dra·mat·ic		drip	
dram·a·tist		drive	
dram·a·tize		dri·vel	
drank		driv·er	
drape		drive·way	
dra·per·y		driz·zle	
dras·tic		droll	
draw		droll·er·y	
draw·back		drom·e·dar·y	
draw·bridge		drone	
draw·er		drool	
drawl		droop	
drawn		drip	
dray		drop	
dread		drop·sy	
dread·ful		dross	
dread·nought		drought	
dream		drove	
dream·er		drown	
dream·i·ly		drow·si·ness	
drear·i·ly		drow·sy	
drear·y		drub	
dredge		drudge	
dreg		drudg·er·y	
drench		drug	
dress		drug·gist	
dress·er		drug·store	
dress·mak·er		drum	
drew		drum·stick	
drib·ble		drunk	
dri·er		drunk·ard	
drift		drunk·en	
drift·wood		dry	
drill		dry·ad	
drink		dry·er	

dry·ly	_del_	dun·ga·ree	_dge_
dry·ness	_di'_	dun·geon	_dyn_
du·al	_dul_	dunk	_dg_
dub	_db_	du·o·dec·i·mal	_dvds·l_
du·bi·ous	_dbx_	du·o·de·nal	_dudnl_
du·cal	_dcl_	du·o·de·num	_dudn_
duc·at	_dcl_	dupe	_dup_
duch·ess	_dC'_	du·plex	_dpx_
duch·y	_dCe_	✓ du·pli·cate	_dpca (dpcl)_
duck	_dc_	du·pli·ca·tion	_dpoj_
duck·ling	_dcq_	du·pli·ca·tor	_dpca_
duct	_dc_	du·plic·i·ty	_dps)_
duc·tile	_dcl_	✓ du·ra·bil·i·ty	_Db)_
dud	_dd_	✓ du·ra·ble	_Db_
dudg·eon	_dyn_	dur·ance	_D/_
due	_du_	du·ra·tion	_Dj_
du·el	_dul_	du·ress	_D'_
du·el·ist	_dul,_	dur·ing	_du_
du·en·na	_duna_	dusk	_dsc_
du·et	_dul_	dust	_d,_
duf·fer	_df_	dust·cloth	_dscl_
dug	_dq_	dust·er	_dS_
duke	_duc_	Dutch	_dC_
duke·dom	_dcd_	du·ti·a·ble	_dleb_
dul·cet	_dlsl_	du·ti·ful	_dlf_
dul·ci·mer	_dls_	du·ty	_du)_
dull	_dl_	dwarf	_dif_
dull·ard	_dlCd_	dwell	_dwl_
dull·ness	_dl'_	dwell·er	_dwl_
du·ly	_dul_	dwin·dle	_dw — l_
dumb	_dn_	dye	_du_
dum·bell	_drbl_	dye·stuff	_dusf_
dum·my	_dre_	dyke	_dic_
dump	_drp_	dy·nam·ic	_dinrc_
dump·ling	_dipq_	dy·na·mite	_dinru_
dun	_dn_	dy·na·mo	_dinro_
dunce	_d/_	dy·nas·ty	_dins)_

dys·en·ter·y	*ds–y*	dys·pep·tic	*dspc*
dys·pep·sia	*dspSa*		

each	*eC*	earth·quake	*Elgc*
ea·ger	*eg*	earth·ward	*Elld*
ea·ger·ness	*eg'*	ease	*ez*
ea·gle	*egl*	ea·sel	*ezl*
ear	*E*	ease·ment	*ez–*
ear·drum	*ED*	✓eas·i·er	*ez/*
earl	*El*	✓eas·i·est	*ez,*
✓ear·li·er	*El*	✓eas·i·ly	*ezl*
✓ear·li·est	*El,*	east	*E*
ear·ly	*El*	East·er	*E/*
ear·mark	*Elc*	east·ern	*Ern*
earn	*En*	east·ward	*Eld*
ear·nest	*En,*	eas·y	*ez*
ear·ring	*Eg*	eas·y·go·ing	*ezg*
ear·shot	*ESl*	eat	*el*
earth	*El*	eaves	*evz*
earth·ly	*Ell*	ebb	*eb*

eb·on·y		ef·face·ment	
e·bul·li·ent		ef·fect	
ec·cen·tric		ef·fec·tive	
ec·cen·tric·i·ty		ef·fec·tu·al	
ec·cle·si·as·tic		ef·fec·tu·ate	
ech·e·lon		ef·fem·i·nate	
ech·o		ef·fer·vesce	
é·clair		ef·fer·ves·cent	
é·clat		ef·fete	
ec·lec·tic		ef·fi·ca·cious	
e·clipse		ef·fi·ca·cy	
e·co·nom·ic		ef·fi·cien·cy	
e·con·o·mist		ef·fi·cient	
e·con·o·my		ef·fi·cient·ly	
ec·sta·sy		ef·fi·gy	
ec·stat·ic		ef·flo·res·cent	
ec·u·men·i·cal		ef·flu·vi·um	
ec·ze·ma		ef·fort	
ed·dy		ef·fron·ter·y	
edge		ef·ful·gent	
edge·ways		ef·fu·sion	
ed·i·ble		ef·fu·sive	
e·dict		egg	
ed·i·fi·ca·tion		egg·head	
ed·i·fice		egg·nog	
ed·i·fy		egg·plant	
ed·it		e·go	
e·di·tion		e·go·ist	
ed·i·tor		e·go·tism	
ed·i·to·ri·al		e·go·tist	
ed·u·cate		e·go·tis·ti·cal	
ed·u·ca·tion		e·gre·gious	
ed·u·ca·tor		e·gress	
e·duce		E·gyp·tian	
eel		ei·der	
ee·rie		eight	
ef·face		eighth	

✓ei·ther		e·lec·tro·plate	
e·jac·u·late		e·lec·tro·scope	
e·ject		e·lec·tro·type	
e·jec·tion		el·e·gance	
eke		el·e·gant	
e·lab·o·rate		el·e·gi·ac	
e·lab·o·ra·tion		el·e·gy	
e·lapse		el·e·ment	
e·las·tic		el·e·men·tal	
e·las·tic·i·ty		el·e·men·ta·ry	
e·late		el·e·phant	
e·la·tion		el·e·phan·tine	
el·bow		el·e·vate	
eld·er		el·e·va·tion	
eld·est		el·e·va·tor	
e·lect		elf	
e·lec·tion		elves	
e·lec·tion·eer		e·lic·it	
e·lec·tive		e·lide	
e·lec·tor		el·i·gi·bil·i·ty	
e·lec·tor·al		✓el·i·gi·ble	
e·lec·tor·ate		e·lim·i·nate	
e·lec·tric		e·lim·i·na·tion	
e·lec·tri·cal		e·li·sion	
e·lec·tri·cian		e·lite	
e·lec·tric·i·ty		e·lix·ir	
e·lec·tri·fi·ca·tion		elk	
e·lec·tri·fy		ell	
e·lec·tro		el·lipse	
e·lec·tro·cute		el·lip·sis	
e·lec·tro·cu·tion		el·lip·ti·cal	
e·lec·trode		elm	
e·lec·trol·y·sis		el·o·cu·tion	
e·lec·tro·lyte		e·lon·gate	
e·lec·tro·mag·net		e·lon·ga·tion	
e·lec·tron		e·lope	
e·lec·tron·ic		el·o·quence	

el·o·quent		em·bro·cate	
else		em·broi·der	
else·where		em·broi·der·y	
e·lu·ci·date		em·broil	
e·lu·ci·da·tion		em·bry·o	
e·lude		em·bry·on·ic	
e·lu·sive		e·mend	
E·ly·si·um		em·er·ald	
e·ma·ci·ate		e·merge	
e·ma·ci·a·tion		e·mer·gen·cy	
em·a·nate		e·mer·i·tus	
em·a·na·tion		e·mer·sion	
e·man·ci·pate		em·er·y	
e·man·ci·pa·tion		e·met·ic	
e·man·ci·pa·tor		em·i·grant	
e·mas·cu·late		em·i·grate	
em·balm		em·i·gra·tion	
em·bank·ment		e·mi·gré	
em·bar·go		em·i·nence	
em·bark		em·i·nent	
em·bar·ka·tion		e·mir	
em·bar·rass		em·is·sar·y	
em·bar·rass·ment		e·mit	
em·bas·sy		e·mol·li·ent	
em·bel·lish		e·mol·u·ment	
em·ber		e·mote	
em·bez·zle		e·mo·tion	
em·bit·ter		em·pa·thy	
em·bla·zon		em·pen·nage	
em·blem		em·per·or	
em·blem·at·ic		em·pha·sis	
em·bod·i·ment		em·pha·size	
em·bod·y		em·phat·ic	
em·bold·en		em·pire	
em·boss		em·pir·i·cal	
em·brace		em·ploy	
em·bra·sure		em·ploy·ee	

✓ em·ploy·er	*py*	en·cy·clo·pe·di·a	*nscpda*
✓ em·ploy·ment	*py—*	✓ end	*e —*
em·po·ri·um	*py*	en·dan·ger	*ndy*
em·pow·er	*pi*	en·dear	*nde*
em·press	*p²*	en·dear·ment	*nde—*
✓ emp·ty	*⌐)*	✓ en·deav·or	*ndv*
e·mu	*eru*	en·dem·ic	*ndrc*
em·u·late	*la*	en·dive	*ndi*
em·u·la·tion	*ly*	✓ end·less	*e — l²*
e·mul·si·fy	*erlsf*	en·dorse	*nDs*
e·mul·sion	*erly*	en·dow	*ndi*
en·a·ble	*nab*	en·dur·ance	*ndu /*
en·act	*nac*	en·dure	*ndu*
en·am·el	*nrl*	en·e·ma	*n ra*
en·am·el·er	*nrl*	en·e·my	*n re*
en·am·or	*nr*	✓ en·er·get·ic	*nyrc*
en·camp	*ncrp*	en·er·gize	*nyz*
en·case	*ncs*	✓ en·er·gy	*nye*
en·ceinte	*ans—*	en·er·vate	*nva*
en·chant	*nC—*	en·fee·ble	*nfb*
en·chant·ment	*nC——*	en·fold	*nfol*
en·chant·ress	*nC—r²*	en·force	*nfs*
en·cir·cle	*nScl*	en·force·a·ble	*nfsb*
en·clave	*nca*	en·force·ment	*nfs—*
en·close	*ncz*	en·forc·er	*nfs*
✓ en·clo·sure	*ncz*	en·fran·chise	*nFCz*
en·co·mi·um	*ncre*	en·gage	*ngf*
en·com·pass	*nkp²*	en·gen·der	*ny—*
en·core	*anco*	en·gine	*nyn*
✓ en·count·er	*nk*	en·gi·neer	*nyne*
en·cour·age	*nCf*	En·glish	*egS (Eng)*
en·croach	*nCC*	en·grain	*ngn*
en·crust	*nC,*	en·grave	*nga*
en·crus·ta·tion	*nCsf*	en·grav·er	*nga*
en·cum·ber	*nkb*	en·gross	*ngo*
en·cum·brance	*nk8/*	✓ en·hance	*nhl*
en·cy·cli·cal	*nsccl*	en·hance·ment	*nhl—*

e·nig·má		en·throne	
e·nig·mat·ic		en·thuse	
en·join		en·thu·si·asm	
en·joy		en·thu·si·as·tic	
en·joy·ment		en·tice	
en·large		en·tire	
en·large·ment		en·tire·ly	
en·light·en		en·ti·tle	
en·list		en·ti·ty	
en·liv·en		en·tomb	
en·mi·ty		en·to·mol·o·gist	
en·no·ble		en·trails	
en·nui		en·trance	
e·nor·mi·ty		en·trant	
e·nor·mous		en·treat	
e·nough		en·treat·y	
en·rage		en·trée	
en·rap·ture		en·trench	
en·rich		en·tre·pre·neur	
en·roll		en·trust	
en·roll·ment		en·try	
en·sconce		e·num·er·ate	
en·shrine		e·nu·mer·a·tion	
en·shroud		e·nu·mer·a·tor	
en·sign		e·nun·ci·ate	
en·slave		e·nun·ci·a·tion	
en·snare		e·nun·ci·a·tor	
en·sue		en·vel·op	
en·tab·la·ture		en·ve·lope	
en·tail		en·vel·op·ment	
en·tan·gle		en·vi·ous	
en·ter		en·vi·ron·ment	
en·ter·ic		en·vis·age	
en·ter·prise		en·voy	
en·ter·tain		en·vy	
en·ter·tain·er		en·zyme	
en·thrall		ep·au·let	

e·phem·er·al		e·qui·nox	
ep·ic		e·quip	
ep·i·cure		eq·ui·ta·ble	
ep·i·cu·re·an		eq·ui·ty	
ep·i·cy·cle		e·quiv·a·lent	
ep·i·dem·ic		e·quiv·o·cal	
ep·i·der·mis		e·quiv·o·cate	
ep·i·glot·tis		e·quiv·o·ca·tor	
ep·i·gram		e·ra	
ep·i·graph		e·rad·i·cate	
ep·i·lep·sy		e·rase	
ep·i·lep·tic		e·ras·er	
ep·i·logue		e·ra·sure	
e·pis·co·pal		ere	
E·pis·co·pa·li·an		e·rect	
ep·i·sode		e·rec·tion	
e·pis·tle		er·mine	
ep·i·taph		e·rode	
ep·i·thet		e·ro·sion	
e·pit·o·me		e·rot·ic	
e·pit·o·mize		err	
ep·poch		er·rand	
ep·ox·y		er·rant	
eq·ua·ble		er·rat·ic	
e·qual		er·ra·ta	
e·qual·i·ty		er·ra·tum	
e·qual·ize		er·ro·ne·ous	
e·qua·nim·i·ty		√er·ror	
e·quate		er·satz	
e·qua·tion		er·u·dite	
e·qua·tor		er·u·di·tion	
e·qua·to·ri·al		e·rupt	
e·ques·tri·an		e·rup·tion	
e·qui·an·gu·lar		er·y·sip·e·las	
e·qui·dis·tant		es·ca·la·tor	
e·qui·lat·er·al		es·ca·pade	
e·qui·lib·ri·um		es·cape	

es·chew	*esCu*	eth·yl	*ell*
es·cort	*esCl*	et·i·quette	*elcl*
es·cutch·eon	*esCCn*	et·y·mol·o·gy	*el lje*
Es·ki·mo	*escro*	eu·ca·lyp·tus	*uclpx*
es·o·ter·ic	*es c*	eu·gen·ics	*ujncs*
es·pecial	*esx*	eu·lo·gize	*llyz*
✓ es·pe·cial·ly	*esx*	eu·lo·gy	*ulje*
es·pi·o·nage	*e senz*	eu·phe·mism	*ufn z*
es·pla·nade	*esnd*	eu·pho·ni·ous	*ufnx*
es·pouse	*esuz*	eu·pho·ri·a	*ufya*
es·prit	*eSe*	eu·re·ka	*urca*
es·quire	*esgu (Esg.)*	Eu·ro·pe·an	*upen*
es·say	*esa*	e·vac·u·ate	*evca*
es·sence	*es /*	e·vac·u·a·tion	*evcj*
es·sen·tial	*esx*	e·vade	*evd*
✓ es·sen·tial·ly	*esx*	e·val·u·ate	*evlua*
✓ es·tab·lish	*esl*	e·val·u·a·tion	*evluj*
✓ es·tab·lish·ment	*esl –*	ev·a·nes·cent	*evns –*
es·tate	*esa*	e·van·gel·ic	*evglc*
es·teem	*ese*	e·van·ge·lism	*evglz*
es·ti·ma·ble	*esrb*	e·van·ge·list	*evgl*
✓ es·ti·mate	*esra (esrl)*	e·vap·o·rate	*evsa*
es·ti·ma·tion	*esrj*	e·vap·o·ra·tion	*evrj*
Es·to·ni·an	*esnen*	e·va·sion	*evj*
es·top	*esp*	e·va·sive	*evsv*
es·trange	*eSj*	eve	*ev*
es·tro·gen	*eSjn*	✓ e·ven	*vn*
es·tu·ar·y	*esCy*	eve·ning	*vn*
et cet·er·a	*elc*	✓ e·ven·ly	*vnl*
etch	*eC*	✓ e·vent	*ev –*
e·ter·nal	*eJnl*	e·ven·tful	*ev – f*
e·ther	*eJ*	e·ven·tu·al	*evCul*
e·the·re·al	*elyl*	e·ven·tu·ate	*evCa*
eth·i·cal	*elcl*	✓ ev·er	*E*
eth·ics	*elcs*	ev·er·more	*Ero*
E·the·o·pi·an	*elepen*	ev·er·y	*E*
eth·nic	*elnc*	ev·er·y·bod·y	*Ebde*

ev·er·y·day		ex·cel·lence	
ev·er·y·one		ex·cel·lent	
ev·er·y·thing		ex·cel·si·or	
ev·er·y·where		ex·cept	
e·vict		ex·cep·tion	
e·vic·tion		ex·cep·tion·al	
ev·i·dence		ex·cep·tion·al·ly	
ev·i·dent		ex·cerpt	
ev·i·dent·ly		ex·cess	
e·vil		ex·ces·sive	
e·vil·ness		ex·change	
e·vince		ex·change·a·ble	
e·vis·cer·ate		ex·cheq·uer	
e·voc·a·tive		ex·cise	
ev·o·ca·tor		ex·ci·sion	
e·voke		ex·cit·a·ble	
ev·o·lu·tion		ex·ci·ta·tion	
e·volve		ex·cite	
ewe		ex·cite·ment	
ew·er		ex·claim	
ex·ac·er·bate		ex·cla·ma·tion	
ex·ac·er·ba·tion		ex·clam·a·to·ry	
ex·act		ex·clude	
ex·act·ly		ex·clu·sion	
ex·ag·ger·ate		ex·clu·sive	
ex·ag·ger·a·tion		ex·com·mu·ni·cate	
ex·ag·ger·a·tor		ex·com·mu·ni·ca·tion	
ex·alt		ex·co·ri·ate	
ex·am·i·na·tion		ex·crete	
ex·am·ine		ex·cre·tion	
ex·am·ple		ex·cru·ci·at·ing	
ex·as·per·ate		ex·cul·pate	
ex·as·per·a·tion		ex·cul·pa·to·ry	
ex·ca·vate		ex·cur·sion	
ex·ca·va·tion		ex·cur·sive	
ex·ceed		ex·cus·a·ble	
ex·cel		ex·cuse	

ex·e·cra·ble		ex·or·cise	
ex·e·crate		ex·o·ter·ic	
ex·e·cute		ex·ot·ic	
ex·e·cu·tion		✓ ex·pand	
ex·e·cu·tion·er		ex·panse	
✓ ex·ec·u·tive		ex·pan·sion	
ex·ec·u·tor		ex par·te	
ex·ec·u·to·ri·al		ex·pa·ti·ate	
ex·em·plar		ex·pa·tri·ate	
ex·em·pla·ry		✓ ex·pect	
ex·em·pli·fy		ex·pect·ant	
✓ ex·empt		ex·pec·ta·tion	
ex·emp·tion		ex·pec·to·rant	
ex·er·cise		ex·pec·to·rate	
ex·ert		ex·pe·di·en·cy	
ex·er·tion		ex·pe·di·ent	
ex·ha·la·tion		ex·pedite	
ex·hale		ex·pe·di·tion	
✓ ex·haust		ex·pe·di·tious	
ex·haus·tion		ex·pel	
ex·hib·it		ex·pend	
ex·hi·bi·tion		ex·pen·di·ture	
ex·hib·i·tor		✓ ex·pense	
ex·hil·a·rate		ex·pen·sive	
ex·hil·a·ra·tion		✓ ex·pe·ri·ence	
ex·hort		ex·pe·ri·enced	
ex·hor·ta·tion		ex·per·i·ment	
ex·hume		ex·per·i·men·tal	
ex·i·gen·cy		ex·pert	
ex·ile		ex·per·tise	
✓ ex·ist		ex·pi·ate	
ex·ist·ence		ex·pi·a·tion	
✓ ex·it		ex·pi·a·to·ry	
ex·o·dus		ex·pi·ra·tion	
ex of·fi·ci·o		ex·pire	
ex·on·er·ate		✓ ex·plain	
ex·or·bi·tant		ex·pla·na·tion	

ex·ple·tive		ex·ten·u·ate	
ex·pli·ca·ble		ex·ten·u·a·tion	
ex·plic·it		ex·te·ri·or	
ex·plode		ex·ter·mi·nate	
ex·ploit		ex·ter·mi·na·tion	
ex·ploi·ta·tion		ex·ter·mi·na·tor	
ex·plor·a·to·ry		ex·ter·nal	
ex·plore		ex·ter·nal·ize	
ex·plor·er		ex·tinct	
ex·plo·sion		ex·tinc·tion	
ex·plo·sive		ex·tin·guish	
ex·po·nent		ex·tir·pate	
ex·port		ex·tol	
ex·por·ter		ex·tort	
ex·po·se		ex·tor·tion	
ex·posé		ex·tra	
ex·po·si·tion		ex·tract	
ex·pos·tu·late		ex·trac·tion	
ex·po·sure		ex·trac·tor	
ex·pound		ex·tra·dite	
ex·press		ex·tra·di·tion	
ex·pressed		ex·tra·ne·ous	
ex·pres·sion		ex·tra·or·di·nar·y	
ex·pres·sive		ex·trav·a·gance	
ex·pro·pri·ate		ex·trav·a·gant	
ex·pul·sion		ex·trav·a·ganz·a	
ex·punge		ex·treme	
ex·pur·gate		ex·treme·ly	
ex·quis·ite		ex·trem·ist	
ex·tant		ex·trem·i·ty	
ex·tem·po·ra·ne·ous		ex·tri·cate	
ex·tem·po·re		ex·trin·sic	
ex·tem·po·rize		ex·tro·vert	
ex·tend		ex·trude	
ex·ten·sion		ex·u·ber·ant	
ex·ten·sive		ex·u·da·tion	
ex·tent		ex·ude	

ex·ult	*xll*	eye·let	*cll*
eye	*c*	eye·lid	*cld*
eye·ball	*cbal*	eye·sight	*csc*
eye·lash	*cld*	eye·wit·ness	*iwl*

fa·ble	*fb*	fac·tion	*fcy*
fa·bric	*fBc*	fac·ti·tious	*fcx*
fab·ri·cate	*fBca*	fac·tor	*fc*
fab·ri·ca·tion	*fBcy*	✓fac·to·ry	*fcy*
fab·u·lous	*fbly*	fac·tu·al	*fcUl*
fa·cade	*fsd*	fac·ul·ty	*fcl)*
face	*fas*	fad	*fd*
fac·et	*fsl*	fade	*fd*
fa·ce·tious	*fsx*	fag·ot	*fgl*
fa·cial	*fx*	Fahr·en·heit	*(F) Fnhc*
fac·ile	*fsl*	fa·ience	*fa/*
fa·cil·i·tate	*fslla*	fail	*fl*
fa·cil·i·ty	*fsl)*	faille	*ful*
fac·sim·i·le	*fcsrl*	✓fail·ure	*fl*
fact	*fc*	faint	*fa—*

faint·ly		fan·ci·ful	
fair		fan·cy	
fair·ly		fan·fare	
fair·y		fang	
fait ac·com·pli		fan·tail	
fair·y·land		fan·tas·tic	
faith		fan·ta·sy	
faithful		far	
fake		far·a·way	
fak·er		farce	
fal·con		fare	
fall		fare·well	
fal·la·cy		far·fetched	
fall·en		fa·ri·na	
fal·li·ble		farm	
fal·low		farm·er	
false		farm·house	
false·hood		far·ri·er	
fal·si·fy		far·row	
fal·set·to		far·see·ing	
fal·si·fi·ca·tion		far·sight·ed	
fal·si·fi·er		✓far·ther	
fal·si·fy		far·thest	
fal·ter		far·thing	
fame		fas·ci·nate	
fa·mil·iar		fas·ci·na·tion	
fa·mil·i·ar·i·ty		fas·ci·na·tor	
fa·mil·iar·ize		fas·cism	
fa·mil·iar·ly		fash·ion	
fam·i·ly		✓fast	
fam·ine		fast·er	
fam·ish		fas·tid·i·ous	
fa·mous		fast·ness	
fa·mous·ly		fat	
fan		fa·tal	
fa·nat·ic		fa·tal·ist	
fa·nat·i·cism		fa·tal·i·ty	

Word	Shorthand	Word	Shorthand
fa·tal·ly		Feb·ru·ar·y	
fate		fe·cund	
fate·ful		fe·cun·di·ty	
fa·ther		fed	
fa·ther·hood		fed·er·al	
fa·ther-in-law		fed·er·ate	
fa·ther·land		fed·er·a·tion	
fa·ther·less		fee	
fath·om		fee·ble	
fa·tigue		feed	
fat·ness		feed·back	
fat·ty		feel	
fat·u·ous		feel·er	
fau·cet		feel·ing·ly	
fault		feet	
fault·less		feign	
fault·y		feint	
faux pas		fe·lic·i·tate	
fa·vor		fe·lic·i·ty	
fa·vor·a·ble		fe·line	
fa·vor·a·bly		fell	
fa·vor·ite		fel·low	
fawn		fel·low·ship	
faze		fel·on	
fe·al·ty		fe·lo·ni·ous	
fear		fel·on·y	
fear·ful·ly		felt	
fear·less		fe·male	
fear·some		fem·i·nine	
fea·si·bil·i·ty		fem·i·nin·i·ty	
fea·si·ble		fe·mur	
feast		fen	
feat		fence	
feath·er		fenc·er	
feath·er·weight		fend	
fea·ture		fend·er	
feb·ri·fuge		fer·ment	

fer·men·ta·tion		fi·an·cée	
fern		fi·as·co	
fern·er·y		fi·at	
fe·ro·cious		fib	
fe·roc·i·ty		fi·ber	
fer·ret		fi·brous	
fer·ric		fick·le	
fer·rous		fic·tion	
fer·rule		fic·ti·tious	
fer·ry		fid·dle	
fer·tile		fi·del·i·ty	
fer·til·i·ty		fidg·et	
fer·ti·lize		fi·du·ci·ar·y	
fer·ti·liz·er		field	
fer·vent		fiend	
fer·vid		fiend·ish	
fer·vor		fierce	
fes·ter		fierce·ness	
fes·ti·val		fi·er·y	
fes·tive		fi·es·ta	
fes·tiv·i·ty		fife	
fes·toon		fifth	
fetch		fight	
fete		fight·er	
fet·id		fig·ment	
fe·tish		fig·ur·a·tive	
fet·ter		fig·ure	
feud		fig·ure·head	
feu·dal		fil·a·ment	
feu·dal·ism		fil·bert	
fe·ver		filch	
fe·ver·ish		file	
few		fil·i·al	
few·er		fil·i·bus·ter	
fey		fil·i·gree	
fez		Fil·i·pi·no	
fi·an·cé		fill	

fil·let	fire·proof
film	fire·side
fil·my	fire·trap
fil·ter	fire·works
filth	fir·kin
filth·i·ness	firm
fil·trate	fir·ma·ment
fin	firm·er
fi·na·gle	firm·ly
✓ fi·nal	firm·ness
fi·na·le	first
fi·nal·ist	first·ly
fi·nance	first·hand
fi·nan·cial	firth
fi·nan·cial·ly	fis·cal
fin·an·cier	fish
finch	fish·er
find	fish·er·man
find·er	fish·hook
fine	fis·sion
fine·ly	fis·sure
fin·er	fist
fin·er·y	fist·ic
fine·spun	fis·tu·la
fi·nesse	fit
fin·est	fit·ful
fin·ger	five
fin·i·cal	fix
fi·nis	fix·ate
fin·ish	fix·a·tion
fi·nite	fix·a·tive
fir	fix·ture
fire	fizz
fire·bug	fiz·zle
fire·fly	flab·by
fire·man	flac·cid
fire·place	flag

flag·el·late		flee	
flag·el·la·tion		fleece	
flag·on		fleec·y	
fla·grant		fleet	
flag·ship		Flem·ish	
flag·staff		flesh	
flail		flesh·i·ness	
flair		flesh·y	
flake		flew	
flam·beau		flex·i·bil·i·ty	
flam·boy·ant		flex·i·ble	
flame		flick	
fla·min·go		flick·er	
flam·ma·ble		fli·er	
flange		flight	
flank		flight·i·ness	
flan·nel		flim·si·ness	
flap		flim·sy	
flap·per		flinch	
flare		fling	
flash		flint	
flash·light		flip	
flash·y		flip·pan·cy	
flat		flip·pant	
flat·ten		flirt	
flat·ter		flir·ta·tion	
flat·ter·y		flir·ta·tious	
flat·u·lent		flit	
flaunt		float	
fla·vor		floc·cu·lent	
flaw		flock	
flax		floe	
flay		flog	
flea		flood	
fleck		flood·light	
fled		floor	
fledg·ling		floor·walk·er	

flop	fly	
flop·py	fly·er	
flo·ral	fly·leaf	
flo·res·cent	fly·wheel	
flor·id	foal	
flor·in	foam	
flo·rist	fob	
floss	fo·cal	
flo·til·la	fo·cus	
flot·sam	fod·der	
flounce	foe	
floun·der	fog	
flour	fo·gy	
flour·ish	foi·ble	
flour·y	foil	
flout	foist	
flow	fold	
flow·er	fold·er	
flow·er·pot	fo·li·age	
flown	fo·li·o	
√ fluc·tu·ate	folk	
fluc·tu·a·tion	folk·song	
flue	fol·li·cle	
flu·ent	fol·low	
fluff	fol·low·er	
fluff·y	fol·ly	
√ flu·id	fo·ment	
fluke	√ fond	
flunk	fon·dant	
flu·o·res·cent	fon·dle	
flu·o·ro·scope	font	
flur·ry	food	
flush	fool	
flus·ter	fool·er·y	
flute	fool·har·dy	
flut·ter	fool·ish	
flux	fools·cap	

foot		fore·hand	
foot·ball		fore·head	
foot·hill		for·eign	
foot·hold		for·eign·er	
foot·lights		fore·knowl·edge	
foot·note		fore·lock	
foot·path		fore·man	
foot·print		fore·most	
foot·sore		fore·noon	
foot·step		fo·ren·sic	
foot·stool		fore·see	
foot·wear		fore·shad·ow	
foot·work		fore·sight	
fop		for·est	
for		fore·stall	
for·age		for·est·er	
for·ay		for·est·ry	
for·bade		fore·tell	
for·bear		fore·thought	
for·bid		fore·told	
for·bid·den		for·ev·er	
for·bore		fore·warn	
force		fore·word	
forced		for·feit	
force·ful		for·fei·ture	
for·ceps		forge	
ford		forg·er	
fore		for·get	
fore·arm		for·get·ful	
fore·cast		for·get·ful·ness	
for·close		for·give	
fore·clo·sure		for·give·ness	
fore·fa·ther		for·got	
fore·fin·ger		for·got·ten	
fore·go		fork	
fore·gone		for·lorn	
fore·ground		form	

for·mal		found	
for·mal·i·ty		foun·da·tion	
for·mal·ly		found·er	
for·mat		found·ling	
form·a·tive		found·ry	
form·er		fount	
for·mer·ly		foun·tain	
for·mi·da·ble		four	
form·less		fourth	
for·mu·la		fowl	
for·mu·late		fox	
for·mu·la·tion		foy·er	
for·ni·ca·tion		fra·cas	
for·sake		frac·tion	
for·sooth		frac·tious	
for·swear		frac·ture	
for·syth·i·a		frag·ile	
fort		frag·ment	
forth		fra·grance	
forth·right		fra·grant	
forth·with		frail	
for·ti·fi·ca·tion		frail·ty	
for·ti·fy		frame	
for·tis·si·mo		frame·work	
for·ti·tude		franc	
fort·night		fran·chise	
for·tress		frank	
for·tu·i·tous		frank·in·cense	
for·tu·nate		fran·tic	
for·tune		frat	
fo·rum		fra·ter·nal	
for·ward		fra·ter·ni·ty	
fos·sil		frat·ri·cide	
fos·ter		fraud	
fought		fraud·u·lence	
foul		fraud·u·lent	
foul·ness		fraught	

fray		frig·id	
freak		fri·gid·i·ty	
freck·le		frill	
free		fringe	
free·dom		frisk	
free·hand		frit·ter	
free·hold		fri·vol·i·ty	
free·ly		friv·o·lous	
free·way		frizz	
freeze		fro	
✓ freight		frock	
freight·er		frog	
French		frol·ic	
fre·net·ic		fro·lic·some	
fren·zy		from	
fre·quen·cy		frond	
fre·quent		front	
fre·quent·ly		fron·tier	
fres·co		fron·tis·piece	
fresh		frost	
fresh·er		frost·bite	
fresh·ly		frost·y	
fresh·man		froth	
fret		frown	
fret·work		frow·zy	
fri·a·ble		froze	
fri·ar		fro·zen	
fric·as·see		fru·gal	
fric·tion		fru·gal·i·ty	
✓ Fri·day		fruit	
friend		fru·i·tion	
friend·less		fruit·less	
friend·ly		✓ frus·trate	
friend·ship		frus·tra·tion	
frig·ate		fry	
fright		fry·er	
fright·ful		fuch·si·a	

fudge		fu·ri·ous	
fu·el		furl	
fu·gi·tive		fur·long	
fugue		fur·lough	
ful·crum		fur·nace	
ful·fill		fur·nish	
full		fur·ni·ture	
full·ness		fu·rore	
ful·ly		fur·ri·er	
ful·mi·nate		fur·row	
ful·some		✓fur·ther	
fum·ble		fur·ther·ance	
fume		✓fur·ther·more	
fu·mi·gate		✓fur·ther·most	
fu·mi·ga·tion		✓fur·thest	
fun		fur·tive	
✓func·tion		fu·ry	
func·tion·ar·y		furze	
fund		fuse	
✓fun·da·men·tal		fu·se·lage	
fu·ner·al		fu·sil·lade	
fu·ne·re·al		fu·sion	
fun·gi·cide		fuss	
fun·gus		fuss·y	
fu·nic·u·lar		fu·tile	
funk		fu·til·i·ty	
fun·nel		✓fu·ture	
fur		fu·tur·ist·ic	
fur·be·low		fu·tu·ri·ty	
fur·bish		fuzz	

gab	
gab·ar·dine	
gab·ble	
ga·ble	
gad	
gad·get	
gaff	
gag	
gage	
gai·e·ty	
gai·ly	
gain	
gain·ful	
gait	
gai·ter	
ga·la	
gal·ax·y	
gale	
gall	
gal·lant	
gal·lant·ry	
gal·ler·y	
gal·ley	
Gal·lic	
gal·li·vant	
gal·lon	
gal·lop	

gal·lows	
gall·stone	
ga·lore	
gal·van·ic	
gal·va·nize	
gam·bit	
gam·ble	
gam·bler	
game	
game·ster	
gam·in	
gam·ut	
gan·der	
gang	
gan·gli·on	
gang·plank	
gan·grene	
gang·ster	
gang·way	
gant·let	
gan·try	
gaol	
gap	
gape	
ga·rage	
garb	
gar·bage	

gar·ble		gave	
gar·den		gav·el	
gar·den·er		gay	
gar·de·ni·a		gaze	
gar·gle		ga·zelle	
gar·goyle		ga·zette	
gar·ish		gaz·et·teer	
gar·land		gear	
gar·lic		geese	
gar·ment		gel·a·tin	
gar·ner		ge·lat·i·nous	
gar·net		gel·id	
gar·nish		gem	
gar·nish·ee		gen·darme	
gar·ni·ture		gen·der	
gar·ret		gene	
gar·ri·son		gen·e·al·o·gy	
gar·ru·li·ty		✓ gen·er·al	
gar·ru·lous		gen·er·a·lis·si·mo	
gar·ter		gen·er·al·i·ty	
gas		gen·er·al·ize	
gas·e·ous		gen·er·ate	
gash		gen·er·a·tion	
gas·ket		gener·a·tor	
gas·light		ge·ner·ic	
gas·o·line		gen·er·os·i·ty	
gasp		gen·er·ous	
gas·tric		gen·er·ous·ly	
gas·tron·o·my		gen·e·sis	
gate		ge·net·ic	
gate·way		gen·ial	
✓ gath·er		ge·ni·al·i·ty	
gaud·y		ge·nie	
gauge		gen·i·tal	
gaunt		gen·i·tive	
gaunt·let		gen·ius	
gauze		gen·o·cide	

gen·teel		gher·kin	
gen·tile		ghet·to	
gen·til·i·ty		ghost	
gen·tle		ghost·ly	
gen·tle·man		ghoul	
gen·tle·men		gi·ant	
gen·tly		gib·ber·ish	
gen·try		gibe	
gen·u·flect		gib·let	
gen·u·ine		gid·di·ness	
ge·nus		gid·dy	
ge·o·det·ic		gift	
ge·og·ra·pher		gi·gan·tic	
ge·o·graph·ic		gig·gle	
ge·og·ra·phy		gild	
ge·ol·o·gist		gill	
ge·ol·o·gy		gilt	
ge·o·met·ric		gim·let	
ge·om·e·try		gim·mick	
ge·ra·ni·um		gin	
ger·i·at·ric		gin·ger	
germ		gin·ger·ly	
Ger·man		ging·ham	
ger·mane		gi·raffe	
ger·mi·cide		gird	
ger·mi·nate		gird·er	
ger·mi·na·tion		gir·dle	
ger·und		girl	
ge·sta·po		girl·hood	
ges·tate		girl·ish	
ges·ta·tion		girth	
ges·tic·u·late		gist	
ges·tic·u·la·tion		give	
ges·ture		giv·en	
get		giv·er	
gey·ser		giz·zard	
ghast·ly		gla·cial	

gla·cier		gloom·y	
glad		glo·ri·fy	
glade		glo·ri·ous	
glad·i·a·tor		glo·ry	
glad·i·o·lus		gloss	
glad·ly		glos·sa·ry	
glam·our		gloss·i·ness	
glam·or·ous		gloss·y	
glance		glove	
gland		glow	
glan·du·lar		glow·er	
glare		glow·worm	
glass		glu·cose	
glass·ful		glue	
glass·ware		glum	
glass·y		glum·ness	
glaze		glut	
gla·zier		glu·ten	
gleam		glu·ti·nous	
glean		glut·ton	
glee		glut·ton·ous	
glee·ful		glut·ton·y	
glen		glyc·er·in	
glide		gnarl	
glid·er		gnash	
glim·mer		gnat	
glimpse		gnaw	
glint		gnome	
glis·ten		go	
glit·ter		goad	
gloam·ing		goal	
gloat		goat	
glob		gob·ble	
globe		gob·bler	
glob·u·lar		gob·let	
gloom		god·child	
gloom·i·ly		god·dess	

god·fa·ther	*gdf*	gour·mand	*gr —*
god·less	*gdl'*	gour·met	*gra*
god·like	*gdlc*	gout	*gul*
god·moth·er	*gd*	gov·ern	*gvn,*
god·par·ent	*gd —*	gov·ern·ess	*gv'*
god·send	*gds —*	gov·ern·ment	*gvl*
god·son	*gdsn*	gov·er·nor	*gvn*
goes	*gs*	gov·er·nor·ship	*gvns*
gog·gle	*ggl*	gown	*gun*
go·ing	*g*	grab	*gb*
goi·ter	*gy*	grace	*gas*
gold	*(au) gol*	grace·ful	*gsf*
gold·en	*goln*	gra·cious	*gx*
golf	*glf*	gra·cious·ly	*gx*
gon·do·la	*g — la*	gra·da·tion	*gdy*
gon·do·lier	*g — le*	✓ grade	*gd*
gone	*gn*	gra·di·ent	*gde —*
gong	*gg*	✓ grad·u·al	*gdul*
good	*g*	grad·u·ate	*gda (gdul)*
good·by	*gb*	grad·u·a·tion	*gdy*
good·ly	*gl*	graft	*gf*
✓ good·ness	*g'*	graft·er	*gf*
goose	*gus*	grain	*gn*
goose·neck	*gsnc*	gram	*gr*
go·pher	*gf*	gram·mar	*gr*
gore	*go*	gram·mar·i·an	*gryn*
gorge	*gy*	gram·mat·i·cal	*grlcl*
gor·geous	*gyx*	gran·a·ry	*gny*
go·ril·la	*gla*	grand	*g —*
gos·pel	*gsl*	grand·child	*g — ch*
gos·sa·mer	*gs*	grand·chil·dren	*g — chn*
gos·sip	*gsp*	grand·daugh·ter	*g — d*
got	*gl*	gran·deur	*gs*
got·ten	*gln*	grand·fa·ther	*g — f*
gouge	*guy*	gran·dil·o·quent	*g — lg —*
gou·lash	*gls*	gran·di·ose	*g — es*
gourd	*gd*	grand·moth·er	*g —*

Word	Shorthand	Word	Shorthand
grand·par·ent		grav·i·ta·tion	
grand·son		grav·i·ty	
grand·stand		gra·vy	
grange		gray	
gran·ite		gray·er	
grant		graze	
gran·tee		grease	
grant·or		greas·y	
gran·u·lar		great	
gran·u·late		great·er	
gran·u·la·tion		great·est	
gran·ule		great·ly	
grape		great·ness	
grape·vine		Gre·cian	
graph		greed·i·ly	
graph·ic		greed·i·ness	
graph·ite		greed·y	
graph·ol·o·gy		green	
grap·ple		green·gage	
grasp		green·gro·cer	
grass		green·horn	
grass·y		green·house	
grate		greet	
grate·ful		gre·gar·i·ous	
grat·i·fi·ca·tion		grem·lin	
grat·i·fi·er		gre·nade	
grat·i·fy		gren·a·dier	
gra·tis		grew	
grat·i·tude		grey	
gra·tu·i·tous		grey·hound	
gra·tu·i·ty		grid	
grave		grid·dle	
grav·el		grief	
grav·er		griev·ance	
grav·est		grieve	
grave·stone		grie·vous	
grav·i·tate		grif·fon	

grill		grub	
grim		grudge	
gri·mace		gru·el	
grim·ly		grue·some	
grin		gruff	
grind		grum·ble	
grind·stone		grump·y	
grip		grunt	
gripe		guar·an·tee	
gris·ly		guar·an·tor	
grist		guar·an·ty	
gris·tle		guard	
grit		guard·house	
griz·zly		guard·i·an	
groan		guar·di·an·ship	
gro·cer		guard·room	
gro·cer·y		guards·man	
grog		gu·ber·na·to·ri·al	
grog·gy		guer·ril·la	
groin		guess	
grom·met		guess·work	
groom		guest	
groove		guf·faw	
grope		guid·ance	
gross		guide	
gross·ly		guild	
gro·tesque		guile	
grouch		guil·lo·tine	
ground		guilt	
ground·less		guilt·i·ness	
group		guilt·less	
grouse		guin·ea	
grove		guise	
grov·el		gui·tar	
grow		gulf	
growl		gull	
growth		gul·li·ble	

gul·ly	*gl*	gus·to	*gso*
gulp	*glp*	gut	*gl*
gum	*g*	gut·ter	*g/l*
gump·tion	*gry*	gut·tur·al	*g*
gun	*gn*	guy	*gi*
gun·boat	*gnbo*	guz·zle	*gzl*
gun·fire	*gnfr*	gym·na·si·um	*jmze*
gun·ner	*gn*	gym·nast	*jm,*
gun·pow·der	*gnped*	gym·nas·tic	*jmsc*
gun·run·ner	*gnrn*	gyp	*jp*
gun·shot	*gnsl*	gyp·sum	*jps*
gun·wale	*gnl*	Gyp·sy	*jpse*
gur·gle	*ggl*	gy·rate	*ja*
gush	*gs*	gy·ra·tion	*j*
gus·set	*gsl*	gy·ro·scope	*jscp*
gust	*g,*		

ha·be·as cor·pus	*hbes Cpx*	ha·bil·i·ment	*hbl–*
hab·er·dash·er	*hBdS*	ha·bil·i·tate	*hblla*
hab·er·dash·er·y	*hBdSy*	hab·it	*hbl*

hab·it·a·ble	*hbtb*	hal·ter	*hl*
hab·it·ant	*hbt –*	halve	*hv*
hab·it·at	*hbtt*	hal·yard	*hllfd*
hab·i·ta·tion	*hblf*	ham	*h*
ha·bit·u·al	*hbCul*	ham·bur·ger	*h Bg*
ha·bit·u·ate	*hbCa*	ham·let	*hrll*
ha·cien·da	*hse —a*	ham·mer	*hr*
hack	*hc*	ham·mock	*hrc*
hack·ney	*hcne*	ham·per	*hrp*
had	*h*	ham·ster	*hrS*
had·dock	*hdc*	ham·string	*hrSg*
had·n't	*h –*	hand	*h —*
hag	*hg*	hand·bag	*h — bg*
hag·gard	*hgfd*	hand·ball	*h — bal*
hag·gle	*hgl*	hand·book	*h — bc*
hail	*hal*	hand·cuff	*h — cf*
hail·storm	*hlS*	hand·ful	*h — f*
hair	*ha*	hand·i·cap	*h — cp*
hair·dress·er	*haDs*	hand·i·work	*h — Urc*
hair·y	*hy*	hand·ker·chief	*hGCf*
hal·cy·on	*hlsen*	han·dle	*h — l*
hale	*hal*	hand·made	*h — rd*
half	*hf*	hand·out	*h — ou*
half·back	*hfbc*	hand·rail	*h — rl*
half·pen·ny	*hfpne*	hand·saw	*h — sa*
half·tone	*hftn*	hand·some	*h — s*
half·way	*hfea*	hand·work	*h — Urc*
hal·i·but	*hlbt*	hand·writ·ing	*h — ru*
hall	*hal*	hand·y	*h — e*
hall·mark	*hl rc*	hang	*hg*
hal·low	*hlo*	hang·ar	*hg*
Hal·low·een	*hlrn*	hang·man	*hg –*
hal·lu·ci·nate	*hlsna*	hank	*hg*
hal·lu·ci·na·tion	*hlsnf*	han·ker	*hg*
hall·way	*hlea*	han·som	*h/*
ha·lo	*hlo*	hap·haz·ard	*hphzd*
halt	*hll*	hap·less	*hpl³*

hap·pen	*hpn*	har·py	*Hpe*
hap·pi·est	*hpe,*	har·ri·dan	*Hdn*
hap·pi·ly	*hpl'*	har·row	*Ho*
hap·pi·ness	*hpe'*	har·ry	*hy*
hap·py	*hpe*	harsh	*HS*
ha·rangue	*Hq*	hart	*Hl*
har·ass	*H'*	har·vest	*Hv,*
har·bin·ger	*Hbg*	har·vest·er	*HvS*
har·bor	*Hb*	has	*as*
hard	*Hd*	hash	*hS*
hard·head	*Hdhd*	hasn't	*as—*
hard·heart·ed	*HdHt*	hasp	*hs*
har·di·ness	*Hde'*	has·sock	*hsc*
hard·ly	*Hdl*	haste	*ha,*
hard·ship	*HdS*	has·ten	*hsn*
hard·tack	*Hdlc*	hast·y	*hs)*
hard·ware	*Hdwa*	hat	*hl*
hard·wood	*Hdwd*	hat·box	*hlbx*
har·dy	*Hde*	hatch	*hC*
hare	*ha*	hatch·er·y	*hCy*
hare·lip	*halp*	hatch·et	*hCl*
ha·rem	*H—*	hatch·way	*hCwa*
hark	*Hc*	hate	*ha*
har·le·quin	*Hlqn*	hate·ful	*haf*
har·lot	*Hll*	hat·rack	*hlrc*
harm	*H—*	ha·tred	*hTd*
harm·ful	*Hf*	hat·stand	*hls—*
harm·less	*Hl'*	hat·ter	*h'*
har·mon·i·ca	*H—mca*	haugh·ty	*h)*
har·mo·ni·ous	*H—mx*	haul	*hal*
har·mo·nize	*H—mz*	haunch	*hC*
har·mo·ny	*H—me*	haunt	*h—*
har·ness	*H'*	have	*v*
harp	*Hp*	ha·ven	*hvn*
harp·ist	*Hp,*	haven't	*v—*
har·poon	*Hpn*	hav·er·sack	*hvsc*
harp·si·chord	*HpsCd*	hav·oc	*hvc*

Word	Shorthand	Word	Shorthand
Ha·wai·ian		heart·break	
hawk		heart·felt	
haw·ser		hearth	
haw·thorn		hearth·stone	
hay		heart·i·ly	
haz·ard		heart·i·ness	
ha·zard·ous		heart·less	
haze		heart·rend·ing	
ha·zel		heart·sick	
ha·zi·ness		heart·string	
ha·zy		heat	
he		heat·er	
head		heath	
head·ache		hea·then	
head·band		heath·er	
head·first		heave	
head·land		heav·en	
head·light		heav·en·ward	
head·long		heav·i·ly	
head·quar·ters		heav·i·ness	
head·room		heav·y	
head·strong		heav·y·set	
head·way		heav·y·weight	
heal		He·brew	
health		heck·le	
health·ful		hect·are	
health·i·ly		hec·tic	
health·i·ness		hec·to·graph	
health·y		hec·tor	
heap		hedge	
hear		hedge·hog	
heard		he·do·nist	
heark·en		heed	
hear·say		heed·less	
hearse		heel	
heart		heft	
heart·ache		he·gem·o·ny	

he·gi·ra		hench·man	
heif·er		hen·na	
height		hep	
height·en		hep·ta·gon	
hei·nous		her	
heir		her·ald	
heir·ess		her·ald·ry	
heir·loom		herb	
held		her·ba·ceous	
hel·i·cal		her·biv·o·rous	
hel·i·cop·ter		herd	
he·li·o·graph		herd·er	
he·li·um		here	
hell		here·a·bout	
hel·lion		here·aft·er	
hel·lo		here·by	
helm		he·red·i·tar·y	
hel·met		he·red·i·ty	
help		here·in	
help·er		here·in·aft·er	
help·ful		her·e·sy	
help·less		her·e·tic	
help·less·ness		here·to·fore	
help·mate		here·up·on	
hem		here·with	
hem·i·sphere		her·it·age	
hem·i·spher·ic		her·met·ic	
hem·lock		her·mit	
he·mo·glo·bin		her·mit·age	
he·mo·phil·i·a		her·ni·a	
hem·or·rhage		he·ro	
hem·or·rhoid		he·ro·ic	
hemp		her·o·in	
hen		her·o·ine	
hence		her·o·ism	
hem·stitch		her·on	
hence·forth		her·ring	

hers	*h//*	high·way	*hura*
her·self	*Hs/*	high·way·man	*huras-*
hes·i·tan·cy	*hzl/*	hi·jack	*hyc*
hes·i·tant	*hzl-*	hike	*hic*
hes·i·tate	*hzta*	hi·lar·i·ous	*hlyx*
hes·i·ta·tion	*hzly*	hi·lar·i·ty	*hL)*
het·er·o·dox	*hdx*	hill	*hl*
het·er·o·ge·ne·ous	*hJgnx*	hill·i·ness	*hl'*
hew	*hu*	hill·ock	*hlc*
hex	*hx*	hill·side	*hlsd*
hex·a·gon	*hugn*	hill·top	*hllp*
hey·day	*hd*	hill·y	*hl*
hi·a·tus	*hulx*	hilt	*hll*
hi·ber·nate	*hBna*	him	*h*
hi·ber·na·tion	*hBny*	him·self	*hs/*
hi·bis·cus	*hbscx*	hind	*hu—*
hic·cup	*hcp*	hin·der	*h—/*
hick	*hc*	hin·drance	*h—r/*
hick·o·ry	*hcy*	hind·sight	*hu—su*
hid	*hd*	hinge	*hy*
hid·den	*hdn*	hint	*h-*
hide	*hd*	hin·ter·land	*h-rl—*
hid·e·ous	*hdx*	hip	*hp*
hie	*hu*	hip·bone	*hpbn*
hi·er·ar·chal	*Hrcl*	hip·po·drome	*hpD°*
hi·er·arch·y	*Hrce*	hip·po·pot·a·mus	*hpplrx*
hi·er·o·glyph·ic	*Hgfc*	hip·ster	*hpS*
high	*hu*	hire	*hu*
high·er	*hu/*	hire·ling	*hulg*
high·est	*hu,*	hir·sute	*Hsl*
high·hand·ed	*huh—=*	his	*s*
high·land	*hul—*	hiss	*h'*
high·light	*hulu*	his·ta·mine	*hsm*
high·ly	*hul*	his·to·ri·an	*hSen*
high·ness	*hu'*	his·tor·ic	*hSc*
high·road	*hurd*	his·tol·o·gy	*hslge*
high·tail	*hull*	his·to·ry	*hSe*

his·tri·on·ic		hol·o·graph	
hit		hol·ster	
hitch		ho·ly	
hith·er		hom·age	
hive		home	
hoard		home·less	
hoarse		home·like	
hoar·y		home·li·ness	
hoax		home·ly	
hob·ble		home·made	
hob·by		home·mak·er	
hob·gob·lin		ho·me·o·path	
hob·nail		home·own·er	
ho·bo		home·sick	
hock		home·spun	
hock·ey		home·stead	
hod		home·ward	
hoe		hom·i·cide	
hog		hom·i·ly	
hoi pol·loi		hom·i·ny	
hogs·head		ho·mo·ge·ne·i·ty	
hoist		ho·mo·ge·ne·ous	
ho·kum		ho·mog·e·nous	
hold		ho·mol·o·gous	
hold·er		hom·o·nym	
hold·o·ver		hone	
hold·up		hon·est	
hole		hon·est·ly	
hole·proof		hon·es·ty	
hole·y		hon·ey	
hol·i·day		honk	
ho·li·ness		hon·ey·comb	
Hol·land·er		hon·ey·dew	
hol·low		hon·ey·moon	
hol·low·ness		hon·ey·suck·le	
hol·ly		hon·or	
hol·o·caust		hon·or·a·ble	

hon·o·rar·i·um		horse·pow·er	
hon·or·ar·y		horse·shoe	
hood		horse·whip	
hood·lum		horse·wom·an	
hoo·doo		hor·ti·cul·ture	
hood·wink		√ hose	
hoof		ho·sier·y	
hook		hos·pi·ta·ble	
hoop		hos·pi·tal	
hoot		hos·pi·tal·i·ty	
hop		host	
hope		hos·tage	
hope·ful		hos·tel	
hope·less		hos·tel·ry	
hope·less·ness		host·ess	
hop·per		hos·tile	
horde		hos·til·i·ty	
hore·hound		hos·tler	
ho·ri·zon		hot	
hor·i·zon·tal		ho·tel	
hor·mone		hot·head	
horn		hot·house	
hor·net		hot·ly	
horn·pipe		hot·ness	
hor·o·scope		hound	
hor·ri·ble		hour	
hor·rid		hour·ly	
hor·rif·ic		house	
hor·ri·fy		house·coat	
hor·ror		house·ful	
horse		house·hold	
horse·back		house·keep·er	
horse·flesh		house·maid	
horse·hair		house·own·er	
horse·hide		house·warm·ing	
horse·man		house·wife	
horse·play		house·work	

hov·el		hu·mid·i·fy	
hov·er		hu·mid·i·ty	
how		hu·mi·dor	
√how·ev·er		hu·mil·i·ate	
howl		hu·mil·i·a·tion	
howl·er		hu·mil·i·ty	
hoy·den		hum·mock	
hub		hu·mor	
hub·bub		hu·mor·ist	
huck·le·ber·ry		hu·mor·ous	
huck·ster		hump	
hud·dle		hu·mus	
hue		hunch	
huff		√ hun·dred	
huff·i·ly		√ hun·dredth	
huff·y		hun·dred·weight	
hug		hung	
huge		Hun·gar·i·an	
Hu·gue·not		hun·ger	
hulk		hun·gri·er	
hull		hun·gri·ly	
hul·la·ba·loo		hun·gry	
hum		hunk	
hu·man		hunt	
hu·mane		hunt·er	
hu·man·ist		hunts·man	
hu·man·i·tar·i·an		hur·dle	
hu·man·i·ty		hur·dy·gur·dy	
hu·man·kind		hurl	
hu·man·ly		hur·ly·bur·ly	
hum·ble		hur·rah	
hum·ble·ness		hur·ri·cane	
hum·bly		hur·ry	
hum·bug		hurt	
hum·ding·er		hurt·ful	
hum·drum		hur·tle	
hu·mid		hus·band	

hus·band·ry		hy·giene	
husk		hy·gi·en·ic	
husk·i·ly		hy·men	
husk·i·ness		hy·me·ne·al	
husk·y		hymn	
hus·sar		hy·per·bo·la	
hus·sy		hy·per·bo·le	
hus·tle		hy·per·sen·si·tive	
hut		hy·phen	
hutch		hy·phen·ate	
hy·a·cinth		hyp·no·sis	
hy·brid		hyp·not·ic	
hy·dran·ge·a		hyp·no·tist	
hy·drant		hy·po·chon·dri·a	
hy·drate		hy·po·chon·dri·ac	
hy·drau·lic		hy·poc·ri·sy	
hy·dro·chlo·ride		hyp·o·crite	
hy·dro·e·lec·tric		hy·po·der·mic	
hy·dro·gen		hy·pot·e·nuse	
hy·drol·y·sis		hy·poth·e·cate	
hy·drom·e·ter		hy·poth·e·sis	
hy·dro·pho·bi·a		hy·poth·e·ses	
hy·dro·plane		hy·po·thet·i·cal	
hy·dro·scope		hys·sop	
hy·dro·stat·ic		hys·te·ri·a	
hy·drous		hys·ter·i·cal	
hy·drox·ide		hys·ter·ics	
hy·e·na			

I	$\mathcal{i}$
i·am·bic	$\mathcal{i}mbc$
i·bex	$\mathcal{i}bx$
i·bis	$\mathcal{i}bs$
ice	$\mathcal{i}s$
ice·berg	$\mathcal{i}sBg$
ice·boat	$\mathcal{i}sbo$
ice·bound	$\mathcal{i}sbr$
ice·box	$\mathcal{i}sbx$
ice·man	$\mathcal{i}s$
i·ci·cle	$\mathcal{i}scl$
i·ci·ly	$\mathcal{i}sl$
i·ci·ness	$\mathcal{i}se'$
i·con	$\mathcal{i}k$
i·con·o·clast	$\mathcal{i}kc,$
i·con·o·scope	$\mathcal{i}kscp$
i·cy	$\mathcal{i}se$
i·de·a	$\mathcal{i}d$
i·de·al	$\mathcal{i}dl$
i·de·al·ism	$\mathcal{i}dlz$
i·de·al·ist	$\mathcal{i}dl,$
i·de·al·is·tic	$\mathcal{i}dlsc$
i·de·al·ize	$\mathcal{i}dlz$
i·de·al·ly	$\mathcal{i}dl$
i·den·ti·cal	$\mathcal{i}d-cl$
i·den·ti·fi·ca·tion	$\mathcal{i}d-fc$
i·den·ti·fy	$\mathcal{i}d-f$
i·den·ti·ty	$\mathcal{i}d-)$
id·e·o·gram	$\mathcal{i}deg$
id·i·o·cy	$\mathcal{i}dese$
id·iom	$\mathcal{i}de$
id·i·o·mat·ic	$\mathcal{i}derlc$
id·i·o·syn·cra·sy	$\mathcal{i}desnCse$
id·i·ot	$\mathcal{i}del$
id·i·ot·ic	$\mathcal{i}delc$
i·dle	$\mathcal{i}dl$
i·dle·ness	$\mathcal{i}dl'$
i·dly	$\mathcal{i}dl$
i·dol	$\mathcal{i}dl$
i·dol·a·trous	$\mathcal{i}dl$
i·dol·a·try	$\mathcal{i}dl$
i·dol·ize	$\mathcal{i}dlz$
i·dyl	$\mathcal{i}dl$
i·dyl·lic	$\mathcal{i}dlc$
if	$\mathcal{f}$
ig·loo	$\mathcal{i}glu$
ig·ne·ous	$\mathcal{i}gnx$
ig·nite	$\mathcal{i}gnc$
ig·ni·tion	$\mathcal{i}ng$
ig·no·ble	$\mathcal{i}gnb$
ig·no·min·i·ous	$\mathcal{i}gn mx$
ig·no·min·y	$\mathcal{i}gn me$
ig·no·ra·mus	$\mathcal{i}gNrx$
ig·no·rance	$\mathcal{i}gN$

✓ig·no·rant	im·mac·u·late	
✓ig·nore	im·ma·nent	
ilk	im·ma·te·ri·al	
✓ill	im·ma·ture	
✓il·le·gal	im·meas·ur·a·ble	
il·leg·i·ble	im·me·di·a·cy	
il·le·git·i·mate	im·me·di·ate	
il·lic·it	im·me·di·ate·ly	
il·lit·er·ate	im·me·mo·ri·al	
✓ ill·ness	im·mense	
il·log·i·cal	im·merse	
ill·tem·pered	im·mi·grant	
il·lu·mi·nate	im·mi·grate	
il·lu·mi·na·tion	im·mi·nence	
il·lu·mine	im·mi·nent	
il·lu·sion	im·mo·bile	
il·lu·sive	im·mo·bi·lize	
il·lu·so·ry	im·mod·er·ate	
il·lus·trate	im·mod·est	
il·lus·tra·tion	im·mo·late	
il·lus·tra·tor	im·mor·al	
il·lus·tri·ous	im·mor·tal	
im·age	im·mov·a·ble	
im·age·ry	im·mune	
im·ag·i·nar·y	im·mu·ni·ty	
im·ag·i·na·tion	im·mu·nize	
im·ag·ine	im·mure	
im·bal·ance	im·mu·ta·ble	
im·be·cile	imp	
im·bed	im·pact	
im·bibe	im·pair	
im·bri·cate	im·pale	
im·bro·glio	im·pal·pa·ble	
im·bue	im·pan·el	
im·i·tate	im·part	
im·i·ta·tion	im·par·tial	
im·i·ta·tor	im·passe	

im·pas·si·ble		im·pla·ca·ble	
im·pas·sion		im·plant	
im·pas·sive		im·ple·ment	
im·pa·tience		im·pli·cate	
im·pa·tient		im·pli·ca·tion	
im·peach		im·plic·it	
im·pec·ca·ble		im·plic·it·ness	
im·pe·cu·ni·ous		im·plore	
im·pede		im·ply	
im·ped·i·ment		im·po·lite	
im·ped·i·men·ta		im·pol·i·tic	
im·pel		im·pon·der·a·ble	
im·pend		im·port	
im·pen·e·tra·ble		im·por·tance	
im·pen·i·tent		im·por·tant	
im·per·a·tive		im·por·ter	
im·per·cep·ti·ble		im·por·tune	
im·per·fect		im·pose	
im·per·fo·rate		im·pos·si·bil·i·ty	
im·pe·ri·al		im·pos·si·ble	
im·per·ri·al·ism		im·pos·tor	
im·per·il		im·po·tent	
im·pe·ri·ous		im·pound	
im·per·ish·a·ble		im·pov·er·ish	
im·per·me·a·ble		im·pre·ca·tion	
im·per·son·al		im·preg·na·ble	
im·per·son·ate		im·preg·nate	
im·per·ti·nence		im·pre·sa·ri·o	
im·per·ti·nent		im·press	
im·per·turb·a·ble		im·pres·sion	
im·per·vi·ous		im·pri·ma·tur	
im·pet·u·ous		im·print	
im·pe·tus		im·pris·on	
im·pi·e·ty		im·prob·a·ble	
im·pinge		im·promp·tu	
im·pi·ous		im·prop·er	
imp·ish		im·pro·pri·e·ty	

✓im·prove	*sv*	in·aus·pi·cious	*nasx*
im·prove·ment	*sv–*	in·bred	*nBd*
im·prov·i·dent	*svd–*	in·cal·cu·la·ble	*nclcll*
im·pro·vise	*svz*	in·ca·les·cent	*ncls–*
im·pru·dent	*sd–*	in·can·des·cent	*nc — s–*
im·pu·dent	*ipd–*	in·can·ta·tion	*nc–ŋ*
im·pugn	*ipn*	in·ca·pa·ble	*ncpb*
im·pulse	*ipls*	in·ca·pac·i·tate	*ncpsta*
im·pu·ni·ty	*ipn)*	in·car·cer·ate	*ncsa*
im·pure	*ipu*	in·car·na·tion	*nlnŋ*
im·pu·ta·tion	*iplŋ*	in·cau·tious	*ncx*
im·pute	*ipu*	in·cen·di·ar·y	*ns — y*
in	*n*	in·cense	*nsl*
in·a·bil·i·ty	*nab)*	in·cen·tive	*ns–v*
in·ac·ces·si·ble	*nfsb*	in·cep·tion	*nspŋ*
in·ac·cu·rate	*nacl*	in·ces·sant	*nss—*
in·ac·tion	*nacŋ*	in·cest	*ns,*
in·ac·tive	*nacv*	✓inch	*in*
in·ad·e·quate	*nadgl*	in·cho·ate	*ncol*
in·ad·mis·si·ble	*narsb*	in·ci·dence	*nsd/*
in·ad·vert·ent	*navt–*	in·ci·den·tal	*nsd–l*
in·ad·vis·a·ble	*navzb*	in·cin·er·ate	*nsNa*
in·al·ien·a·ble	*naenb*	in·cin·er·a·tor	*nsNa/*
in·ane	*nn*	in·cip·i·ent	*nspe–*
in·an·i·mate	*narl*	in·cise	*nsz/*
in·an·i·ty	*nn)*	in·ci·sor	*nsz/*
in·ap·pli·ca·ble	*napcb*	in·cite	*nsi*
in·ap·pro·pri·ate	*naspel*	in·ci·vil·i·ty	*nsvl)*
in·apt·i·tude	*napld*	in·clem·ent	*nc–*
in·ar·tic·u·late	*nlcll*	in·cline	*ncin*
in·as·much	*nzrc*	✓in·clude	*ncd*
in·at·ten·tion	*nalŋ*	in·cog·ni·to	*ncgnlo*
in·at·ten·tive	*nal–v*	in·cog·ni·zant	*ncgnz–*
in·au·di·ble	*nadb*	in·co·her·ent	*ncH–*
in·au·gu·ral	*naGl*	in·come	*nk*
in·au·gu·rate	*naGa*	in·com·men·su·rate	*nk/rl*
in·au·gu·ra·tion	*naGŋ*	in·com·mode	*nkd*

in·com·mu·ni·ca·ble	*nkncb*	in·cum·bent	*nkb —*
in·com·mu·ni·ca·do	*nkncdo*	in·cur	*nc*
in·com·pa·ra·ble	*nkpb*	in·cur·a·ble	*ncub*
in·com·pat·i·ble	*nkplb*	in·cu·ri·ous	*ncyx*
in·com·pe·tent	*nkpl —*	in·cur·sion	*nCj*
in·com·plete	*nkpe*	in·debt·ed	*ndt*
in·com·pre·hen·si·ble	*nkph/b*	in·de·cen·cy	*nds /*
in·con·clu·sive	*nkcsv*	in·de·cent	*ndo —*
in·con·gru·ous	*nkGj*	in·de·ci·sion	*ndsj*
in·con·se·quen·tial	*nksgx*	in·de·ci·sive	*ndssv*
in·con·sid·er·ate	*nksl*	in·dec·o·rous	*ndCx*
in·con·sist·ent	*nkss —*	in·deed	*ndd*
in·con·sol·a·ble	*nkslb*	in·de·fat·i·ga·ble	*ndflgb*
in·con·spic·u·ous	*nkscx*	in·de·fea·si·ble	*ndfzb*
in·con·stant	*nks —*	in·de·fin·a·ble	*ndfib*
in·con·test·a·ble	*nklsb*	in·def·i·nite	*ndfn*
in·con·ti·nent	*nkln —*	in·del·i·ble	*ndllb*
in·con·tro·vert·i·ble	*nkTvib*	in·del·i·cate	*ndlcl*
in·con·ven·ience	*nkvn /*	in·dem·ni·fy	*nd mf*
in·con·ven·ient	*nkvn —*	in·dem·ni·ty	*nd m)*
in·cor·po·rate	*nCpa*	in·dent	*nd —*
in·cor·po·re·al	*nCpyl*	in·den·ture	*ndC /*
in·cor·rect	*nkc*	in·de·pend·ence	*ind /*
in·cor·ri·gi·ble	*nCjb*	in·de·pen·dent	*ind*
in·cor·rupt·i·ble	*nCpb*	in·de·scrib·a·ble	*ndesb*
in·crease	*nCs*	in·de·struct·i·ble	*nd Scb*
in·cred·i·ble	*nCdb*	in·de·ter·mi·nate	*nd ml*
in·cred·u·lous	*nCdlx*	↓in·dex	*ndx*
in·cre·ment	*nC —*	In·di·an	*nden*
in·crim·i·nate	*nC ma*	in·di·cate	*ndca*
in·crust	*nC,*	in·dic·a·tive	*ndcv*
in·crus·ta·tion	*nCsj*	in·dict	*ndi*
in·cu·bate	*ncba*	in·dif·fer·ent	*ndf —*
in·cu·ba·tor	*ncba*	in·dig·e·nous	*ndfnx*
in·cu·bus	*ncbx*	in·di·gent	*ndj —*
in·cul·cate	*nclca*	in·di·gest·i·ble	*ndjsb*
in·cul·pate	*nclpa*	in·di·ges·tion	*ndjsCn*

in·dig·nant	*ndgn —*	in·el·e·gant	*neg—*
in·dig·ni·ty	*ndgn)*	in·el·i·gi·ble	*nejb*
in·di·go	*ndg*	in·e·luc·ta·ble	*nlcb*
in·di·rect	*nD*	in·ept	*np*
in·dis·creet	*ndsCe*	in·e·qual·i·ty	*negl)*
in·dis·cre·tion	*ndsCj*	in·eq·ui·ty	*neg)*
in·dis·crim·i·nate	*ndeCml*	in·e·rad·i·ca·ble	*nerdcb*
in·dis·pen·sa·ble	*nds/b*	in·ert	*nl*
in·dis·posed	*ndsz*	in·er·tia	*nla*
in·dis·pu·ta·ble	*ndsub*	in·es·ti·ma·ble	*neerb*
in·dis·so·lu·ble	*ndslb*	in·ev·i·ta·ble	*nevlb*
in·dis·tinct	*ndsq*	in·ex·act	*nec*
in·dite	*nde*	in·ex·cus·a·ble	*neczb*
in·di·vid·u·al	*ndv*	in·ex·haust·i·ble	*nesb*
in·di·vid·u·al·ist	*ndv,*	in·ex·o·ra·ble	*nlb*
in·di·vid·u·al·i·ty	*ndv)*	in·ex·pen·sive	*nep/v*
in·di·vis·i·ble	*ndvzb*	in·ex·pe·ri·ence	*nepy/*
in·doc·tri·nate	*ndcrna*	in·ex·pert	*nepl*
in·do·lent	*ndl —*	in·ex·pli·ca·ble	*nepcb*
in·dom·i·ta·ble	*ndrlb*	in·ex·press·i·ble	*nessb*
In·do·ne·sian	*ndnj*	in·ex·tri·ca·ble	*netcb*
in·doors	*ndos*	in·fal·li·ble	*nflb*
in·du·bi·ta·ble	*ndblb*	in·fa·mous	*nfrx*
in·duce	*nds*	in·fan·cy	*nf/*
in·duct	*ndc*	in·fant	*nf—*
in·dulge	*ndlj*	in·fan·tile	*nf—l*
in·du·rate	*ndl*	in·fan·try	*nf—re*
in·dus·tri·al	*ndSel*	in·fat·u·ate	*nfCa*
in·dus·tri·al·ist	*ndSel,*	in·fect	*nfc*
in·dus·tri·ous	*ndSr*	in·fec·tion	*nfcj*
in·dus·try	*ndSe*	in·fec·tious	*nfcx*
in·e·bri·ate	*nBa (nBl)*	in·fer	*nf*
in·ef·fa·ble	*nfb*	in·fe·ri·or	*nfy*
in·ef·face·a·ble	*nefsb*	in·fe·ri·or·i·ty	*nfy)*
in·ef·fec·tive	*nefcv*	in·fer·nal	*ntnl*
in·ef·fec·tu·al	*nefCul*	in·fer·no	*ntno*
in·ef·fi·cient	*nefs—*	in·fest	*nf,*

in·fi·del		in·ges·tion	
in·fi·del·i·ty		in·glo·ri·ous	
in·field		in·got	
in·fil·trate		in·grain	
in·fi·nite		in·grate	
in·fin·i·tes·i·mal		in·gra·ti·ate	
in·fin·i·tive		in·grat·i·tude	
in·fin·i·ty		in·gre·di·ent	
in·firm		in·gress	
in·flame		in·grown	
in·flam·ma·tion		in·hab·it	
in·flate		in·hab·it·ant	
in·flect		in·ha·la·tion	
in·flex·i·ble		in·hale	
in·flict		in·her·ent	
in·flow		in·her·it	
in·flu·ence		in·hib·it	
in·flu·en·tial		in·hos·pi·ta·ble	
in·flu·en·za		in·hu·man	
in·flux		in·im·i·cal	
in·form		in·im·i·ta·ble	
in·for·mal		in·iq·ui·tous	
in·for·mal·i·ty		in·i·tial	
in·form·ant		in·i·ti·ate	
in·for·ma·tion		in·i·ti·a·tive	
in·frac·tion		in·i·tial·ize	
in·fran·gi·ble		in·ject	
in·fra·red		in·junc·tion	
in·fre·quent		in·jure	
in·fringe		in·ju·ri·ous	
in·fu·ri·ate		in·ju·ry	
in·fuse		in·jus·tice	
in·fu·sion		ink	
in·gen·ious		ink·ling	
in·ge·nue		ink·stain	
in·ge·nu·i·ty		ink·stand	
in·gen·u·ous		ink·well	

in·laid		in·sa·ti·a·ble	
in·land		in·scribe	
in·lay		in·scrip·tion	
in·let		in·scru·ta·ble	
in·mate		in·sect	
in·most		in·sec·ti·cide	
inn		in·se·cure	
in·nate		in·se·cu·ri·ty	
√ in·ner		in·sen·sate	
in·ner·most		in·sen·si·ble	
inn·keep·er		in·sen·si·tive	
in·no·cence		in·sen·ti·ent	
in·no·cent		in·sep·a·ra·ble	
in·noc·u·ous		in·sert	
in·no·vate		in·ser·tion	
in·nu·en·do		in·side	
in·nu·mer·a·ble		in·sid·i·ous	
in·oc·u·late		in·sight	
in·of·fen·sive		in·sig·ni·a	
in·op·er·a·ble		in·sig·nif·i·cant	
in·op·por·tune		in·sin·cere	
in·or·di·nate		in·sin·u·ate	
in·or·gan·ic		in·sip·id	
in·put		in·sist	
in·quest		in·sist·ence	
in·qui·e·tude		in·so·far	
in·quire		in·sole	
in·quir·y		in·so·lent	
in·qui·si·tion		in·sol·u·ble	
in·quis·i·tive		in·sol·vent	
in·quis·i·tor		in·som·ni·a	
in·road		in·so·much	
in·rush		in·sou·ci·ance	
in·sa·lu·bri·ous		in·spect	
in·sane		in·spec·tor	
in·san·i·tar·y		in·spi·ra·tion	
in·san·i·ty		in·spire	

in·sta·bil·i·ty		in·tagl·io	
in·stall		in·take	
in·stal·la·tion		in·tan·gi·ble	
in·stance		in·te·ger	
in·stant		in·te·gral	
in·stan·ta·ne·ous		in·te·grate	
in·stant·ly		in·teg·ri·ty	
in·stead		in·teg·u·ment	
in·step		in·tel·lect	
in·sti·gate		in·tel·lec·tu·al	
in·still		in·tel·li·gence	
in·stinct		in·tel·li·gent	
in·stinc·tive		in·tel·li·gent·ly	
in·sti·tute		in·tem·per·ate	
in·sti·tu·tion		in·tend	
in·struct		in·tense	
in·struc·tion		in·ten·si·fy	
in·struc·tor		in·ten·si·ty	
in·stru·ment		in·tent	
in·stru·men·tal		in·ten·tion	
in·stru·men·ta·tion		in·ter	
in·sub·or·di·nate		in·ter·act	
in·suf·fer·a·ble		in·ter·cede	
in·suf·fi·cient		in·ter·cept	
in·su·lar		in·ter·ces·sion	
in·su·late		in·ter·change	
in·su·la·tor		in·ter·col·le·gi·ate	
in·sult		in·ter·com	
in·su·per·a·ble		in·ter·course	
in·sup·port·a·ble		in·ter·dict	
in·sur·a·ble		in·ter·est	
in·sur·ance		in·ter·fere	
in·sure		in·ter·fer·ence	
in·sur·gent		in·ter·im	
in·sur·mount·a·ble		in·te·ri·or	
in·sur·rec·tion		in·ter·ject	
in·tact		in·ter·line	

in·ter·loc·u·tor		in·ti·mate	
in·ter·lop·er		in·ti·ma·tion	
in·ter·lude		in·tim·i·date	
in·ter·mar·riage		in·to	
in·ter·me·di·ate		in·tol·er·a·ble	
in·ter·mi·na·ble		in·tol·er·ant	
in·ter·mis·sion		in·to·na·tion	
in·ter·mit·tent		in·tox·i·cant	
in·ter·mix		in·tox·i·cate	
in·tern		in·trac·ta·ble	
in·ter·nal		in·tran·si·gent	
in·ter·na·tion·al		in·tran·si·tive	
in·ter·ne·cine		in·tra·state	
in·ter·po·late		in·tra·ve·nous	
in·ter·pose		in·trep·id	
in·ter·pret		in·tri·cate	
in·ter·pre·ta·tion		in·trigue	
in·ter·reg·num		in·trin·sic	
in·ter·ro·gate		in·tro·duce	
in·ter·ro·ga·tion		in·tro·duced	
in·ter·rupt		in·tro·duc·tion	
in·ter·rup·tion		in·tro·duc·to·ry	
in·ter·sect		in·tro·spec·tion	
in·ter·sperse		in·tro·vert	
in·ter·state		in·trude	
in·ter·stice		in·tru·sion	
in·ter·twine		in·tu·i·tion	
in·ter·ur·ban		in·tu·i·tive	
in·ter·val		in·un·date	
in·ter·vene		in·ure	
in·ter·ven·tion		in·vade	
in·ter·view		in·val·id	
in·ter·weave		in·val·u·a·ble	
in·ter·wo·ven		in·var·i·a·ble	
in·tes·tate		in·va·sion	
in·tes·tine		in·vec·tive	
in·ti·ma·cy		in·veigh	

in·vei·gle		I·rish	
in·vent		irk	
in·ven·tion		i·ron	
in·ven·tor		i·ron·i·cal	
in·ven·to·ry		ir·ra·di·ate	
in·vert		ir·ra·tion·al	
in·vest		ir·rec·on·cil·a·ble	
in·ves·ti·gate		ir·re·deem·a·ble	
in·ves·ti·ga·tion		ir·re·duc·i·ble	
in·ves·ti·ga·tor		ir·ref·ra·ga·ble	
in·ves·ti·ture		ir·ref·u·ta·ble	
in·vest·ment		ir·reg·u·lar	
in·vet·er·ate		ir·rel·e·vant	
in·vid·i·ous		ir·re·li·gious	
in·vig·or·ate		ir·re·me·di·a·ble	
in·vin·ci·ble		ir·rep·a·ra·ble	
in·vi·o·late		ir·re·press·i·ble	
in·vis·i·ble		ir·re·proach·a·ble	
in·vi·ta·tion		ir·re·sist·i·ble	
in·vite		ir·res·o·lute	
in·vo·ca·tion		ir·re·spec·tive	
in·voice		ir·re·spon·si·ble	
in·voke		ir·retriev·a·ble	
in·vol·un·tar·y		ir·rev·er·ent	
in·volve		ir·re·vers·i·ble	
in·vul·ner·a·ble		ir·rev·o·ca·ble	
in·ward		ir·ri·gate	
i·o·dine		ir·ri·ga·tion	
i·on		ir·ri·ta·ble	
i·o·ta		ir·ri·tant	
ip·so fac·to		ir·ri·tate	
Ir·a·ni·an		ir·ri·ta·tion	
i·ras·ci·ble		is	
i·rate		i·sin·glass	
ire		is·land	
ir·i·des·cent		isle	
i·rid·i·um		is·n't	

i·so·late	*csla*	itch	
i·so·la·tion	*isly*	i·tem	
i·sos·ce·les	*csslz*	i·tem·ize	
i·so·tope	*islp*	it·er·ate	
Is·ra·el	*izrel*	i·tin·er·ant	
is·sue	*isu*	i·tin·er·ar·y	
isth·mus	*usrx*	its	
it	*l*	√ it·self	
I·tal·ian	*illn*	i·vo·ry	*wy*
i·tal·ic	*ille*	i·vy	*we*

jab		ja·lop·y	
ja·bot		jal·ou·sie	
jack		jam	
jack·al		jamb	
jack·et		jam·bo·ree	
jack·knife		jan·gle	
jac·quard		jan·i·tor	
jade		Jan·u·ar·y	
jag		Jap·a·nese	
jag·uar		jar	
jail		jar·di·niere	

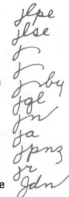

jar·gon		jilt	
jas·mine		jin·gle	
jas·per		jin·go	
jaun·dice		jinx	
jaunt		jit·ter	
jaunt·y		job	
jave·lin		job·ber	
jaw		jock·ey	
jay		jo·cose	
jazz		joc·u·lar	
jeal·ous		joc·und	
jeans		jog	
jeer		join	
Je·ho·vah		joint	
je·june		joint·ly	
jell		joist	
jel·ly		joke	
jeop·ard·ize		jok·er	
jeop·ard·y		jol·li·ty	
jer·e·mi·ad		jol·ly	
jerk		jolt	
jerk·y		jon·quil	
jer·kin		josh	
jer·sey		jos·tle	
jest		jot	
Jes·u·it		jounce	
jet		jour·nal	
jet·sam		jour·nal·ism	
jet·ti·son		jour·nal·ist	
jet·ty		jour·ney	
jew·el		jo·vi·al	
jew·el·er		jowl	
jew·el·ry		joy	
jib		joy·ful	
jibe		joy·ous	
jif·fy		ju·bi·lant	
jig		ju·bi·la·tion	

ju·bi·lee		junc·ture	
judge		June	
judg·ment		jun·gle	
ju·di·ca·ture		jun·ior	
ju·di·cial		ju·ni·per	
ju·di·ci·ar·y		junk	
ju·di·cious		jun·ta	
ju·do		ju·ris·dic·tion	
jug		ju·ris·pru·dence	
jug·ger·naut		ju·rist	
jug·gle		ju·ror	
jug·u·lar		ju·ry	
juice		√ just	
juic·i·ness		just·ly	
juic·y		jus·tice	
ju·jit·su		jus·ti·fi·ca·tion	
ju·jube		jus·ti·fy	
juke·box		just·ness	
ju·lep		jut	
Ju·ly		jute	
jum·ble		ju·ve·nile	
jump		jux·ta·po·si·tion	
junc·tion			

ka·bob	*cbb*	key·board	*ceBd*
kai·ser	*cz*	key·note	*cenl*
ka·lei·do·scope	*cldscp*	key·stone	*cesn*
kan·ga·roo	*cgu*	kha·ki	*cce*
ka·o·lin	*caln*	khan	*cn*
ka·pok	*cpc*	khe·dive	*cde*
ka·put	*cpl*	kick	*cc*
ka·ra·te	*c')*	kid	*cd*
kar·ma	*cra*	kid·nap	*cdnp*
kay·ak	*cic*	kid·ney	*cdne*
kedge	*cy*	kill	*cl*
keel	*cel*	kiln	*cln*
keen	*cn*	kil·o	*clo*
keen·ness	*cn'*	kil·o·cy·cle	*clscl* (kc)
keep	*cp*	kil·o·gram	*clg* (kg)
keep·sake	*cpsc*	kil·o·me·ter	*clv* (km)
keg	*cg*	kil·o·volt	*clvl*
kelp	*clp*	kil·o·watt	*clvll* (kw)
ken·nel	*cnl*	kilt	*cll*
kept	*cp*	ki·mo·no	*cma*
ker·nel	*cnl*	kin	*cn*
ker·o·sene	*csn*	kind	*ci*
ketch	*cC*	kin·der·gar·ten	*c——rgln*
ketch·up	*clp*	kind·est	*ci,*
ket·tle	*cll*	kind·heart·ed	*ciHt*
ket·tle·drum	*clld*	kin·dle	*c——l*
key	*ce*	kind·li·ness	*cil'*

133

kind·ly	*cil*	knead	*md*
kind·ness	*ci'*	knee	*ne*
kin·dred	*c — rd*	kneel	*nel*
ki·net·ic	*cnlc*	knell	*nl*
king	*cq*	knew	*nu*
king·dom	*cgd*	knick·knack	*ncnc*
kink	*cg*	knife	*nif*
kin·ship	*cnS*	knight	*ni*
kins·man	*cnz —*	knit	*nl*
ki·osk	*cesc*	knives	*nuz*
kip·per	*cp*	knob	*nb*
kis·met	*czrl*	knock	*nc*
kiss	*c'*	knock·out	*ncou*
kit	*cl*	knoll	*nol*
kitch·en	*cCn*	knot	*n*
kitch·en·ette	*cCnl*	know	*no*
kitch·en·ware	*cCnra*	know-how	*nohu*
kite	*ci*	knowl·edge	*nlj*
kith	*cl*	known	*no*
kit·ten	*cln*	knuck·le	*ncl*
klep·to·ma·ni·ac	*cp mec*	ko·dak	*cdc*
knack	*nc*	Ko·re·an	*Cen*
knap·sack	*npsc*	ko·sher	*cS*
knave	*na*		

lab	*lb*	lade	*ld*
✓ la·bel	*lb*	la·dle	*ldl*
la·bi·al	*lbel*	la·dy	*lde*
✓ la·bor	*lb*	lag	*lg*
lab·o·ra·to·ry	*l3ly*	la·ger	*lg*
la·bor·er	*l3'*	lag·gard	*lgd*
la·bo·ri·ous	*lbyx*	la·goon	*lgn*
la·bur·num	*l3n*	laid	*ld*
lab·y·rinth	*l3nl*	lain	*ln*
lac	*lc*	lair	*la*
lace	*las*	laird	*ld*
lac·er·ate	*lsa*	la·i·ty	*la)*
lac·er·a·tion	*lsj*	lake	*lc*
lach·ry·mal	*lcrl*	lamb	*l*
lach·ry·mose	*lcrs*	lam·baste	*lrba,*
lack	*lc*	lam·ben·cy	*lrb/*
lack·a·dai·si·cal	*lcdzcl*	lam·bent	*lrb—*
lack·ey	*lce*	lamb·skin	*lrscn*
la·con·ic	*lkc*	lame	*la*
lac·quer	*lc*	la·ment	*l—*
la·crosse	*lCs*	lam·en·ta·tion	*l—1*
lac·ta·tion	*lcj*	lam·i·nate	*lma*
lac·te·al	*lcel*	lamp	*lrp*
lac·tic	*lcc*	lam·poon	*lrpn*
la·cu·na	*lcna*	lam·prey	*lrpe*
lad	*ld*	lance	*l/*
lad·der	*ld*	lan·cet	*l/c*

land	*l —*	lar·ynx	*lgs*
lan·dau	*l — ⌣*	las·civ·i·ous	*lsvx*
land·hold·er	*l — hol*	lash	*lS*
land·la·dy	*l — lde*	lass	*l'*
land·lord	*l —ld*	las·si·tude	*lsld*
land·mark	*l — ⌐c*	√last	*l,*
land·own·er	*l — on*	last·ly	*lsl*
land·scape	*l — scp*	latch	*lC*
lane	*ln*	late	*la*
lan·guage	*lg*	late·ly	*lal*
lan·guid	*lgvd*	late·ness	*la'*
lan·guish	*lgvs*	la·tent	*ll —*
lan·guor	*lg*	⌐ lat·er	*la e*
lank	*lg*	lat·er·al	*lT*
lan·o·lin	*lnln*	⌐ lat·est	*la,*
lan·tern	*l— rn*	lath	*ll*
lan·yard	*lnlfd*	lathe	*lal*
La·o·tian	*lg*	lath·er	*lT*
lap	*lp*	lat·i·tude	*lttd*
la·pel	*lpl*	⟍ lat·ter	*l*
lap·i·dar·y	*lpdy*	lat·tice	*lls*
lapse	*lps*	Lat·vi·an	*llven*
lar·ce·nous	*lsnx*	laud	*ld*
lar·ce·ny	*lsne*	laud·a·ble	*ldb*
lard	*ld*	lau·da·num	*ldn*
large	*lg*	laugh	*lf*
large·ly	*lgl*	laugh·a·ble	*lfb*
large·ness	*lg'*	laugh·ter	*lf*
larg·er	*lg*	launch	*lC*
lar·gess	*lg'*	laun·der	*l —*
larg·est	*lg,*	laun·dress	*l — r'*
lar·i·at	*lyl*	laun·dry	*l — re*
lark	*lc*	lau·re·ate	*lyl*
lark·spur	*lcs*	lau·rel	*ll*
lar·va	*lva*	la·va	*lva*
lar·vàe	*lve*	lav·a·to·ry	*lvly*
lar·yn·gi·tis	*lgls*	lave	*la*

lav·en·der		lech·er·ous	
lav·ish		lec·tern	
law		lec·ture	
law·ful		led	
law·less		ledge	
law·mak·er		led·ger	
lawn		leech	
law·suit		leer	
law·yer		lee·way	
lax		left	
lax·a·tive		leg	
lax·i·ty		leg·a·cy	
lay		le·gal	
lay·er		le·gal·i·ty	
lay·ette		le·gal·ize	
lay·man		leg·ate	
lay·out		leg·a·tee	
la·zy		le·ga·tion	
lead		le·ga·to	
lead·en		leg·end	
lead·er		leg·end·ar·y	
lead·er·ship		leg·er·de·main	
leaf		leg·horn	
leaf·let		leg·i·bil·i·ty	
league		leg·i·ble	
leak		le·gion	
leak·age		leg·is·late	
lean		leg·is·la·tion	
leap		leg·is·la·tor	
learn		leg·is·la·ture	
lease		le·git·i·ma·cy	
lease·hold		le·git·i·mate	
leash		lei·sure	
least		lei·sure·ly	
leath·er		lem·on	
leave		lem·on·ade	
leav·en		lend	

length		lewd	
length·en		lex·i·cog·ra·pher	
length·i·er		lex·i·cog·ra·phy	
length·wise		lex·i·con	
length·y		li·a·bil·i·ty	
le·ni·ence		li·a·ble	
le·ni·ent		li·ai·son	
lens		li·ar	
lent		li·ba·tion	
len·til		li·bel	
le·o·nine		li·bel·ous	
leop·ard		lib·er·al	
le·o·tard		lib·er·al·i·ty	
lep·ro·sy		lib·er·al·ize	
le·sion		lib·er·ate	
less		lib·er·a·tion	
les·see		lib·er·a·tor	
less·en		lib·er·tine	
less·er		lib·er·ty	
les·son		li·bid·i·nous	
lest		li·bi·do	
let		li·brar·i·an	
le·thal		li·brar·y	
le·thar·gic		li·bret·to	
leth·ar·gy		lice	
let·ter		li·cense	
let·ter·head		li·cen·tious	
let·ter·press		li·chen	
let·tuce		lic·it	
lev·ee		lick	
lev·el		lic·o·rice	
lev·er		lid	
le·ver·age		lie	
le·vi·a·than		liege	
lev·i·ta·tion		li·en	
lev·i·ty		lieu	
lev·y		lieu·ten·ant	

life		lime·wa·ter	
life·boat		lim·i·nal	
life·less		lim·it	
life·like		lim·i·ta·tion	
life·line		lim·it·less	
life·long		limn	
life·sav·er		lim·ou·sine	
life·time		limp	
lift		lim·pet	
lift·off		lim·pid	
lig·a·ment		linch·pin	
lig·a·ture		line	
light		lin·e·age	
light·en		lin·e·al	
light·er		lin·e·a·ment	
light·house		lin·e·ar	
light·ly		lin·en	
light·ning		lin·er	
light·ship		lin·ger	
light·weight		lin·ge·rie	
lig·ne·ous		lin·go	
lig·nite		lin·guist	
like		lin·i·ment	
like·able		link	
like·li·hood		li·no·le·um	
like·ly		lin·seed	
like·ness		lint	
like·wise		lin·tel	
li·lac		li·on	
lilt		li·on·ess	
lil·y		lip	
limb		liq·ue·fac·tion	
lim·ber		liq·ue·fy	
lime		li·queur	
lime·light		liq·uid	
lim·er·ick		liq·ui·date	
lime·stone		liq·ui·da·tion	

liq·uor		liv·er	
lisle		liv·id	
lisp		liz·ard	
lis·some		load	
list		loaf	
lis·ten		loam	
list·less		loan	
lit		loathe	
lit·a·ny		loath·some	
li·ter		loaves	
lit·er·a·cy		lob·by	
lit·er·al		lobe	
lit·er·al·ly		lob·ster	
lit·er·ar·y		lo·cal	
lit·er·ate		lo·cal·ity	
lit·e·ra·ti		lo·cal·ize	
lit·er·a·ture		lo·cate	
lithe		lo·ca·tion	
lithe·some		lock	
lith·i·um		lock·jaw	
lith·o·graph		lock·out	
li·thog·ra·pher		lock·smith	
li·thog·ra·phy		lo·co·mo·tion	
Lith·u·a·ni·an		lo·co·mo·tive	
lit·i·gant		lo·cus	
lit·i·gate		lo·cust	
lit·i·ga·tion		lo·cu·tion	
li·ti·gious		lode	
lit·mus		lode·stone	
lit·ter		lodge	
lit·tle		loft	
lit·ur·gy		loft·y	
liv·a·ble		log	
live		log·a·rithm	
live·li·hood		loge	
live·long		log·gia	
live·ly		log·ic	

log·i·cal		loud	
lo·gi·cian		loud·speak·er	
lo·gy		lounge	
loin		louse	
loin·cloth		lout	
loi·ter		lou·ver	
loll		lov·a·ble	
lol·li·pop		love	
lone		love·li·ness	
lone·li·ness		love·ly	
lone·ly		love·sick	
lone·some		low	
long		low·born	
long·boat		low·brow	
lon·gev·i·ty		low·er	
long·hand		low·est	
lon·gi·tude		low·land	
long·shore·man		lox	
look		loy·al	
look·out		loy·al·ty	
loom		loz·enge	
loon		lub·ber	
loop		lu·bri·cant	
loop·hole		lu·bri·cate	
loose		lu·bri·cious	
loose·ly		lu·cid	
lo·qua·cious		lu·cid·i·ty	
lord		luck	
lore		luck·i·er	
lor·gnette		luck·y	
lor·ry		lu·cra·tive	
lose		lu·cre	
loss		lu·cu·bra·tion	
lost		lu·di·crous	
lot		lug	
lo·tion		lug·gage	
lot·ter·y		lu·gu·bri·ous	

luke·warm		lush	
lull		lust	
lull·a·by		√ lus·ter	
lum·ba·go		√ lus·trous	
lum·ber		lust·y	
lu·mi·nar·y		lute	
lu·mi·nous		Lu·ther·an	
lump		lux·u·ri·ant	
lu·na·cy		lux·u·ri·ate	
lu·nar		lux·u·ri·ous	
lu·na·tic		lux·u·ry	
√ lunch		ly·ce·um	
lunch·eon		lye	
lunch·room		lymph	
lu·nette		lym·phat·ic	
lung		lynch	
lunge		lynx	
lurch		lyre	
lure		ly·on·naise	
lu·rid		lyr·ic	
lurk		lyr·i·cal	
lus·cious			

ma·ca·bre		mag·got	
mac·ad·am		mag·ic	
mac·a·ro·ni		ma·gi·cian	
mac·a·roon		mag·is·te·ri·al	
mace		mag·is·trate	
mac·er·ate		mag·na·nim·i·ty	
mac·er·a·tion		mag·nan·i·mous	
mach		mag·nate	
ma·che·te		mag·ne·sia	
mach·i·na·tion		mag·ne·si·um	
ma·chine		mag·net	
ma·chin·er·y		mag·net·ic	
ma·chin·ist		mag·ne·tism	
mack·er·el		mag·ne·tize	
mack·i·naw		mag·ne·to	
mac·ro·cosm		mag·ni·fi·ca·tion	
ma·cron		mag·nif·i·cence	
mad		mag·nif·i·cent	
mad·am		mag·ni·fy	
made		mag·ni·tude	
ma·de·moi·selle		mag·no·li·a	
ma·dras		mag·num	
mad·ri·gal		mag·pie	
mael·strom		ma·ha·ra·ja	
mae·stro		ma·hog·a·ny	
mag·a·zine		maid	
ma·gen·ta		maid·en	

maid·en·hair		mal·for·ma·tion	
maid·serv·ant		mal·formed	
mail		mal·ice	
mail·a·ble		ma·li·cious	
mail·bag		ma·lign	
mail·box		ma·lig·nan·cy	
mail·man		ma·lig·nant	
maim		ma·lin·ger	
main		mall	
main·land		mal·lard	
main·ly		mal·le·a·ble	
main·stay		mal·let	
main·tain		mal·low	
main·te·nance		mal·nu·tri·tion	
ma·jes·tic		mal·oc·clu·sion	
maj·es·ty		mal·o·dor·ous	
ma·jol·i·ca		mal·prac·tice	
maj·or		malt	
ma·jor·do·mo		malt·ose	
ma·jor·i·ty		mal·treat	
make		ma·ma	
make·shift		mam·mal	
mal·a·chite		mam·mon	
mal·ad·just·ment		mam·moth	
mal·ad·min·is·ter		man	
mal·a·droit		man·a·cle	
mal·a·dy		man·age	
ma·laise		man·age·a·ble	
ma·lar·i·a		man·age·ment	
mal·con·tent		man·ag·er	
male		man·a·ge·ri·al	
mal·e·dic·tion		man·ci·ple	
mal·e·fac·tion		man·da·mus	
mal·e·fac·tor		man·da·rin	
ma·lef·ic		man·date	
ma·lev·o·lent		man·da·to·ry	
mal·fea·sance		man·di·ble	

man·do·lin		man·teau	
man·drel		man·tel	
mane		man·til·la	
ma·neu·ver		man·tle	
ma·neu·ver·a·bil·i·ty		man·u·al	
man·ga·nese		man·u·fac·ture	
mange		man·u·fac·tur·er	
man·ger		man·u·mis·sion	
man·gle		ma·nure	
man·go		man·u·script	
man·grove		man·y	
man·han·dle		Ma·o·ri	
man·hole		map	
man·hood		ma·ple	
ma·ni·a		mar	
ma·ni·ac		mar·a·schi·no	
man·i·cure		mar·a·thon	
man·i·fest		ma·raud	
man·i·fes·to		mar·ble	
man·i·fold		mar·ble·ize	
man·i·kin		march	
ma·nip·u·late		mar·che·sa	
ma·nip·u·la·tion		mar·che·se	
ma·nip·u·la·tor		mar·chion·ess	
man·kind		mare	
man·ly		mar·ga·rine	
man·na		mar·gin	
man·ne·quin		mar·gin·al	
man·ner		mar·gi·na·li·a	
man·ner·ism		mar·grave	
man·nish		mar·i·gold	
man·or		ma·ri·na	
ma·no·ri·al		mar·i·nade	
manse		mar·i·nate	
man·ser·vant		ma·rine	
man·sion		mar·i·ner	
man·slaugh·ter		mar·i·o·nette	

mar·i·tal		mash	
mar·i·time		mask	
mar·jo·ram		mas·och·ism	
mark		mas·och·ist	
mark·er		ma·son	
mar·ket		mas·quer·ade	
✓ mar·ket·a·ble		mass	
marl		mas·sa·cre	
mar·lin		mas·sage	
mar·ma·lade		mas·seur	
mar·mo·set		mas·seuse	
mar·mot		mas·sif	
ma·roon		mas·sive	
mar·quee		mast	
mar·que·try		mas·ter	
mar·quis		mas·ter·ful	
mar·quise		mas·ter·piece	
mar·riage		mas·ter·y	
mar·riage·a·ble		mast·head	
mar·row		mas·ti·cate	
mar·ry		mas·ti·ca·tion	
marsh		mas·tiff	
mar·shal		mas·to·don	
marsh·mal·low		mas·toid	
mart		mat	
mar·ten		mat·a·dor	
mar·tial		match	
mar·tial·ly		match·book	
mar·ti·net		match·less	
mar·tyr		match·mak·er	
mar·tyr·dom		mate	
mar·vel		ma·te·ri·al	
mar·vel·ous		ma·te·ri·al·ism	
mas·ca·ra		ma·te·ri·al·ist	
mas·cot		ma·te·ri·al·ize	
mas·cu·line		ma·ter·nal	
mas·cu·lin·i·ty		ma·ter·ni·ty	

math·e·mat·i·cal		may·be	
math·e·ma·ti·cian		May·day	
math·e·mat·ics		may·hem	
mat·i·nee		may·on·naise	
ma·tri·arch		may·or	
ma·tri·arch·y		may·or·al·ty	
mat·rices		maze	
ma·tric·u·late		ma·zur·ka	
ma·tric·u·la·tion		me	
mat·ri·mo·ni·al		mead	
mat·ri·mo·ny		mead·ow	
ma·trix		mea·ger	
ma·tron		meal	
ma·tron·ly		mean	
mat·ter		me·an·der	
mat·tock		mean·ness	
mat·tress		meant	
mat·u·rate		mean·time	
mat·u·ra·tion		mean·while	
ma·ture		mea·sles	
ma·tu·ri·ty		mea·sly	
ma·tu·tin·al		meas·ur·a·ble	
mat·zo		meas·ure	
maud·lin		meas·ure·ment	
maul		meas·ur·er	
maun·der		meat	
mau·so·le·um		me·a·tus	
mauve		mec·ca	
mav·er·ick		me·chan·ic	
maw		me·chan·i·cal	
mawk·ish		mech·a·nism	
max·il·la		med·al	
max·il·lar·y		me·dal·lion	
max·im		med·dle	
max·i·mum		med·dle·some	
may		me·di·a	
ma·ya		me·di·al	

me·di·an	*den*	mel·o·dra·ma	
me·di·ate	*da*	mel·o·dy	
me·di·a·tion	*dy*	mel·on	
me·di·a·tor	*da*	melt	
med·i·ca·ble	*dcb*	✓mem·ber	
med·i·cal	*dcl*	mem·ber·ship	
me·dic·a·ment	*dc–*	mem·brane	
med·i·cate	*dca*	mem·bra·nous	
med i·ca·tion	*dcy*	me·men·to	
me·dic·i·nal	*dsnl*	mem·o	
med·i·cine	*dsn*	mem·oir	
me·di·e·val	*devl*	mem·o·ra·bil·ia	
me·di·o·cre	*dec*	mem·o·ra·ble	
me·di·oc·ri·ty	*deC)*	mem·o·rand·um	
med·i·tate	*dla*	me·mo·ri·al	
med·i·ta·tion	*dly*	me·mo·ri·al·ize	
me·di·um	*de*	mem·o·rize	
med·ley	*dl*	mem·o·ry	
meek	*ec*	men	
meer·schaum		men·ace	
meet	*e*	mé·nage	
meg·a·cy·cle	*gscl*	me·nag·er·ie	
meg·a·phone	*gfn*	mend	
meg·a·ton	*gln*	men·da·cious	
mel·an·cho·li·a	*lncla*	men·di·cant	
mel·an·chol·y	*lncl*	me·ni·al	
Mel·a·ne·sian	*lny*	me·nin·ges	
mé·lange	*lnz*	men·in·gi·tis	
mel·a·noid	*lnyd*	men·o·pause	
meld	*ld*	men's	
me·lee	*la*	men·ses	
mel·io·rate	*lEa*	men·stru·al	
mel·io·ra·tion	*lEy*	men·stru·ate	
mel·lif·lu·ous	*lfx*	men·stru·a·tion	
mel·low	*lo*	men·sur·a·ble	
me·lo·de·on	*lden*	men·su·ra·tion	
me·lo·di·ous	*ldx*	men·tal	

men·tal·i·ty		mes·mer·ism	
men·tal·ly		mes·mer·ize	
men·thol		mess	
men·tion		mes·sage	
men·tor		mes·sen·ger	
men·u		mes·si·ah	
me·phi·tic		mes·sieurs	
mer·can·tile		mes·sy	
mer·ce·nar·y		mes·ti·zo	
mer·cer·ize		met	
✓mer·chan·dise		me·tab·o·lism	
mer·chant		met·al	
mer·chant·man		✓me·tal·lic	
mer·ci·ful		✓met·al·loid	
mer·ci·less		met·al·lur·gy	
mer·cu·ri·al		met·a·mor·phic	
mer·cu·ry		met·a·mor·pho·ses	
mer·cy		met·a·mor·pho·sis	
mere		met·a·phor	
mere·ly		met·a·phor·i·cal	
mer·e·tri·cious		met·a·phys·i·cal	
✓merge		met·a·phys·ics	
merg·er		me·tas·ta·sis	
me·rid·i·an		met·a·tar·sal	
me·ringue		mete	
me·ri·no		me·te·or	
mer·it		me·te·or·ite	
mer·i·to·ri·ous		me·te·or·ol·o·gist	
mer·maid		me·te·or·ol·o·gy	
mer·man		me·ter	
mer·ri·ly		meth·od	
mer·ri·ment		me·thod·i·cal	
mer·ry		Meth·od·ist	
me·sa		meth·od·ize	
més·al·li·ance		meth·od·ol·o·gy	
mesh		meth·yl·ate	
me·si·al		me·tic·u·lous	

Word	Shorthand	Word	Shorthand
mé·tier		mid·year	
met·ric		mien	
met·ri·cal		miff	
met·ro·nome		might	
me·trop·o·lis		might·i·ness	
me·tro·pol·i·tan		might·y	
met·tle		mi·gnon·ette	
met·tle·some		mi·graine	
Mex·i·can		mi·grate	
mez·za·nine		mi·gra·tion	
mez·zo·so·pra·no		mi·ka·do	
mi·as·ma		milch	
mi·ca		mild	
mice		mil·dew	
mi·crobe		mild·ly	
mi·cro·bi·al		mile	
mi·cro·cosm		mile·age	
mi·cro·or·gan·ism		mile·post	
mi·cro·phone		mile·stone	
mi·cro·scope		mi·lieu	
mi·cro·scop·ic		mil·i·tant	
mi·cro·sec·ond		mil·i·ta·rist	
mi·cro·wave		mil·i·tar·y	
mid		mil·i·tate	
mid·aft·er·noon		mi·li·tia	
mid·course		milk	
mid·day		milk·sop	
mid·den		mill	
mid·dle		mil·len·ni·um	
midg·et		mill·er	
mid·land		mil·let	
mid·night		mil·li·gram	(mg)
mid·ship·man		mil·li·me·ter	(mm)
mid·sum·mer		mil·li·ner	
mid·way		mil·li·ner·y	
mid·week		mil·lion	
mid·wife		mil·lion·aire	

mil·lionth		min·ute·ly	
mil·li·sec·ond		mi·nu·ti·ae	
mill·stone		mir·a·cle	
mim·e·o·graph		mi·rac·u·lous	
mim·ic		mi·rage	
mim·ic·ry		mire	
mi·mo·sa		mir·ror	
min·a·ret		mirth	
min·a·to·ry		mis·ad·ven·ture	
mince		mis·an·thrope	
mind		mis·ap·pli·ca·tion	
mind·ful		mis·ap·pre·hen·sion	
mine		mis·ap·pro·pri·ate	
min·er		mis·be·got·ten	
min·er·al		mis·be·have	
min·er·al·o·gy		mis·be·lief	
min·gle		mis·cal·cu·late	
min·i·a·ture		mis·ce·ge·na·tion	
min·i·mal		mis·cel·la·ne·ous	
min·i·mize		mis·cel·la·ny	
min·i·mum		mis·chance	
min·ion		mis·chief	
min·is·cule		mis·chie·vous	
min·is·ter		mis·ci·ble	
min·is·trant		mis·con·cep·tion	
min·i·track		mis·con·duct	
mink		mis·con·struc·tion	
min·now		mis·con·strue	
mi·nor		mis·cre·ant	
mi·nor·i·ty		mis·cue	
min·ster		mis·deal	
min·strel		mis·deed	
mint		mis·de·mean·or	
min·u·end		mis·di·rect	
min·u·et		mi·ser	
mi·nus		mis·er·a·ble	
min·ute		mis·er·y	

mis·fea·sance		mis·tle·toe	
mis·fire		mis·took	
mis·fit		mis·tral	
mis·for·tune		mis·treat	
mis·giv·ing		mis·tress	
mis·gov·ern		mis·tri·al	
mis·guide		mis·trust	
mis·hap		mist·y	
mis·in·form		mis·un·der·stand	
mis·in·ter·pret		mis·un·der·stood	
mis·judge		mis·use	
mis·lay		mite	
mis·lead		mi·ter	
mis·man·age		mit·i·gate	
mis·no·mer		mit·i·ga·tor	
mi·sog·y·nous		mitt	
mis·place		mit·ten	
mis·print		mit·ti·mus	
mis·pro·nounce		mix	
mis·quo·ta·tion		mix·er	
mis·read		mix·ture	
mis·reck·on		miz·zen	
mis·rep·re·sent		miz·zle	
mis·rule		mne·mon·ic	
miss		moan	
missed		moat	
mis·shap·en		mob	
mis·sile		mo·bile	
mis·sile·man		mo·bil·i·ty	
mis·sion		mo·bi·lize	
mis·sion·ar·y		mob·ster	
mis·sive		moc·ca·sin	
mis·spell		mo·cha	
mis·state		mock	
mist		mock·er·y	
mis·take		mode	
mis·step		mod·el	

mod·er·ate		mo·lest	
mod·er·a·tion		mo·les·ta·tion	
mod·er·a·tor		mol·li·fi·ca·tion	
mod·ern		mol·li·fy	
mod·er·ni·ty		mol·lusk	
mod·ern·ize		mol·ly·cod·dle	
mod·est		molt	
mod·es·ty		mol·ten	
mod·i·cum		mo·lyb·de·num	
mod·i·fi·a·ble		mo·ment	
mod·i·fi·ca·tion		mo·men·tar·y	
mod·i·fi·er		mo·men·tous	
mod·i·fy		mo·men·tum	
mod·ish		mon·arch	
mo·diste		mon·arch·ism	
mod·u·lar		mon·arch·y	
mod·u·late		mon·as·ter·y	
mod·u·la·tion		mo·nas·tic	
mod·ule		mon·au·ral	
mod·u·lus		Mon·day	
mo·dus vi·ven·di		mon·e·tar·y	
mo·gul		mon·ey	
mo·hair		Mon·go·lian	
Mo·ham·med·an		mon·grel	
moi·e·ty		mon·i·tor	
moil		mon·i·tress	
moist		monk	
mois·ten		mon·key	
mois·ture		mon·key·shine	
mo·lar		mon·o·chrome	
mo·las·ses		mon·o·cle	
mold		mo·nog·a·mous	
mold·er		mo·nog·a·my	
mold·y		mon·o·gram	
mole		mon·o·graph	
mo·lec·u·lar		mo·nog·y·ny	
mol·e·cule		mon·o·lith	

mon·o·logue		moot	
mon·o·ma·ni·a		mop	
mon·o·plane		mope	
mo·nop·o·list		mop·pet	
mo·nop·o·lize		mo·raine	
mo·nop·o·ly		mor·al	
mon·o·syl·la·ble		mo·rale	
mon·o·tone		mor·al·ist	
mo·not·o·nous		mor·al·i·ty	
mon·ox·ide		mor·al·ize	
mon·sieur		mo·rass	
mon·si·gnor		mor·a·to·ri·um	
mon·soon		mor·bid	
mon·ster		mor·bid·i·ty	
mon·stros·i·ty		mor·dant	
mon·strous		more	
mon·tage		more·o·ver	
month		mo·res	
month·ly		morgue	
mon·u·ment		mor·i·bund	
mon·u·men·tal		Mor·mon	
mood		morn	
mood·i·ness		morn·ing	
mood·y		mo·roc·co	
moon		mo·ron	
moon·beam		mo·rose	
moon·light		mor·phi·a	
moon·light·er		mor·phine	
moon·lit		mor·row	
moon·rise		mor·sel	
moon·scape		mor·tal	
moon·shine		mor·tal·i·ty	
moon·stone		mor·tar	
moor		mor·tar·board	
moor·age		mort·gage	
Moor·ish		mort·ga·gee	
moose		mort·ga·gor	

mor·ti·cian		mo·tor·man	
mor·ti·fi·ca·tion		mot·tle	
mor·ti·fy		mot·to	
mor·tise		mound	
mor·tu·ar·y		mount	
mo·sa·ic		moun·tain	
mo·sey		moun·tain·eer	
Mos·lem		mount·ain·ous	
mosque		moun·te·bank	
mos·qui·to		mourn	
moss		mourn·ful	
moss·back		mouse	
moss·i·ness		mousse	
most		mous·y	
mote		mouth	
mo·tel		mouth·ful	
moth		mouth·piece	
moth·er		mov·a·ble	
moth·er·hood		move	
moth·er·in·law		mov·er	
moth·er·land		move·ment	
moth·er·ly		mov·ie	
moth·proof		mow	
mo·tif		mow·er	
mo·tile		mown	
mo·tion		Mr.	
mo·tion·less		Mrs.	
mo·ti·vate		much	
mo·tive		mu·ci·lage	
mot·ley		mu·ci·lag·i·nous	
mo·tor		muck	
mo·tor·boat		muck·rak·er	
mo·tor·cade		mu·cous	
mo·tor·car		mu·cus	
mo·tor·cy·cle		mud	
mo·tor·ist		mud·di·ness	
mo·tor·ize		mud·dle	

mud·dy		mum	
mud·guard		mum·ble	
mud·sling·er		mum·mi·fy	
mu·ez·zin		mum·my	
muff		mumps	
muf·fin		munch	
muf·fle		mun·dane	
muf·fler		mu·nic·i·pal	
muf·ti		mu·nic·i·pal·i·ty	
mug		mu·nif·i·cence	
mug·ger		mu·nif·i·cent	
mug·wump		mu·ni·tion	
mu·lat·to		mu·ral	
mul·ber·ry		mur·der	
mulch		mur·der·er	
mulct		mur·der·ous	
mule		murk	
mull		mur·mur	
mul·lion		mur·mur·ous	
mul·ti·far·i·ous		mur·rain	
mul·ti·form		mus·ca·tel	
mul·ti·graph		mus·cle	
mul·ti·lat·er·al		mus·cu·lar	
Mul·tim·eter		mus·cu·lar·i·ty	
mul·ti·mil·lion·aire		mus·cu·la·ture	
mul·ti·ped		muse	
mul·ti·ple		mu·sette	
mul·ti·plex		mu·se·um	
mul·ti·pli·a·ble		mush	
mul·ti·pli·cand		mush·room	
mul·ti·pli·ca·tion		mush·y	
mul·ti·plic·i·ty		mu·sic	
mul·ti·pli·er		mu·si·cal	
mul·ti·ply		mu·si·cian	
mul·ti·stage		musk	
mul·ti·tude		mus·ket	
mul·ti·tu·di·nous		mus·ket·eer	

musk·rat		mu·tu·al	
Mus·lim		mu·tu·al·ly	
mus·lin		muz·zle	
muss		my	
mus·sel		my·o·pi·a	
must		my·op·ic	
mus·tache		myr·i·ad	
mus·tang		myr·mi·don	
mus·tard		myrrh	
mus·ter		my·self	
mus·ti·ness		mys·te·ri·ous	
mus·ty		mys·ter·y	
mu·ta·ble		mys·tic	
mu·tate		mys·ti·cal	
mu·ta·tion		mys·ti·cism	
mute		mys·ti·fi·ca·tion	
mu·ti·late		mys·ti·fy	
mu·ti·la·tion		mys·tique	
mu·ti·nous		myth	
mu·ti·ny		myth·i·cal	
mut·ter		my·thol·o·gy	
mut·ton			

nab	*nb*	nar·co·tism	*nclz*
na·bob	*nbb*	nar·rate	*na*
na·celle	*nsl*	nar·ra·tion	*ny*
na·cre	*nc*	nar·ra·tive	*nv*
na·cre·ous	*ncx*	nar·ra·tor	*na*
na·dir	*nd*	✓ nar·row	*no*
nag	*nq*	nar·row·ly	*nol*
nag·ger	*ng*	na·sal	*nzl*
nail	*nal*	na·sal·i·ty	*nzl)*
na·ive	*ne*	na·sal·ize	*nzlz*
na·ive·té	*nela*	nas·cent	*ns—*
na·ked	*ncd*	nas·ti·ly	*nsl*
nam·by·pam·by	*nbp-be*	nas·ti·ness	*nse'*
✓ name	*na*	na·stur·tium	*nSS*
name·less	*nal'*	nas·ty	*ns)*
name·ly	*nal*	na·tal	*nll*
name·sake	*nasc*	na·tant	*nt—*
nap	*np*	na·ta·to·ri·al	*nttyl*
nape	*nap*	na·ta·to·ri·um	*ntty*
na·per·y	*npy*	✓ na·tion	*ny*
naph·tha	*npta*	na·tion·al	*nyl*
nap·kin	*npcn*	na·tion·al·i·ty	*nyl)*
na·po·le·on	*nplen*	na·tion·al·ize	*nylz*
Na·po·le·on·ic	*nplenc*	na·tion·al·ly	*nyl*
nar·cis·sist	*nss,*	na·tive	*nv*
nar·cis·sus	*nssx*	na·tive·ly	*nvl*
nar·cot·ic	*nclc*	na·tiv·i·ty	*nv)*

nat·ty		neb·u·lar	
nat·u·ral		neb·u·lous	
nat·u·ral·ism		nec·es·sar·i·ly	
nat·u·ral·ist		nec·es·sar·y	
nat·u·ral·ize		ne·ces·si·tate	
nat·u·ral·ly		ne·ces·si·tous	
nat·u·ral·ness		ne·ces·si·ty	
na·ture		neck	
naught		neck·lace	
naugh·ti·ness		neck·tie	
naugh·ty		ne·crop·o·lis	
nau·se·a		ne·cro·sis	
nau·se·ate		nec·tar	
nau·seous		nec·tar·ine	
nau·ti·cal		née	
nau·ti·lus		need	
Nav·a·ho		need·ful	
na·val		need·i·est	
nave		need·i·ness	
nav·i·gate		nee·dle	
nav·i·ga·tion		need·less	
nav·i·ga·tor		need·y	
na·vy		ne·far·i·ous	
nay		ne·gate	
Na·zi		ne·ga·tion	
Ne·an·der·thal		neg·a·tive	
near		neg·a·tiv·ism	
near·er		neg·lect	
near·est		neg·lect·ful	
near·ly		neg·li·gee	
near·ness		neg·li·gence	
near·sight·ed		neg·li·gent	
neat		neg·li·gi·ble	
neat·er		ne·go·ti·a·bil·i·ty	
neat·ness		ne·go·ti·a·ble	
neb·u·la		ne·go·ti·ate	
neb·u·lae		ne·go·ti·a·tion	

ne·go·ti·a·tor		✓neu·tral	
Ne·gro		neu·tral·i·ty	
neigh		neu·tral·ize	
✓neigh·bor		neu·tron	
neigh·bor·hood		✓nev·er	
neigh·bor·ly		✓nev·er·the·less	
✓nei·ther		new	
nem·e·sis		new·com·er	
ne·on		new·el	
ne·o·lith·ic		new·ly	
ne·o·phyte		new·ness	
ne·o·plasm		news	
ne·o·ter·ic		news·cas·ter	
neph·ew		news·pa·per	
ne·phri·tis		news·pa·per·man	
nep·o·tism		news·print	
nerve		news·stand	
nerve·less		✓next	
nerv·ous		nib	
nerv·y		nib·ble	
nest		nib·lick	
nes·tle		nice	
net		nice·ly	
neth·er		ni·ce·ty	
neth·er·most		niche	
net·tle		nick	
net·work		nick·el	
neu·ral		nick·el·o·de·on	
neu·ral·gia		nick·er	
neu·ras·the·ni·a		nick·name	
neu·ri·tis		nic·o·tine	
neu·rol·o·gist		nif·ty	
neu·rol·o·gy		Ni·ge·ri·an	
neu·ron		niece	
neu·ro·sis		nig·gard	
neu·rot·ic		nig·gard·ly	
neu·ter		nig·gle	

nigh	
night	
night·cap	
night·fall	
night·gown	
night·in·gale	
night·ly	
night·mare	
night·time	
ni·hil·ist	
ni·hil·is·tic	
nil	
nim·ble	
nim·bus	
nin·com·poop	
nine	9
ninth	9
nip	
nip·ple	
nir·va·na	
ni·sei	
ni·ter	
ni·trate	
ni·tric	
ni·tride	
ni·tri·fy	
ni·trite	
ni·tro·gen	
ni·tro·glyc·er·in	
ni·trous	
nit·wit	
no	
no·bil·i·ty	
no·ble	
no·ble·man	
no·ble·wom·an	
no·bly	

no·bod·y	
noc·tur·nal	
noc·turne	
nod	
nod·u·lar	
node	
nod·ule	
✓noise	
noise·less	
nois·i·ly	
noi·some	
nois·y	
no·mad	
no·mad·ic	
no·men·cla·ture	
nom·i·nal	
nom·in·al·ly	
nom·i·nate	
nom·i·na·tion	
nom·i·na·tor	
nom·i·nee	
nonce	
non·cha·lance	
non·cha·lant	
non·com·bat·ant	
non·com·mit·tal	
non com·pos men·tis	
non·con·duc·tor	
non·con·form·ist	
non·de·script	
✓none	
non·en·ti·ty	
non·ex·ist·ent	
non·fea·sance	
non·in·ter·ven·tion	
non·join·der	
non·pa·reil	

non·par·ti·san		not	
non·plus		no·ta·bil·i·ty	
√non·sense		no·ta·ble	
non·stop		no·ta·bly	
non·sup·port		no·tar·i·al	
non·un·ion		√no·ta·rize	
noo·dle		√no·ta·ry	
nook		no·ta·tion	
noon		notch	
noon·day		note	
noon·time		note·book	
noose		note·wor·thy	
nor		noth·ing	
Nor·dic		no·tice	
norm		no·tice·a·ble	
√nor·mal		no·ti·fi·ca·tion	
nor·mal·i·ty		no·ti·fy	
nor·mal·ly		no·tion	
Norse		no·tion·al	
√north		no·to·ri·e·ty	
north·east		no·to·ri·ous	
north·eas·ter		not·with·stand·ing	
north·east·ern		noun	
north·er·ly		nour·ish	
north·ern		no·va	
North·ern·er		nov·el	
north·ward		nov·el·ette	
north·west		nov·el·ist	
north·west·ern		nov·el·ty	
Nor·we·gian		No·vem·ber	
nose		no·ve·na	
nose·bleed		nov·ice	
nose·gay		no·vi·ti·ate	
nose·piece		No·vo·cain	
nos·tal·gi·a		now	
nos·tril		now·a·days	
nos·trum		no·where	

nox·ious	*ncx*	nu·mer·ic·al	*n cl*
noz·zle	*nzl*	nu·mer·ous	*n r*
nu·ance	*nu /*	nu·mis·mat·ics	*nzlcs*
nub	*nb*	nu·mis·ma·tist	*nzrl,*
nub·bin	*nbn*	num·skull	*nscl*
nu·bile	*nb*	nun	*nn*
nu·cle·ar	*nce*	nun·cio	*n/o*
nu·cle·a·tion	*ncj*	nun·cu·pa·tive	*nncpv*
nu·cle·us	*ncx*	nun·ner·y	*nny*
nude	*nd*	nup·tial	*npx*
nudge	*nj*	nurse	*Ns*
nu·di·ty	*nd)*	nurs·er·y	*Nsy*
nug·get	*ngl*	nurs·ling	*Nslg*
nui·sance	*ns /*	nur·ture	*nc*
null	*nl*	nut	*nl*
nul·li·fi·ca·tion	*nlfcj*	nut·meg	*nlmg*
nul·li·fi·er	*nlf*	nu·tri·ent	*nte*
nul·li·fy	*nlf*	nu·tri·tion	*nt1*
numb	*n*	nu·tri·tious	*nt x*
num·ber	*no*	nu·tri·tive	*ntv*
num·ber·less	*nol'*	nut·shell	*nlsl*
numb·ness	*n'*	nuz·zle	*nzl*
nu·mer·al	*n l*	ny·lon	*nln*
nu·mer·ate	*n la*	nymph	*nf*
nu·mer·a·tor	*n la*		

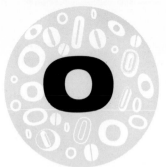

oaf	*of*	ob·jec·tive	*obv*
oak	*oc*	ob·jec·tive·ly	*obvl*
oa·kum	*ok*	ob·jec·tiv·i·ty	*obv)*
oar	*o*	ob·jec·tor	*obj*
oar·lock	*olc*	ob·jur·gate	*objga*
o·a·sis	*oss*	ob·jur·ga·tion	*objgj*
oat	*ol*	ob·late	*oba*
oat·cake	*olcc*	ob·li·gate	*obga*
oat·meal	*olrl*	ob·li·ga·tion	*obgj*
ob·bli·ga·to	*obglo*	ob·lig·a·to·ry	*obgly*
ob·du·ra·cy	*obDse*	o·blige	*obj*
ob·du·rate	*obDl*	o·blig·er	*obj*
o·be·di·ence	*obde /*	o·blique	*obc*
o·be·di·ent	*obde –*	ob·lit·er·ate	*obTa*
o·bei·sance	*obs /*	ob·lit·er·a·tion	*obTj*
ob·e·lisk	*oblsc*	ob·liv·i·on	*obven*
o·bese	*obs*	ob·liv·i·ous	*obvr*
o·bes·i·ty	*obs)*	ob·long	*obq*
o·bey	*oba*	ob·lo·quy	*obqe*
ob·fus·cate	*obfsca*	ob·nox·ious	*obncr*
ob·fus·ca·tion	*obfscj*	o·boe	*obo*
o·bi	*obe*	o·bo·ist	*obo,*
o·bit	*obl*	ob·scene	*obsn*
o·bit·u·ar·y	*obCy*	ob·scen·i·ty	*obsn)*
ob·ject	*ob*	ob·scu·ra·tion	*obsCj*
ob·jec·tion	*oby*	ob·scure	*obscu*
ob·jec·tion·a·ble	*objb*	ob·scu·ri·ty	*obscu)*

ob·se·qui·ous		oc·clude	
ob·se·quy		oc·clu·sion	
ob·serv·ance		oc·cult	
ob·serv·ant		oc·cult·ism	
ob·ser·va·tion		oc·cu·pan·cy	
ob·ser·va·to·ry		✓oc·cu·pant	
✓ob·serve		oc·cu·pa·tion	
ob·serv·er		oc·cu·py	
ob·sess		✓oc·cur	
ob·ses·sion		o·cean	
ob·so·les·cence		o·cean·go·ing	
ob·so·lete		o·ce·lot	
ob·sta·cle		o·cher	
ob·stet·ri·cal		o·clock	
ob·ste·tri·cian		oc·ta·gon	
ob·sti·na·cy		oc·tag·o·nal	
ob·sti·nate		oc·tan·gu·lar	
ob·strep·er·ous		oc·tant	
ob·struct		oc·tave	
ob·struc·tion		oc·ta·vo	
ob·tain		Oc·to·ber	
ob·tain·a·ble		oc·to·ge·nar·i·an	
ob·trude		oc·to·pus	
ob·tru·sion		oc·u·lar	
ob·tru·sive		oc·u·list	
ob·tuse		odd	
ob·verse		odd·ball	
ob·ver·sion		odd·i·ty	
ob·vi·ate		odd·ly	
ob·vi·ous		ode	
oc·ca·sion		o·di·ous	
oc·ca·sion·al		o·di·um	
oc·ca·sion·al·ly		o·dom·e·ter	
oc·ci·dent		o·dor	
oc·ci·den·tal		o·dor·if·er·ous	
oc·cip·i·tal		o·dor·less	
oc·ci·put		o·dor·ous	

od·ys·sey	*odse*	old·ness	*ol'*
of	*v*	old·ster	*olS*
off	*of*	o·le·ag·i·nous	*olejnx*
off·beat	*ofbe*	o·le·o·graph	*olegf*
of·fal	*ofl*	o·le·o·mar·ga·rine	*ole gn*
off·cast	*ofc,*	ol·fac·to·ry	*ofcy*
of·fend	*of___*	ol·i·garch·y	*ogce*
of·fend·er	*of___/*	ol·ive	*ov*
of·fense	*of/*	O·lym·pic	*ol pc*
of·fen·sive	*of/v*	o·me·ga	*o rga*
of·fer	*of*	om·e·let	*o rll*
of·fer·to·ry	*ofly*	o·men	*o m*
off·hand	*ofh___*	om·i·nous	*o mx*
of·fice	*ofs*	o·mis·sion	*o ry*
of·fi·cer	*ofs/*	o·mit	*oril*
of·fi·cial	*ofx*	om·ni·bus	*o mbx*
of·fi·cial·ly	*ofx*	om·ni·far·i·ous	*o mfyx*
of·fi·ci·ate	*ofSa*	om·nip·o·tence	*o mpl/*
of·fi·ci·a·tor	*ofSa*	om·nip·o·tent	*o mpl-*
of·fi·cious	*ofx*	om·nis·cience	*o mS/*
off·set	*ofsl*	om·nis·cient	*o mS-*
off·shoot	*ofSu*	om·niv·o·rous	*o mUx*
off·shore	*ofSo*	on	*o*
off·spring	*ofSg*	once	*c/*
of·ten	*ofn*	on·com·ing	*ok*
of·ten·times	*ofnlrs*	one	*1*
o·gle	*ogl*	one·ness	*1'*
o·gre	*og*	on·er·ous	*oNx*
ohm	*o*	one·self	*1 s/*
oil	*yl*	on·ion	*onn*
oil·cloth	*ylcl*	on·ion·skin	*onnscn*
oil·i·ness	*yl'*	on·look·er	*olc*
oil·skin	*ylscn*	on·ly	*nl*
oil·y	*yl*	on·rush	*orS*
oint·ment	*y___*	on·set	*osl*
old	*ol*	on·slaught	*osl*
old·er	*ol*	on·to	*ol*

o·nus		opt	
on·ward		op·tic	
on·yx		op·ti·cal	
oo·dles		op·ti·cian	
ooze		op·ti·mism	
o·pac·i·ty		op·ti·mist	
o·pal		op·ti·mis·tic	
o·pal·es·cent		op·ti·mum	
o·paque		op·tion	
o·pen		op·tion·al	
o·pen·er		op·tom·e·trist	
o·pen·ly		op·tom·e·try	
op·er·a		op·u·lence	
op·er·a·ble		op·u·lent	
op·er·ate		o·pus	
op·er·a·tion		or	
op·er·a·tor		or·a·cle	
op·er·et·ta		o·rac·u·lar	
oph·thal·mi·a		o·ral	
oph·thal·mo·scope		or·ange	
o·pi·ate		or·ange·ade	
o·pine		o·ra·tion	
o·pin·ion		or·a·tor	
o·pin·ion·at·ed		or·a·tor·i·cal	
o·pi·um		or·a·to·ri·o	
op·po·nent		orb	
op·por·tune		or·bic·u·lar	
op·por·tu·ni·ty		or·bit	
op·pos·a·ble		or·chard	
op·pose		or·ches·tra	
op·po·site		or·ches·trate	
op·po·si·tion		or·chid	
op·press		or·dain	
op·pres·sion		or·deal	
op·pres·sor		or·der	
op·pro·bri·ous		or·der·li·ness	
op·pro·bri·um		or·der·ly	

or·di·nal	*odnl*	or·tho·don·tia	*oldCa*
or·di·nance	*odn/*	or·tho·dox	*oldx*
or·di·nar·i·ly	*odnl*	or·thog·ra·pher	*olgf*
or·di·nar·y	*odny*	or·tho·graph·ic	*olgfc*
or·di·nate	*odnl*	or·thog·ra·phy	*olgfe*
ord·nance	*odn/*	or·tho·pe·dic	*olpdc*
ore	*o*	os·cil·late	*osla*
or·gan	*ogn*	os·cil·la·tion	*osly*
or·gan·ic	*ognc*	os·cil·la·tor	*osla*
or·gan·ism	*ognz*	os·cil·lo·scope	*oslscp*
or·gan·ist	*ogn,*	os·cu·late	*oscla*
or·gan·i·za·tion	*og*	os·cula·tion	*oscly*
or·gan·ize	*og*	os·mi·um	*(Os) ozne*
or·gy	*oje*	os·mo·sis	*osrss*
o·ri·ent	*oe –*	os·o·phone	*osfn*
o·ri·en·tal	*oe – l*	os·prey	*osae*
o·ri·en·tate	*oe – a*	os·se·ous	*osx*
ori·en·ta·tion	*oe – 1*	os·si·fi·ca·tion	*osfcy*
or·i·fice	*ofs*	os·si·fy	*osf*
ori·gin	*ojn*	os·ten·si·ble	*oo/b*
o·rig·i·nal	*ojnl*	os·ten·ta·tion	*os – 1*
o·rig·i·nal·i·ty	*ojnl)*	os·ten·ta·tious	*os – x*
o·rig·i·nal·ly	*ojnl*	os·te·o·path	*osepl*
o·rig·i·nate	*ojna*	os·te·op·a·thist	*osepl,*
o·rig·i·na·tion	*ojny*	os·te·op·a·thy	*oseple*
o·rig·i·na·tor	*ojna*	os·tra·cism	*oSsz*
o·ri·ole	*olel*	os·tra·cize·	*oSsz*
or·i·son	*osn*	os·trich	*oSC*
or·mo·lu	*orlu*	√oth·er	*J*
or·na·ment	*on –*	√oth·er·wise	*Jwz*
or·na·men·tal	*on – l*	ouch	*ouc*
or·nate	*ona*	√ought	*al*
or·ner·y	*ony*	ounce	*oz*
or·ni·thol·o·gy	*onlje*	our	*r*
o·ro·tund	*ol –*	√our·selves	*rs/*
or·phan	*ofn*	oust	*ou,*
or·phan·age	*ofny*	oust·er	*ou'S*

out		out·smart	
out·bid		out·spo·ken	
out·board		out·stand·ing	
out·break		out·stay	
out·burst		out·ward	
out·cast		out·wear	
out·class		out·weigh	
out·come		out·wit	
out·cry		out·worn	
out·do		o·val	
out·door		o·val·ly	
out·er		o·va·ry	
out·field		o·va·tion	
out·fit		ov·en	
out·go·ing		o·ver	
out·grow		o·ver·all	
out·growth		o·ver·awe	
out·land·ish		o·ver·bal·ance	
out·last		o·ver·bear	
out·law		o·ver·board	
out·lay		o·ver·build	
out·let		o·ver·came	
out·line		o·ver·cast	
out·live		o·ver·charge	
out·look		o·ver·coat	
out·ly·ing		o·ver·come	
out·post		o·ver·do	
out·pour		o·ver·draft	
out·put		o·ver·draw	
out·rage		o·ver·due	
out·ra·geous		o·ver·flow	
out·rank		o·ver·hand	
out·right		o·ver·hang	
out·sell		o·ver·haul	
out·set		o·ver·head	
out·side		o·ver·hear	
out·skirts		o·ver·look	

over·night	*One*	o·ver·whelm	*Owl*
over·power	*Opu*	o·ver·work	*Orc*
√ over·pro·duc·tion	*OPdcf*	o·ver·wrought	*Orl*
o·ver·reach	*OrC*	o·void	*ovyd*
o·ver·ride	*Ord*	o·vule	*ovl*
o·ver·rule	*Orl*	o·vum	*ovm*
o·ver·run	*Orn*	owe	*o*
o·ver·see	*Ose*	owl	*oul*
o·ver·shad·ow	*OSdo*	own	*on*
o·ver·shoe	*OSu*	own·er	*on*
o·ver·sight	*Osu*	√ own·er·ship	*onS*
o·ver·sleep	*Osp*	ox	*ox*
o·ver·stay	*Osa*	ox·al·ic	*xlc*
o·ver·step	*Osp*	ox·ford	*xfd*
o·vert	*ovl*	ox·i·da·tion	*xdj*
o·ver·take	*Olc*	ox·ide	*xd*
o·ver·threw	*Oru*	ox·i·dize	*xdz*
o·ver·throw	*Oro*	ox·y·gen	*(o) xyn*
o·ver·tone	*Oln*	ox·y·gen·ate	*xyna*
o·ver·ture	*OC*	oys·ter	*yS*
o·ver·turn	*Orn*	o·zone	*ozn*
o·ver·weight	*Owa*		

pab·u·lum	*pbl*	pag·eant·ry	*pj—re*
pace	*pas*	pag·i·na·tion	*pjny*
pace·mak·er	*psrc*	pa·go·da	*pgda*
pac·er	*ps*	paid	*pd*
pach·y·derm	*pcD*	pail	*pal*
pa·cif·ic	*psfc*	pain	*pn*
pac·i·fi·er	*psf*	pain·ful	*pnf*
pac·i·fism	*psfz*	pain·less	*pnl'*
pac·i·fist	*psf*	pains·tak·ing	*pnsc*
pac·i·fy	*psf*	paint	*pa—*
pack	*pc*	paint·er	*pa—*
pack·age	*pcj*	pair	*pr*
pack·er	*pc*	pais·ley	*pzl*
pack·et	*pcl*	pa·ja·ma	*pjra*
pack·sack	*pcsc*	Pak·i·stan·i	*pcsne*
pack·sad·dle	*pcsdl*	pal	*pl*
pact	*pc*	pal·ace	*pls*
pad	*pd*	pal·at·a·ble	*pllb*
pad·dle	*pdl*	pal·a·tal	*plrl*
pad·dock	*pdc*	pal·ate	*pll*
pad·dy	*pde*	pa·la·tial	*plr*
pad·lock	*pdlc*	pal·a·tine	*plun*
pa·dre	*pDa*	pa·lav·er	*plv*
pa·gan	*pgn*	pale	*pal*
pa·gan·ism	*pgnz*	pale·ness	*pl'*
page	*p*	pal·ette	*pll*
pag·eant	*pj—*	pal·frey	*plfe*

171

pal·i·sade	*plsd*	pan·nier	*pn*
pall	*pal*	pan·o·ply	*pnp*
pall·bear·er	*plba*	pan·o·ra·ma	*pnra*
pal·li·ate	*pla*	pan·o·ram·ic	*pnrc*
pal·li·a·tive	*plev*	pan·sy	*pnze*
pal·lid	*pld*	pant	*p—*
pal·lor	*pl*	pan·ta·loon	*p—ln*
palm	*pn*	pan·the·ism	*pnlez*
pal·mate	*plra*	pan·the·on	*pnlen*
pal·met·to	*plrlo*	pan·ther	*pn*
palm·is·try	*pSe*	pan·to·mime	*p—ru*
pal·o·mi·no	*plmo*	pan·try	*p—re*
pal·pa·ble	*plpb*	pa·pa·cy	*ppse*
pal·pate	*plpa*	pa·pal	*pp*
pal·pi·tate	*plpla*	pa·per	*pp*
pal·pi·ta·tion	*plply*	pa·pier-mâ·ché	*p—Sa*
pal·sy	*plze*	pa·poose	*pps*
pal·try	*ple*	pap·ri·ka	*pSca*
pam·per	*p—p*	pa·py·rus	*pex*
pam·phlet	*pfl*	par	*pr*
pan	*pn*	par·a·ble	*Sb*
pan·a·ce·a	*pnsa*	pa·rab·o·la	*Sbla*
pan·a·ma	*pnra*	par·a·bol·ic	*Sblc*
Pan-A·mer·i·can	*pnl*	par·a·chute	*SSu*
pan·chro·ma·tic	*pnCrlc*	pa·rade	*Sd*
pan·cre·as	*pnCes*	par·a·dise	*Sds*
pan·cre·a·tic	*pnCelc*	par·a·dox	*Sdx*
pan·dem·ic	*p——rc*	par·a·dox·i·cal	*Sdxcl*
pan·de·mo·ni·um	*p——men*	par·af·fin	*Sfn*
pan·der	*p—/*	par·a·gon	*Sgn*
pane	*pn*	par·a·graph	*Sgf*
pan·e·gyr·ic	*pnJc*	par·al·lel	*Sll*
pan·e·gy·rize	*pnJz*	par·al·lel·o·gram	*Sllg*
pan·el	*pnl*	pa·ral·y·sis	*Sss*
pang	*pg*	par·a·lyt·ic	*Sllc*
pan·ic	*pnc*	par·a·lyze	*Slz*
pan·jan·drum	*pj——rs*	par·a·me·ter	*Sr*

par·a·mount		par·lay	
par·a·mour		par·ley	
par·a·noi·a		par·lous	
par·a·pet		par·lia·ment	
par·a·pher·na·li·a		par·lia·men·ta·ry	
par·a·phrase		par·lor	
par·a·pleg·ic		pa·ro·chi·al	
par·a·site		par·o·dy	
par·a·sit·ic		pa·role	
par·a·sol		par·ox·ysm	
par·a·troop·er		par·quet	
par·boil		par·ri·cide	
par·cel		par·rot	
par·cel post		par·ry	
parch		parse	
parch·ment		par·si·mo·ni·ous	
par·don		par·si·mo·ny	
par·don·a·ble		pars·ley	
pare		pars·nip	
par·e·gor·ic		par·son	
par·ent		part	
pa·ren·tal		par·take	
pa·ren·the·ses		par·terre	
pa·ren·the·sis		par·tial	
par·en·thet·i·cal		par·ti·al·i·ty	
pa·re·sis		par·tial·ly	
par·fait		par·tic·i·pant	
pa·ri·ah		par·tic·i·pate	
pa·ri·e·tal		par·tic·i·pa·tion	
par·ish		par·tic·i·pa·tor	
pa·rish·ion·er		par·ti·cip·i·al	
Pa·ri·sian		par·ti·ci·ple	
par·i·ty		par·ti·cle	
park		par·tic·u·lar	
par·ka		par·tic·u·lar·i·ty	
park·way		par·tic·u·lar·ize	
par·lance		par·tic·u·lar·ly	

par·ti·san		pas·time	
par·ti·san·ship		pas·tor	
par·ti·tion		pas·to·ral	
part·ly		pas·to·ral·ly	
part·ner		pas·tor·ate	
part·ner·ship		pas·tor·ship	
par·took		pas·try	
par·tridge		pas·tur·age	
par·ty		pas·ture	
par·ve·nu		past·y	
pas·chal		pat	
pa·sha		patch	
✓ pass		patch·work	
pass·a·ble		patch·y	
pas·sage		pate	
pass·book		pa·tel·la	
pas·sé		pat·en	
passed		✓ pat·ent	
pas·sel		pat·ent·a·ble	
pas·sen·ger		pat·ent·ee	
pass·er		pa·ter·fa·mil·i·as	
pas·sion		pa·ter·nal	
pas·sion·ate		pa·ter·nal·ism	
pas·sion·less		pa·ter·nal·ly	
pas·sive		pa·ter·ni·ty	
pass·key		path	
Pass·o·ver		pa·thet·ic	
pass·port		path·find·er	
pass·word		path·less	
✓ past		path·o·gen·ic	
paste		path·o·log·ic	
pas·tel		path·o·log·i·cal	
past·ern		pa·thol·o·gist	
pas·teur·i·za·tion		pa·thol·o·gy	
pas·teur·ize		pa·thos	
pas·tiche		path·way	
pas·tille		✓ pa·tience	

pa·tient	
pat·i·na	
pa·ti·o	
pat·ois	
pa·tri·arch	
pa·tri·ar·chal	
pa·tri·arch·ate	
pa·tri·arch·y	
pa·tri·cian	
pat·ri·cide	
pat·ri·mo·ny	
pa·tri·ot	
pa·tri·ot·ic	
pa·tri·ot·ism	
✓ pa·trol	
pa·trol·man	
pa·tron	
pa·tron·age	
pa·tron·ize	
pa·troon	
pat·sy	
pat·ter	
pat·tern	
pat·ty	
pau·ci·ty	
paunch	
pau·per	
pau·per·ism	
pau·per·ize	
pause	
pave	
pave·ment	
pa·vil·ion	
paw	
pawn	
pawn·bro·ker	
pawn·shop	

pay	
pay·a·ble	
pay·ee	
pay·er	
pay·mas·ter	
pay·ment	
pay·roll	
pea	
peace	
peace·a·ble	
peace·ful	
peace·mak·er	
peach	
pea·cock	
pea·hen	
peak	
peal	
pea·nut	
pear	
pearl	
pearl·y	
peas·ant	
peas·ant·ry	
peat	
peb·ble	
pe·can	
pec·ca·ble	
pec·ca·dil·lo	
pec·can·cy	
pec·cant	
peck	
pec·tin	
pec·to·ral	
pec·u·late	
pec·u·la·tion	
pec·u·la·tor	
pe·cu·liar	

pe·cu·liar·i·ty	*pc ꝇ*	pel·let	*pll*
pe·cu·liar·ly	*pcꝯl*	pel·lu·cid	*plsd*
pe·cu·ni·ar·y	*pcny*	pelt	*pll*
ped·a·gog·ic	*pdgjc*	pel·vis	*plvs*
ped·a·gog·i·cal	*pdgjcl*	pen	*pn*
ped·a·gog·ics	*pdgjcs*	pe·nal	*pnl*
ped·a·gogue	*pdgg*	pe·nal·i·za·tion	*pnlzj*
ped·a·go·gy	*pdgje*	pe·nal·ize	*pnlz*
ped·al	*pdl*	pen·al·ty	*pnl'*
ped·ant	*pd–*	pen·ance	*pn/*
pe·dan·tic	*pd–c*	pence	*pl*
ped·ant·ry	*pd–re*	pen·chant	*pC–*
ped·dle	*pdl*	pen·cil	*pll*
ped·dler	*pdl*	pend·ant	*p—·–*
ped·es·tal	*pdsl*	pen·du·lous	*p—lx*
pe·des·tri·an	*pdSen*	pen·du·lum	*p—lr*
pe·di·at·ric	*pdetc*	pen·e·tra·bil·i·ty	*pnꝵb)*
pe·di·a·tri·cian	*pdet1*	pen·e·tra·ble	*pnꝵb*
ped·i·gree	*pdge*	√ pen·e·trate	*pnꝵa*
ped·i·ment	*pd–*	pen·e·tra·tion	*pnꝵ1*
pe·dom·e·ter	*pdɤ*	pen·e·tra·tive	*pnꝵv*
peek	*pec*	pen·guin	*pgꝵn*
peel	*pel*	pen·i·cil·lin	*pnsln*
peen	*pn*	pen·in·su·la	*pn/la*
peep	*pep*	pen·in·su·lar	*pn/l*
peer	*pe*	pen·i·tence	*pnl/*
peer·age	*pej*	pen·i·tent	*pnl–*
peer·ess	*pe',*	pen·i·ten·tia·ry	*pnlCy*
peer·less	*pel'*	pen·man·ship	*pn—ms*
peeve	*pe*	pen·nant	*pn–*
pee·vish	*peS*	pen·ni·less	*pnl'*
peg	*pq*	pen·ny	*pne*
pei·gnoir	*pnɤr*	pen·ny·weight	*pner–a*
pe·jo·ra·tive	*pJv*	pen·ny·wise	*pnez*
pe·koe	*pco*	pe·no·log·i·cal	*pnljcl*
pelf	*plf*	pe·nol·o·gist	*pnlj'*
pel·i·can	*plcn*	pe·nol·o·gy	*pnlje*

pen·sion		per·cept	
pen·sion·ar·y		per·cep·ti·ble	
pen·sion·er		per·cep·tion	
pen·sive		per·cep·tive	
pent		per·cep·tu·al	
pen·ta·gon		perch	
pen·tag·o·nal		per·chance	
pent·house		per·cip·i·ence	
pen·tode		per·cip·i·en·cy	
pe·nult		per·cip·i·ent	
pe·nul·ti·mate		per·co·late	
pen·um·bra		per·co·la·tion	
pe·nu·ri·ous		per·co·la·tor	
pen·u·ry		per·cus·sion	
pe·on		per·cus·sive	
pe·on·age		per di·em	
pe·o·ny		per·di·tion	
peo·ple		per·e·gri·nate	
pep		per·e·gri·na·tion	
pep·per		per·emp·to·ri·ly	
pep·per·mint		per·emp·to·ri·ness	
pep·per·y		per·emp·to·ry	
pep·sin		per·en·ni·al	
pep·tic		per·fect	
per		per·fect·i·ble	
per·am·bu·late		per·fec·tion	
per·am·bu·la·tion		per·fec·tion·ism	
per·am·bu·la·tor		per·fect·ly	
per·am·bu·la·to·ry		per·fec·to	
per an·num		per·fid·i·ous	
per·cale		per·fi·dy	
per cap·i·ta		per·fo·rate	
per·ceiv·a·ble		per·fo·ra·tion	
per·ceive		per·fo·ra·tor	
per·cent		per·force	
per·cent·age		per·form	
per·cent·ile		per·form·ance	

per·form·er		per·me·ate	
per·fume		per·me·a·tion	
per·fum·er		per·me·a·tive	
per·fum·er·y		per·mis·si·ble	
per·func·to·ry		per·mis·sion	
✓ per·haps		per·mis·sive	
per·i·car·di·um		per·mit	
per·i·gee		per·mu·ta·tion	
per·il		per·ni·cious	
per·il·ous		per·o·rate	
per·im·e·ter		per·o·ra·tion	
per·i·ne·al		per·ox·ide	
per·i·ne·um		per·pen·dic·u·lar	
pe·ri·od		per·pe·trate	
pe·ri·od·ic		per·pe·tra·tion	
pe·ri·od·i·cal		per·pe·tra·tor	
per·i·pa·tet·ic		per·pet·u·al	
pe·riph·er·al		per·pet·u·al·ly	
pe·riph·er·y		per·pet·u·ate	
pe·riph·ra·sis		per·pet·u·a·tion	
per·i·phras·tic		per·pet·u·a·tor	
per·i·scope		per·pe·tu·i·ty	
per·i·scop·ic		per·plex	
per·ish		per·plex·i·ty	
per·ish·a·ble		per·qui·site	
per·i·win·kle		per se	
per·jure		per·se·cute	
per·jur·er		per·se·cu·tion	
per·ju·ry		per·se·cu·tor	
perk		per·se·ver·ance	
perk·y		per·se·vere	
per·ma·nence		Per·sian	
per·ma·nen·cy		per·si·flage	
↓ per·ma·nent		per·sim·mon	
per·man·ga·nate		per·sist	
per·me·a·bil·i·ty		per·sist·ence	
per·me·a·ble		per·sist·ent	

per·snick·e·ty		per·va·sive	
√ per·son		per·verse	
per·son·a·ble		per·ver·sion	
per·son·age		per·ver·si·ty	
per·son·al		per·ver·sive	
per·son·al·i·ty		per·vert	
per·son·al·ize		per·vert·i·ble	
per·son·al·ly		per·vi·ous	
per·son·i·fi·ca·tion		pes·ky	
per·son·i·fy		pes·si·mism	
per·son·nel		pes·si·mist	
per·spec·tive		pes·si·mis·tic	
per·spi·ca·cious		pest	
per·spi·cac·i·ty		pes·ter	
per·spi·cu·i·ty		pes·ti·cide	
per·spic·u·ous		pes·tif·er·ous	
per·spi·ra·tion		pes·ti·lence	
per·spir·a·to·ry		pes·ti·lent	
per·spire		pes·ti·len·tial	
per·suade		pes·tle	
per·sua·si·ble		pet	
per·sua·sion		pet·al	
per·sua·sive		pet·it	
pert		pe·tite	
per·tain		√ pe·ti·tion	
per·ti·na·cious		pe·ti·tion·ar·y	
per·ti·nac·i·ty		pe·ti·tion·er	
per·ti·nence		pet·ri·fac·tion	
per·ti·nent		pet·ri·fac·tive	
per·turb		pet·ri·fi·ca·tion	
per·turb·a·ble		pet·ri·fy	
per·tur·ba·tion		pet·rol	
pe·rus·al		pet·ro·la·tum	
pe·ruse		pe·tro·le·um	
pe·rus·er		pet·ro·log·ic	
per·vade		pe·tro·lo·gy	
per·va·sion		pet·ti·coat	

pet·ti·fog		phi·lol·o·gy	
pet·ti·fog·ger		phi·los·o·pher	
pet·ti·ly		phil·o·soph·ic	
pet·ti·ness		phi·los·o·phy	
√ pet·ty		phil·ter	
pet·u·lance		phlegm	
pet·u·lant		phleg·mat·ic	
pew		pho·bia	
pew·ter		phoe·nix	
pfen·nig		√ phone	
pha·lan·ges		pho·net·ic	
pha·lanx		pho·ne·ti·cian	
phan·tasm		pho·no·graph	
phan·tas·ma·go·ri·a		pho·no·graph·ic	
phan·tom		pho·ny	
phar·oah		phos·phate	
phar·ma·ceu·tic		phos·pho·resce	
phar·ma·cist		phos·pho·res·cence	
phar·ma·col·o·gy		phos·pho·res·cent	
phar·ma·cy		phos·phor·ic	
phase		phos·pho·rus	
pheas·ant		pho·to	
phe·nom·e·na		pho·to·e·lec·tric	
phe·nom·e·nal		pho·to·gen·ic	
phe·nom·e·non		pho·to·graph	
phi·al		pho·tog·ra·pher	
phi·lan·der		pho·to·graph·ic	
phi·lan·der·er		pho·tog·ra·phy	
phil·an·throp·ic		pho·to·gra·vure	
phi·lan·thro·pist		pho·tom·e·ter	
phi·lan·thro·py		pho·to·play	
phi·lat·e·ly		pho·to·stat	
phil·har·mon·ic		pho·to·syn·the·sis	
phil·lip·ic		phrase	
phil·is·tine		phra·se·ol·o·gy	
Phil·ip·pine		phre·net·ic	
phi·lol·o·gist		phre·nol·o·gist	

phre·nol·o·gy		pid·dle	
phy·lum		pid·gin	
phys·ic		pie	
phys·i·cal		piece	
phy·si·cian		piece·meal	
phys·i·cist		piece·work	
phys·ics		pie·crust	
phys·i·og·no·my		pie·pan	
phys·i·og·ra·phy		pier	
phys·i·ol·o·gist		pierce	
phys·i·ol·o·gy		pi·e·ty	
phys·i·o·ther·a·py		pif·fle	
phy·sique		pig	
pi·a·nis·si·mo		pi·geon	
pi·an·ist		pi·geon·hole	
pi·an·o		pig·ment	
pi·as·ter		pig·men·tar·y	
pi·az·za		pig·men·ta·tion	
pi·ca		pig·my	
pic·a·dor		pig·pen	
pic·a·resque		pig·skin	
pic·a·yune		pike	
pic·co·lo		pik·er	
pick		pi·las·ter	
pick·ax		pil·chard	
pick·er		pile	
pick·er·el		pil·fer	
pick·et		pil·grim	
pick·le		pil·grim·age	
pic·nic		pill	
pi·cot		pil·lage	
pic·to·e·lec·tric		pil·lar	
pic·to·graph		pil·lion	
pic·tog·ra·phy		pil·lo·ry	
pic·to·ri·al		pil·low	
pic·ture		pil·low·case	
pic·tur·esque		pi·lot	

pim·ple	*pmp*	pitch·er	*pC*
pin	*pn*	pit·e·ous	*plx*
pince-nez	*p/na*	pit·fall	*plfal*
pin·cer	*pV*	pith	*pl*
pinch	*pC*	pith·i·ness	*ple'*
pinch·er	*pC*	pith·y	*ple*
pine	*pin*	pit·i·a·ble	*pleb*
pine·ap·ple	*pinap*	pit·i·ful	*plf*
pin·feath·er	*pnf*	pit·i·less	*ple'*
pin·head	*pnhd*	pit·tance	*pl/*
pin·hole	*pnhl*	pi·tu·i·tar·y	*pluty*
pin·ion	*pnn*	pit·y	*p)*
pink	*pg*	piv·ot	*pvl*
pin·na·cle	*pncl*	piv·ot·al	*pvll*
pi·noch·le	*pncl*	pix·ie	*pee*
pint	*(pl) pi-*	pla·ca·bil·i·ty	*pcb)*
pin·up	*pnp*	pla·ca·ble	*pcb*
pi·o·neer	*pine*	plac·ard	*pCd*
pi·ous	*px*	pla·cate	*pca*
pip	*pp*	pla·ca·to·ry	*pcly*
pipe	*pip*	place	*pl*
pipe·line	*ppli*	pla·ce·bo	*pCbo*
pi·quan·cy	*pc/*	place·ment	*pl-*
pi·quant	*pc-*	plac·id	*psd*
pique	*pec*	pla·cid·i·ty	*psd)*
pi·qué	*pca*	plack·et	*pcl*
pi·ra·cy	*pse*	pla·gi·a·rism	*pJz*
pi·rate	*pl*	pla·gi·a·rist	*pJ'*
pi·rat·i·cal	*plcl*	pla·gi·a·rize	*pJz*
pir·ou·ette	*pivl*	plague	*pag*
pis·ca·to·ri·al	*psclyl*	plaid	*pd*
pis·ta·chi·o	*psdo*	plain	*pn*
pis·til	*psl*	plain·ly	*pnl*
pis·tol	*psl*	plain·ness	*pn'*
pis·ton	*psn*	plains·man	*pnsr-*
pit	*pl*	plaint	*pa-*
pitch	*pC*	plain·tiff	*pa-f*

plain·tive		play·ful	
plait		play·ground	
plan		play·house	
plane		play·mate	
plan·et		play·room	
plan·e·tar·i·um		play·thing	
plan·e·tar·y		play·time	
plan·gent		play·wright	
plank		pla·za	
plan·ner		plea	
plant		plead	
plan·ta·tion		plead·er	
plant·er		plead·ing·ly	
plaque		pleas·ant	
plas·ma		pleas·ant·ry	
plas·ter		please	
plas·ter·er		pleas·ur·a·ble	
plas·tic		pleas·ure	
plas·tic·i·ty		pleat	
plate		plebe	
pla·teau		ple·be·ian	
plat·en		pleb·i·scite	
plat·form		plec·trum	
plat·i·num	(PL)	pledge	
plat·i·tude		ple·na·ry	
plat·i·tu·di·nous		plen·i·po·ten·ti·ar·y	
pla·ton·ic		plen·i·tude	
pla·toon		plen·te·ous	
plat·ter		plen·ti·ful	
plau·dit		plen·ty	
plau·si·bil·i·ty		pleth·o·ra	
plau·si·ble		pleu·ra	
play		pleu·ri·sy	
play·bill		plex·us	
play·boy		pli·a·bil·i·ty	
play·er		pli·a·ble	
play·fel·low		pli·an·cy	

pli·ant		ply	
pli·ers		pneu·mat·ic	
plight		pneu·mo·ni·a	
plinth		pneu·mon·ic	
plod		poach	
plod·der		pock	
plop		pock·et	
plot		pock·et·book	
plot·ter		pock·mark	
plow		pod	
plow·er		po·di·a·try	
pluck		po·di·um	
plug		po·em	
plum		po·et	
plum·age		po·et·ic	
plumb		po·et·i·cal	
plumb·er		po·et·ry	
plume		po·grom	
plum·met		poign·an·cy	
plump		poign·ant	
plump·er		poin·set·ti·a	
plump·ness		point	
plun·der		point·er	
plun·der·er		point·less	
plunge		poise	
plung·er		poi·son	
plunk		poi·son·ous	
plu·per·fect		poke	
plu·ral		po·lar	
plu·ral·ism		po·lar·i·ty	
plu·ral·i·ty		po·lar·i·za·tion	
plu·ral·ize		po·lar·ize	
plus		pole	
plush		po·lem·ic	
plu·toc·ra·cy		po·lice	
plu·to·crat		po·lice·man	
plu·to·crat·ic		pol·i·cy	

pol·i·cy·hold·er		pom·mel	
po·li·o		pomp	
pol·ish		pom·pa·dour	
po·lite		pom·pa·no	
po·lite·ness		pom·pos·i·ty	
po·li·tesse		pomp·ous	
pol·i·tic		pon·cho	
po·lit·i·cal		pond	
po·lit·i·cal·ly		pon·der	
pol·i·ti·cian		pon·der·a·ble	
pol·i·ty		pon·der·ous	
pol·ka		pone	
poll		pon·iard	
pol·len		pon·tiff	
pol·li·nate		pon·tif·i·cal	
poll·ster		pon·tif·i·cate	
✓ pol·lute		pon·toon	
✓ pol·lu·tion		po·ny	
po·lo		poo·dle	
po·lo·naise		pool	
pol·y·an·dry		poor	
pol·y·an·thus		poor·ly	
pol·y·chro·mat·ic		poor·ness	
pol·y·clin·ic		pop	
po·lyg·a·mist		pop·corn	
po·lyg·a·mous		pope	
po·lyg·a·my		pop·er·y	
pol·y·glot		pop·gun	
pol·y·gon		pop·in·jay	
pol·y·graph		pop·lar	
pol·y·mer		pop·py	
Pol·y·ne·sian		pop·py·cock	
pol·yp		pop·u·lace	
pol·y·phon·ic		✓ pop·u·lar	
pol·y·syl·lab·ic		pop·u·lar·i·ty	
pol·y·tech·nic		pop·u·lar·ize	
po·made		pop·u·lar·ly	

pop·u·late	*ppla*	✓po·si·tion	*pz/*
✓pop·u·la·tion	*pply*	pos·i·tive	*pzv*
pop·u·lous	*pplx*	pos·i·tron	*pz-n*
por·ce·lain	*osln*	pos·se	*pse*
porch	*pC*	pos·sess	*pz'*
por·cine	*sun*	po·sessed	*pz,*
por·cu·pine	*scpin*	pos·ses·sion	*pz/*
pore	*po*	pos·ses·sive	*pzsv*
po·rif·er·ous	*poft*	pos·ses·sor	*pzs*
pork	*sc*	pos·si·bil·i·ty	*psb)*
por·nog·ra·phy	*sngfe*	pos·si·ble	*psb*
✓po·rous	*pox*	pos·si·bly	*psb*
por·poise	*sps*	✓ post	*po,*
por·ridge	*sy*	post·age	*psy*
port	*sl*	post·al	*psl*
port·a·ble	*slb*	post·al card	*psl Cd*
por·tage	*sly*	post card	*po, Cd*
por·tal	*sll*	post·date	*psda*
por·tend	*sl—*	post·di·lu·vi·an	*psdlven*
por·tent	*sl-*	post·er	*pS*
por·ten·tous	*slCx*	pos·te·ri·or	*psy*
por·ter	*s*	pos·ter·i·ty	*pS)*
port·fo·li·o	*slflo*	pos·tern	*pSn*
por·ti·co	*slco*	post·grad·u·ate	*psgda*
por·ti·ere	*sle*	post·haste	*psha,*
por·tion	*sy*	post·hu·mous	*psCx*
port·li·ness	*sll'*	post·man	*psr—*
port·ly	*sll*	post·mark	*ps1c*
port·man·teau	*sls-o*	post·mas·ter	*psS*
por·trait	*sTa*	post·me·rid·i·an	*(p.m.) psden*
por·trai·ture	*sTC*	post·mor·tem	*psu*
por·tray	*sta*	post of·fice	*po*
por·tray·al	*stal*	post·paid	*pspd*
Por·tu·guese	*sCg3*	post·pone	*pspn*
pose	*p3*	post·pone·ment	*pspn-*
po·seur	*pz/*	post·script	*(p.s.) psscp*
posh	*ps*	pos·tu·lant	*pscl-*

pos·tu·late		pow·er·less	
pos·tu·la·tion		prac·ti·ca·bil·i·ty	
pos·ture		prac·ti·ca·ble	
po·sy		prac·ti·cal	
pot		prac·ti·cal·i·ty	
po·ta·ble		prac·ti·cal·ly	
pot·ash		✓prac·tice	
po·tas·si·um		prac·ti·tion·er	
po·ta·tion		prag·mat·ic	
po·ta·to		prag·mat·i·cal	
pot·boil·er		prag·ma·tism	
po·ten·cy		prag·ma·tist	
po·tent		prai·rie	
po·ten·tate		praise	
✓po·ten·tial		pra·line	
po·ten·ti·al·i·ty		prance	
po·ten·tial·ly		prank	
po·tent·ly		prank·ish	
poth·er		prate	
po·tion		prat·tle	
pot·pour·ri		prawn	
pot·tage		pray	
pot·ter		prayer	
pot·ter·y		prayer·ful	
pouch		preach	
poul·tice		preach·er	
poul·try		pre·am·ble	
pounce		pre·car·i·ous	
pound		pre·cau·tion	
pound·age		pre·cau·tion·ar·y	
pour		pre·cau·tious	
pout		pre·cede	
pov·er·ty		pre·ced·ence	
pow·der		pre·ced·ent	
pow·der·y		pre·cept	
pow·er		pre·cep·tive	
pow·er·ful		pre·cep·tor	

pre·cep·to·ry		pre·dis·pose	
pre·cinct		pre·dis·po·si·tion	
pre·cious		pre·dom·i·nance	
prec·i·pice		pre·dom·i·nant	
pre·cip·i·tance		pre·dom·i·nate	
pre·cip·i·tant		pre·em·i·nence	
pre·cip·i·tate		pre·em·i·nent	
pre·cip·i·ta·tion		pre·empt	
pre·cip·i·ta·tor		pre·emp·to·ry	
pre·cip·i·tous		preen	
pré·cis		pre·fab·ri·cate	
pre·cise		pref·ace	
pre·ci·sion		pref·a·to·ry	
pre·clude		pre·fect	
pre·clu·sion		pre·fec·ture	
pre·clu·sive		pre·fer	
pre·co·cious		pre·fer·ence	
pre·coc·i·ty		pre·fer·en·tial	
pre·con·ceive		pre·fix	
pre·con·cep·tion		preg·na·ble	
pre·cur·sive		preg·nan·cy	
pre·cur·sor		preg·nant	
pre·cur·so·ry		pre·hen·sile	
pred·a·tor		pre·his·tor·ic	
pred·a·to·ry		prej·u·dice	
pre·de·cease		prej·u·di·cial	
pred·e·ces·sor		prel·ate	
pre·des·tine		pre·lim·i·nar·y	
pre·de·ter·mine		prel·ude	
pre·dic·a·ment		pre·ma·ture	
pred·i·cate		pre·ma·tu·ri·ty	
pred·i·ca·tion		pre·med·i·tate	
pre·dict		pre·med·i·ta·tion	
pre·dict·a·ble		pre·mi·er	
pre·dic·tion		prem·ise	
pre·dic·tor		pre·mi·um	
pre·di·lec·tion		pre·mo·ni·tion	

pre·mon·i·to·ry	pre·side
pre·na·tal	pres·i·den·cy
pre·oc·cu·pa·tion	pres·i·dent
pre·oc·cu·py	pres·i·den·tial
pre·or·dain	pres·id·i·um
pre·paid	press
prep·a·ra·tion	pressed
pre·par·a·tive	press·man
pre·par·a·to·ry	press·room
✓ pre·pare	pres·sure
pre·par·ed·ness	pres·sur·ize
pre·pay	pres·ti·dig·i·ta·tion
pre·pay·ment	pres·ti·dig·i·ta·tor
pre·pon·der·ance	pres·tige
pre·pon·der·ant	pre·sum·a·ble
pre·pon·der·ate	pre·sume
prep·o·si·tion	pre·sum·ed·ly
prep·o·si·tion·al	pre·sump·tion
pre·pos·sess	pre·sum·tive
pre·pos·ses·sion	pre·sump·tu·ous
pre·pos·ter·ous	pre·sup·pose
pre·req·ui·site	pre·sup·po·si·tion
pre·rog·a·tive	pre·tend
pres·age	pre·tend·er
Pres·by·te·ri·an	pre·tense
pre·sci·ent	pre·ten·sion
pre·scribe	pre·ten·tious
pre·scrip·tion	pre·ter·nat·u·ral
pres·ence	pre·text
pres·ent	pret·ti·ly
pre·sent·a·ble	pret·ti·ness
pres·en·ta·tion	pret·ty
pre·sen·ti·ment	pret·zel
pres·ent·ly	pre·vail
pres·er·va·tion	prev·a·lence
pre·serv·a·tive	prev·a·lent
pre·serve	pre·var·i·cate

pre·var·i·ca·tion		prim·rose	
pre·var·i·ca·tor		prince	
pre·vent		prince·ly	
pre·vent·a·ble		prin·cess	
pre·ven·tion		prin·ci·pal	
pre·ven·tive		prin·ci·pal·i·ty	
pre·view		prin·ci·pal·ly	
pre·vi·ous		prin·ci·pal·ship	
pre·vi·ous·ly		prin·ci·ple	
pre·vi·sion		print	
prey		print·a·ble	
price		print·er	
price·less		pri·or	
prick		pri·or·ess	
prick·le		pri·or·i·ty	
prick·ly		prism	
pride		pris·mat·ic	
priest		pris·on	
priest·ess		pris·on·er	
priest·hood		pris·tine	
priest·ly		pri·va·cy	
prig		pri·vate	
prim		pri·va·teer	
pri·ma·cy		pri·vate·ly	
pri·ma don·na		pri·va·tion	
pri·ma fa·ci·e		priv·i·lege	
pri·mal		priv·y	
pri·ma·ri·ly		prize	
pri·ma·ry		prob·a·bil·i·ty	
prime		prob·a·ble	
prim·er		prob·a·bly	
pri·me·val		pro·bate	
prim·i·tive		pro·ba·tion	
pri·mo·gen·i·tor		pro·ba·tion·al	
pri·mo·gen·i·ture		pro·ba·tion·ar·y	
pri·mor·di·al		pro·ba·tion·er	
primp		probe	

prob·i·ty		pro·duc·tion	
prob·lem		pro·duc·tive	
prob·lem·at·ic		pro·duc·tiv·i·ty	
prob·lem·at·i·cal		pro·fan·a·to·ry	
pro·bos·cis		pro·fane	
pro·ce·dure		pro·fan·i·ty	
pro·ceed		pro·fess	
proc·ess		pro·fes·sion	
proc·ess·or		pro·fes·sion·al	
pro·ces·sion		pro·fes·sion·al·ism	
pro·ces·sion·al		pro·fes·sor	
pro·claim		pro·fes·so·ri·al	
proc·la·ma·tion		pro·fes·sor·ship	
pro·cliv·i·ty		prof·fer	
pro·cras·ti·nate		pro·fi·cien·cy	
pro·cras·ti·na·tion		pro·fi·cient	
pro·cras·ti·na·tor		pro·file	
pro·cre·ate		prof·it	
pro·cre·a·tion		prof·it·a·ble	
pro·cre·a·tive		prof·it·eer	
proc·tor		prof·li·ga·cy	
proc·to·ri·al		prof·li·gate	
pro·cur·a·ble		pro·found	
proc·u·ra·tion		pro·fun·di·ty	
proc·u·ra·tor		pro·fuse	
proc·u·ra·to·ry		pro·fu·sion	
pro·cure		pro·gen·i·tor	
pro·cure·ment		prog·e·ny	
pro·cur·er		prog·no·sis	
pro·cur·ess		prog·nos·tic	
prod·i·gal		prog·nos·ti·cate	
prod·i·gal·i·ty		prog·nos·ti·ca·tion	
pro·di·gious		pro·gram	
prod·i·gy		pro·gram·mer	
pro·duce		pro·gress	
pro·duc·i·ble		pro·gressed	
prod·uct		pro·gres·sion·al	

pro·gres·sive		prompt·ly	
pro·hib·it		prompt·ness	
pro·hi·bi·tion		pro·mul·gate	
pro·hi·bi·tion·ist		pro·mul·ga·tion	
pro·hib·i·tive		prone	
pro·ject		prong	
pro·jec·tile		pro·noun	
pro·jec·tion		pro·nounce	
pro·jec·tor		pro·nounce·a·ble	
pro·late		pro·nounce·ment	
pro·le·tar·i·an		pro·nun·ci·a·tion	
pro·le·tar·i·at		proof	
pro·lif·ic		proof·read·er	
pro·lix		prop	
pro·lix·i·ty		prop·a·gan·da	
pro·logue		prop·a·gan·dist	
pro·long		prop·a·gate	
pro·lon·gate		prop·a·ga·tion	
pro·lon·ga·tion		prop·a·ga·tor	
prom		pro·pel	
prom·e·nade		pro·pel·lant	
prom·e·nad·er		pro·pel·ler	
prom·i·nence		pro·pense	
prom·i·nent		pro·pen·si·ty	
pro·mis·cu·i·ty		prop·er	
pro·mis·cu·ous		prop·er·ly	
prom·ise		prop·er·ty	
prom·ised		proph·e·cy	
prom·is·so·ry		proph·e·si·er	
prom·on·to·ry		proph·e·sy	
pro·mote		proph·et	
pro·mot·er		pro·phet·ic	
pro·mo·tion		pro·phy·lac·tic	
pro·mo·tive		pro·pin·qui·ty	
prompt		pro·pi·ti·ate	
prompt·er		pro·pi·ti·a·tor	
promp·ti·tude		pro·pi·ti·a·to·ry	

pro·pi·tious		pros·y	
pro·po·nent		pro·tag·o·nist	
pro·por·tion		pro·tect	
pro·por·tion·al		pro·tec·tion	
pro·por·tion·ate		pro·tec·tive	
pro·pos·al		pro·tec·tor	
pro·pose		pro·tec·tor·ate	
prop·o·si·tion		pro·té·gé	
prop·o·si·tion·al		pro·te·in	
pro·pound		pro tem	
pro·pri·e·tar·y		pro·test	
pro·pri·e·tor		Prot·es·tant	
pro·pri·e·ty		Prot·es·tant·ism	
pro·pul·sion		pro·tes·ta·tion	
pro·pul·sive		pro·to·col	
pro ra·ta		pro·ton	
pro·rate		pro·to·plasm	
pro·sa·ic		pro·to·plast	
pro·sce·ni·um		pro·to·type	
pro·scribe		pro·tract	
pro·scrip·tion		pro·trac·tile	
prose		pro·trac·tion	
pros·e·cute		pro·trac·tor	
pros·e·cu·tion		pro·trude	
pros·e·cu·tor		pro·tru·sion	
pros·e·lyte		pro·tru·sive	
pros·pect		pro·tu·ber·ance	
pro·spec·tive		pro·tu·ber·ant	
pro·spec·tus		pro·tu·ber·ate	
pros·per		proud	
pros·per·i·ty		prov·a·ble	
pros·per·ous		prove	
pros·tate		prov·en	
pros·ti·tute		prov·en·der	
pros·ti·tu·tion		prov·er	
pros·trate		prov·erb	
pros·tra·tion		pro·ver·bi·al	

pro·vide		psy·che	
prov·i·dence		psy·chi·a·try	
prov·i·dent		psy·chic	
prov·i·den·tial		psy·cho·a·nal·y·sis	
prov·ince		psy·cho·an·a·lyze	
pro·vin·cial		psy·cho·log·i·cal	
pro·vin·cial·ism		psy·chol·o·gist	
pro·vin·cial·ly		psy·chol·o·gize	
pro·vi·sion		psy·chol·o·gy	
pro·vi·sion·al		psy·cho·path	
pro·vi·sion·ar·y		psy·cho·sis	
pro·vi·so		psy·cho·so·mat·ic	
pro·vi·so·ry		pub·er·ty	
prov·o·ca·tion		pub·lic	
pro·voc·a·tive		pub·li·ca·tion	
pro·voke		pub·li·cist	
prov·ost		pub·lic·i·ty	
prow		pub·lic·ly	
prow·ess		pub·lish	
prowl		pub·lish·er	
prox·i·mal		puce	
prox·i·mate		puck·er	
prox·im·i·ty		pud·ding	
prox·i·mo		pud·dle	
prox·y		pueb·lo	
prude		pudg·y	
pru·dence		pu·er·ile	
pru·dent		puff	
pru·den·tial		pug	
prud·ish		pu·gil·ism	
prune		pu·gil·ist	
pru·ri·ence		pu·gil·is·tic	
pru·ri·ent		pug·na·cious	
pry		pug·nac·i·ty	
psalm		pu·is·sance	
pseu·do		pu·is·sant	
pseu·do·nym		pul·chri·tude	

pul·chri·tu·di·nous		pun·ish·ment	
pull		pu·ni·tive	
pul·let		pun	
pul·ley		punk	
Pull·man		pun·ster	
pul·mo·nar·y		punt	
pul·mo·tor		pu·ny	
pulp		pup	
pulp·i·ness		pu·pil	
pul·pit		pup·pet	
pulp·y		pup·pet·ry	
pul·sate		pup·py	
pul·sa·tion		pur·blind	
pulse		pur·chas·a·ble	
pul·ver·ize		pur·chase	
pul·ver·iz·er		pur·chased	
pum·ice		pur·chas·er	
pum·mel		pure	
pump		pu·ree	
pump·per·nick·el		pure·ly	
pump·kin		pure·ness	
pun		pur·ga·tive	
punch		pur·ga·to·ry	
pun·cheon		purge	
punc·til·i·o		pu·ri·fi·ca·tion	
punc·til·i·ous		pu·ri·fi·er	
punc·tu·al		pu·ri·fy	
punc·tu·al·i·ty		pur·ism	
punc·tu·al·ly		pur·ist	
punc·tu·ate		pu·ri·tan	
punc·tu·a·tion		pu·ri·tan·i·cal	
punc·ture		pu·ri·ty	
pun·dit		purl	
pun·gen·cy		pur·lieu	
pun·gent		pur·loin	
pun·ish		pur·ple	
pun·ish·a·ble		pur·plish	

pur·port		pu·tre·fac·tion	
pur·pose		pu·tre·fy	
pur·pose·ly		pu·tres·cence	
purr		pu·tres·cent	
purse		pu·trid	
purs·er		putt	
pur·su·al		put·tee	
pur·su·ant		putt·er	
pur·sue		put·ty	
pur·suit		puz·zle	
pur·vey		pyg·my	
pur·vey·or		py·lon	
pur·view		py·or·rhe·a	
pus		pyr·a·mid	
push		pyre	
pu·sil·lan·i·mous		py·rom·e·ter	
pus·tu·lant		py·ro·ma·ni·ac	
pus·tu·lar		py·ro·tech·nic	
pus·tule		py·rox·y·lin	
put		pyr·rhic	
pu·ta·tive			

Q

quack		quan·ti·ta·tive	
quack·er·y		quan·ti·ty	
quad		quan·tum	
quad·ran·gle		quar·an·tine	
quad·ran·gu·lar		quar·rel	
quad·rant		quar·rel·some	
quad·ren·ni·al		quar·ry	
quad·ren·ni·um		quart	
quad·ri·lat·er·al		quar·ter	
qua·drille		quar·ter·ly	
quad·ril·lion		quar·tet	
quad·roon		quar·to	
quad·ru·ped		quartz	
quad·ru·ple		quash	
quad·ru·plet		qua·si	
quad·ru·pli·cate		quat·rain	
quaff		qua·ver	
quag·mire		quay	
quaint		queen	
quake		queer	
Quak·er		quell	
qual·i·fi·ca·tion		quench	
qual·i·fy		quer·u·lous	
qual·i·ta·tive		que·ry	
qual·i·ty		quest	
qualm		ques·tion	
quan·da·ry		ques·tion·a·ble	

ques·tion·er		quin·tet	
ques·tion·ing·ly		quip	
ques·tion·naire		quire	
queue		quirk	
quib·ble		quis·ling	
quick		quit	
quick·en		quit·claim	
quick·ly		quite	
quick·ness		quit·tance	
quick·sand		quiv·er	
quick·sil·ver		qui vive	
qui·es·cence		quix·ot·ic	
qui·es·cent		quiz	
qui·et		quiz·zi·cal	
qui·et·ly		quon·dam	
qui·et·ness		quo·rum	
qui·e·tude		quo·ta	
qui·e·tus		quot·a·ble	
quill		quo·ta·tion	
quilt		quote	
qui·nine		quo·tient	
quint·es·sence			

rab·bi	rbi
rab·bit	rbl
rab·ble	rb
rab·id	rbd
ra·bi·es	rbz
rac·coon	rcn
race	ras
rac·er	rs
ra·cial	rx
rac·ism	rsz
rack	rc
rack·et	rcl
rack·e·teer	rcle
rac·on·teur	rklu
ra·dar	rdr
ra·dar·scope	rⅮscp
ra·di·al	rdel
ra·di·ance	rde/
ra·di·ant	rde—
ra·di·ant·ly	rde—l
ra·di·ate	rda
ra·di·a·tion	rdy
ra·di·a·tor	rda
rad·i·cal	rdcl
rad·i·cal·ism	rdclz
rad·i·cal·ly	rdcl
ra·di·i	rdi

ra·di·o	rdo
ra·di·o·ac·tive	rdoacv
ra·di·o·gram	rdog
ra·di·o·graph	rdogf
ra·di·ol·o·gy	rdelje
ra·di·o·tel·e·gram	rdollg
ra·di·o·tel·e·graph	rdollgf
ra·di·o·tel·e·phone	rdolel
rad·ish	rdb
ra·di·um	(Ra) rde
ra·di·us	rdx
raf·fia	rfa
raf·fle	rfl
raft	rf
raft·er	rf
rag	rg
rag·a·muf·fin	rgfn
rage	raj
ra·gout	rgu
raid	rd
rail	ral
rail·ler·y	rly
rail·road	rr
rail·way	ry
rai·ment	ra—
✓rain	rn
rain·bow	rnbo

199

rain·coat	*rnco*	rap	*rp*
rain·drop	*rnDp*	ra·pa·cious	*rpx*
rain·fall	*rnfal*	ra·pac·i·ty	*rps)*
rain·y	*rne*	rape	*rap*
✓ raise	*rz*	rap·id	*rpd*
rai·sin	*rzn*	ra·pid·i·ty	*rpd)*
ra·ja	*rja*	ra·pid·ly	*rpdl*
rake	*rc*	ra·pi·er	*rpe*
rak·ish	*rcs*	rap·ine	*rpn*
ral·ly	*rl*	rap·port	*rpo*
ram	*r*	rap·proche·ment	*rℓC–*
ram·ble	*rrb*	rap·scal·lion	*rpscln*
ram·bunc·tious	*rrbgx*	rapt	*rp*
ram·e·kin	*rcn*	rap·ture	*rpC*
ram·i·fi·ca·tion	*rfcj*	rap·tur·ous	*rpCrx*
ram·i·fy	*rf*	✓ rare	*ra*
ramp	*rp*	rar·e·fac·tion	*rafcj*
ramp·age	*rpj*	rar·e·fy	*raf*
ramp·ant	*rp–*	rare·ly	*ral*
ram·part	*rpt*	rare·ness	*ra'*
ram·rod	*rrd*	rar·i·ty	*ra)*
ram·shack·le	*rScl*	ras·cal	*rscl*
ran	*rn*	ra·scal·i·ty	*rscl)*
ranch	*rC*	rash	*rs*
ran·cid	*r/d*	rash·er	*rs*
ran·cor	*rg*	rash·ly	*rsl*
ran·cor·ous	*rgx*	rasp	*rs*
✓ ran·dom	*r——*	rasp·ber·ry	*rzby*
rang	*rg*	rat	*rl*
range	*rj*	rat·a·ble	*rab*
rang·y	*rje*	ratch·et	*rCl*
ra·ni	*rne*	rate	*ra*
rank	*rg*	rath·er	*r*
ran·kle	*rgl*	rat·i·fi·ca·tion	*rlfcj*
ran·sack	*rnsc*	rat·i·fy	*rlf*
ran·som	*r/*	ra·tio	*rSo*
rant	*r–*	ra·ti·oc·i·na·tion	*rlesnj*

ra·tion	*r/ *	re·al·i·za·tion	*rlz/*
ra·tion·al	*rjl*	re·al·ize	*rlz*
ra·tion·al·ize	*rglz*	re·al·ly	*rl*
rat·tan	*rln*	realm	*rl*
rat·tle	*rll*	re·al·tor	*rl*
rau·cous	*rcx*	re·al·ty	*rl)*
rav·age	*ruj*	ream	*re*
rave	*ra*	ream·er	*re*
rav·en	*run*	re·an·i·mate	*rara*
rav·en·ous	*runx*	re·ap·point	*rapy–*
ra·vine	*run*	reap	*rep*
rav·ish	*ruf*	rear	*re*
raw	*ra*	re·ar·range	*rarj*
ray	*ra*	rea·son	*rzn*
ray·on	*ran*	rea·son·a·ble	*rznb*
raze	*rz*	rea·son·a·bly	*rznb*
ra·zor	*rz*	re·as·sur·ance	*rasu /*
reach	*rec*	re·as·sure	*rasu*
re·act	*rac*	re·bate	*rba*
re·ac·tor	*rac*	re·bel	*rbl*
re·ac·tion	*racj*	re·bel·lion	*rbln*
re·ac·tion·ar·y	*racjy*	re·bel·lious	*rblx*
read	*rd*	re·birth	*rbl*
read·a·ble	*rdb*	re·bound	*rb––*
read·er	*rd*	re·buff	*rbf*
read·i·ly	*rdl*	re·buke	*rbc*
read·i·ness	*rde'*	re·bus	*rbx*
read·out	*rdou*	re·but	*rbl*
re·ad·just·ment	*rajs–*	re·but·tal	*rbll*
read·y	*rde*	re·cal·ci·trant	*rclsJ–*
re·af·firm	*raf*	re·call	*rcl*
re·a·gent	*raj–*	re·cant	*rc–*
real	*rl*	re·ca·pit·u·late	*rcpCla*
re·al·ism	*rlz*	re·ca·pit·u·la·tion	*rcpClj*
re·al·ist	*rl,*	re·cap·ture	*rcpC*
re·al·is·tic	*rlsc*	re·cede	*rsd*
re·al·i·ty	*rl)*	re·ceipt	*rse*

re·ceiv·a·ble	*rseb*	rec·om·pense	*rkp/*
re·ceive	*rse*	rec·on·cile	*rksl*
re·ceiv·er·ship	*rs€8*	rec·on·cil·i·a·tion	*rksly*
re·cent	*rs–*	rec·on·dite	*rkdi*
re·cent·ly	*rs–l*	re·con·nais·sance	*rkz/*
re·cep·ta·cle	*rspcl*	rec·on·noi·ter	*rkij*
re·cep·tion	*rspj*	re·con·quer	*rkc*
re·cep·tive	*rspv*	re·con·sid·er	*rks*
re·cess	*rs'*	re·con·sti·tute	*rkslu*
re·ces·sion·al	*rsjl*	re·con·struct	*rkSc*
re·ces·sive	*rssv*	re·con·struc·tion	*rkScj*
rec·i·pe	*rspe*	rec·ord	*rCd*
re·cip·i·ent	*rspe–*	re·cord·er	*rCd*
re·cip·ro·cal	*rspcl*	re·coup	*rcp*
re·cip·ro·cate	*rspca*	re·course	*rCs*
re·cip·ro·ca·tion	*rspcj*	re·cov·er	*rcv*
rec·i·proc·i·ty	*rsps)*	re·cov·er·y	*rcvy*
re·cit·al	*rsil*	rec·re·ant	*rCe–*
rec·i·ta·tion	*rsly*	re·cre·ate	*rCa*
re·cite	*rsi*	rec·re·a·tion	*rCj*
reck·less	*rcl'*	re·crim·i·na·tion	*rCmj*
reck·on	*rcn*	re·cru·des·cence	*rCds/*
re·claim	*rca*	re·cruit	*rCu*
rec·la·ma·tion	*rcy*	✓ rec·tan·gle	*rcgl*
re·cline	*rcin*	rec·tan·gu·lar	*rcgl*
re·cluse	*rcs*	rec·ti·fi·ca·tion	*rcfcj*
rec·og·ni·tion	*rcgnj*	rec·ti·fy	*rcf*
rec·og·niz·a·ble	*rcgnzb*	rec·ti·fi·er	*rcf*
re·cog·ni·zance	*rcgnz/*	rec·ti·lin·e·ar	*rclne*
rec·og·nize	*rcgnz*	rec·ti·tude	*rcld*
re·coil	*rcyl*	rec·tor	*rc*
rec·ol·lect	*rcc*	rec·to·ry	*rcy*
rec·ol·lec·tion	*rccj*	rec·tum	*rc*
re·com·mence	*rk/*	re·cum·bent	*rkb–*
rec·om·mend	*rk—*	re·cu·per·ate	*rcpa*
✓ rec·om·men·da·tion	*rk—j*	re·cu·per·a·tion	*rcpj*
re·com·mit	*rkl*	re·cur	*rc*

re·cur·rence		re·fin·er	
re·cur·rent		re·fin·er·y	
red		re·fit	
✓ re·deem		re·flect	
re·deem·a·ble		re·flec·tion	
re·deem·er		re·flec·tor	
re·demp·tion		re·flex	
re·di·rect		re·flex·ive	
✓ re·dis·trib·ute		re·form	
red·o·lence		ref·or·ma·tion	
red·o·lent		re·form·a·to·ry	
re·doubt·a·ble		re·fract	
re·dound		re·frac·tion	
re·dress		re·frac·to·ry	
re·duce		re·frain	
re·duced		re·fresh	
re·duc·tion		re·fresh·ment	
re·dun·dan·cy		re·frig·er·ant	
re·dun·dant		re·frig·er·ate	
reed		re·frig·er·a·tion	
reef		re·frig·er·a·tor	
reef·er		ref·uge	
reek		ref·u·gee	
reel		re·ful·gent	
re·e·lect		re·fund	
re·en·act		re·fur·bish	
re·en·force		re·fus·al	
re·en·list		re·fuse	
re·en·ter		ref·u·ta·ble	
re·es·tab·lish		ref·u·ta·tion	
re·ex·am·i·na·tion		re·fute	
re·fer		re·gain	
ref·er·ee		re·gal	
ref·er·ence		re·gale	
ref·er·en·dum		re·ga·li·a	
re·fine		✓ re·gard	
re·fine·ment		re·gard·less	

re·gat·ta	*rgla*	rein·deer	*rnde*
re·gen·cy	*ry/*	re·in·force	*rnfs*
re·gen·er·ate	*ryNa*	re·in·force·ment	*rnfs–*
re·gen·er·a·tive	*ryNv*	re·in·sert	*rnSl*
re·gent	*ry–*	re·in·state	*rnsa*
reg·i·cide	*rysd*	re·in·sure	*rnSu*
re·gime	*rze*	re·it·er·ate	*ruʲa*
reg·i·men	*rym*	re·it·er·a·tion	*ru/*
reg·i·ment	*ry–*	re·ject	*ryc*
reg·i·men·ta·tion	*ry–/*	re·jec·tion	*rycj*
re·gion	*ryn*	re·joice	*ryys*
re·gion·al	*rynl*	re·join	*ryyn*
✓ reg·is·ter	*ry5*	re·join·der	*ryy—/*
reg·is·trar	*rySr*	re·ju·ve·nate	*ryvna*
reg·is·tra·tion	*ry5j*	re·lapse	*rlps*
reg·is·try	*rySe*	✓ re·late	*rla*
reg·nant	*rgm–*	✓ re·la·tion	*rlj*
re·gress	*rg'*	✓ re·la·tion·ship	*rlj8*
re·gressed	*rg,*	rel·a·tive	*rlv*
re·gres·sion	*rgj*	rel·a·tive·ly	*rlvl*
re·gret	*rgl*	re·lax	*rlx*
re·gret·ful	*rglf*	re·lax·a·tion	*rlxj*
re·gret·ta·ble	*rglb*	re·lay	*rla*
↓ reg·u·lar	*reg*	re·lease	*rls*
reg·u·lar·i·ty	*reg)*	re·leased	*rle,*
reg·u·lar·ly	*reg*	rel·e·gate	*rlga*
↓ reg·u·late	*rega*	re·lent	*rl–*
reg·u·la·tion	*reg*	re·lent·less	*rl–l'*
re·gur·gi·tate	*rgjla*	rel·e·vance	*rlv/*
re·ha·bil·i·tate	*rhblla*	rel·e·vant	*rlv–*
re·hash	*rh8*	re·li·a·ble	*rleb*
re·hears·al	*rHsl*	re·li·ance	*rle/*
re·hearse	*rHs*	rel·ic	*rlc*
reign	*rn*	rel·ict	*rlc*
↓ re·im·burse	*rubs*	re·lief	*rlf*
rein	*rn*	re·lieve	*rle*
re·in·car·na·tion	*rnCnj*	re·li·gion	*rlyn*

re·li·gious		re·mu·ner·a·tive	
re·lin·quish		re·nais·sance	
rel·i·quar·y		re·nal	
rel·ish		rend	
re·luc·tance		ren·der	
re·luc·tant		ren·dez·vous	
re·ly		ren·di·tion	
re·main		ren·e·gade	
re·main·der		re·nege	
re·mand		re·new	
re·mark		re·new·a·ble	
re·mark·a·ble		re·new·al	
re·me·di·al		ren·net	
rem·e·dy		re·nom·i·nate	
re·mem·ber		re·nounce	
re·mem·brance		ren·o·vate	
re·mind		ren·o·va·tion	
re·mind·er		re·nown	
rem·i·nis·cence		rent	
rem·i·nis·cent		rent·al	
re·miss		re·nun·ci·a·tion	
re·mis·sion		re·oc·cu·py	
re·mit		re·o·pen	
re·mit·tance		re·or·gan·i·za·tion	
re·mit·tent		re·or·gan·ize	
rem·nant		re·pair	
re·mon·strance		rep·a·ra·tion	
re·mon·strate		rep·ar·tee	
re·mon·stra·tion		re·past	
re·morse		re·pay	
re·morse·less		re·peal	
re·mote		re·peat	
re·mov·a·ble		re·peat·er	
re·mov·al		re·pel	
re·move		re·pel·lent	
re·mu·ner·ate		re·pent	
re·mu·ner·a·tion		re·pen·tance	

re·pen·tant	*rp – –*	✓re·pro·duc·tion	*rᔆdcʸ*
re·per·cus·sion	*rᔆcʸ*	re·proof	*rᔍ*
rep·er·toire	*rpᔏᔎ*	re·prove	*rᔍᔝ*
rep·er·to·ry	*rᔗᔓ*	rep·tile	*rpl*
✓rep·e·ti·tion	*rplʸ*	rep·til·i·an	*rplen*
rep·e·ti·tious	*rplx*	re·pub·lic	*rpl*
re·pine	*rpᔌn*	re·pub·li·can	*rpbn*
✓re·place	*rpl*	re·pu·di·ate	*rpda*
re·place·a·ble	*rplb*	re·pu·di·a·tion	*rpdᔒ*
re·place·ment	*rpl –*	re·pug·nance	*rpgn/*
✓re·plen·ish	*rpnᔆ*	re·pug·nant	*rpgn –*
re·plen·ish·ment	*rpnᔆ –*	re·pulse	*rpls*
re·plete	*rpe*	re·pul·sion	*rplʸ*
re·plev·in	*rpᔝn*	re·pul·sive	*rplsᔝ*
rep·li·ca	*rpca*	rep·u·ta·ble	*rplb*
✓re·ply	*rpᔌ*	✓rep·u·ta·tion	*rplʸ*
✓re·port	*rᔆᔎ*	re·pute	*rpᔌ*
re·port·er	*rᔍ*	✓re·quest	*rᵠᵎ*
re·pose	*rpᶾ*	re·qui·em	*rᵠe*
re·pos·i·to·ry	*rpᶾᔓ*	✓re·quire	*rᵠᔌ*
re·pos·sess	*rpᶾ²*	re·quire·ment	*rᵠᔌ –*
re·pos·sessed	*rpᶾ₂₎*	req·ui·site	*rᵠzl*
rep·re·hend	*rᔍh——*	req·ui·si·tion	*rᵠzʸ*
rep·re·hen·si·ble	*rᔍh/b*	re·quit·al	*rᵠll*
rep·re·sent	*rep*	re·quite	*rᵠᔌ*
rep·re·sen·ta·tion	*repʸ*	✓re·sale	*rᔆ*
rep·re·sent·a·tive	*rep₎*	re·scind	*rᔆ——*
re·press	*rᔍᵖ²*	re·scis·sion	*rᔆʸ*
re·pressed	*rᔍᵖₛʸ*	res·cue	*rscᔌ*
re·pres·sion	*rᔆʸ*	re·search	*rᔆC*
re·prieve	*rᔆe*	✓re·sem·blance	*rᶾᔎb/*
rep·ri·mand	*rᔍᵖ——*	✓re·sem·ble	*rᶾᔎb*
re·print	*rᔍᵖ—*	re·sent	*rᶾ –*
re·pris·al	*rᔆᶾl*	re·sent·ful	*rᶾ –f*
re·proach	*rᔆC*	re·sent·ment	*rᶾ – –*
rep·ro·bate	*rᔆba*	✓res·er·va·tion	*rᶾᔝʸ*
re·pro·duce	*rᔆdᔆ*	re·serve	*rᶾᔝ*

res·er·voir	res·pi·ra·tor
re·set	re·spir·a·to·ry
re·side	res·pite
res·i·dence	re·splend·ent
res·i·dent	re·spond
res·i·den·tial	re·spond·ent
re·sid·u·al	re·sponse
re·sid·u·ar·y	re·spon·si·bil·i·ty
res·i·due	re·spon·si·ble
re·sid·u·um	re·spon·sive
re·sign	rest
res·ig·na·tion	res·tau·rant
re·sil·i·ence	res·tau·ra·teur
re·sil·ient	res·ti·tu·tion
res·in	res·tive
res·in·ous	rest·less
re·sist	res·to·ra·tion
re·sist·ance	re·stor·a·tive
re·sist·ant	re·store
re·sis·tor	re·strain
re·so·lute	re·straint
res·o·lu·tion	re·strict
re·solve	re·stric·tion
res·o·nance	re·sult
res·o·nant	re·sult·ant
res·o·na·tor	re·sume
re·sort	ré·su·mé
re·sound	re·sump·tion
re·source	re·sur·gence
re·source·ful	res·ur·rect
re·spect	res·ur·rec·tion
re·spect·a·bil·i·ty	re·sus·ci·tate
re·spect·a·ble	re·sus·ci·ta·tion
re·spect·ful	re·tail
re·spect·ful·ly	re·tail·er
re·spect·ive	re·tain
res·pi·ra·tion	re·tain·er

re·tal·i·ate	*rlla*	rev·el	*rvl*
re·tal·i·a·to·ry	*rllfy*	rev·e·la·tion	*rvlf*
re·tard	*rtd*	re·venge	*rvy*
re·tar·da·tion	*rtdy*	rev·e·nue	*rvnu*
retch	*rC*	re·ver·ber·ate	*rVBa*
re·ten·tion	*rly*	re·ver·ber·a·tion	*rVBy*
re·ten·tive	*rl-v*	re·vere	*rve*
ret·i·cence	*rls/*	rev·er·ence	*rV/*
ret·i·cent	*rls-*	rev·er·end	*rV—*
ret·i·cule	*rlcl*	rev·er·ent	*rV-*
ret·i·na	*rlna*	rev·er·en·tial	*rVx*
ret·i·nue	*rlnu*	rev·er·ie	*rvy*
re·tire	*rlu*	√ re·verse	*rVs*
re·tire·ment	*rlu-*	√ re·vers·i·ble	*rVsb*
re·tort	*rtl*	re·ver·sion	*rVy*
re·touch	*rlC*	re·vert	*rVl*
re·tract	*rTc*	re·view	*rvu*
re·tract·a·ble	*rTcb*	re·view·er	*rvu*
re·trac·tion	*rTcy*	re·vile	*rvl*
re·treat	*rTe*	re·vise	*rvz*
re·trench	*rTC*	re·vi·sion	*rvy*
ret·ri·bu·tion	*rTby*	re·vi·so·ry	*rvzy*
re·trieve	*rTe*	re·vi·tal·ize	*rvllz*
ret·ro·ac·tive	*rTacv*	re·viv·al	*rvvl*
ret·ro·cede	*rTsd*	re·vive	*rvv*
ret·ro·ces·sion	*rTsy*	re·viv·i·fy	*rvvf*
ret·ro·grade	*rTgd*	rev·o·ca·ble	*rvcb*
ret·ro·gres·sion	*rTgy*	rev·o·ca·tion	*rvcy*
ret·ro·spect	*rTsc*	re·voke	*rvc*
ret·ro·spec·tive	*rTscv*	re·volt	*rvll*
√ re·turn	*rTn*	rev·o·lu·tion	*rvly*
re·turn·a·ble	*rTnb*	rev·o·lu·tion·ar·y	*rvlyy*
re·un·ion	*runx*	rev·o·lu·tion·ize	*rvlyz*
re·u·nite	*runl*	re·volve	*rvlv*
rev	*rv*	re·volv·er	*rvlv*
re·veal	*rvl*	re·vue	*rvu*
re·veil·le	*rvl*	re·vul·sion	*rvly*

✓ re·ward

rhap·so·dy

rhe·o·stat

rhet·o·ric

rhe·tor·i·cal

rheu·mat·ic

rheu·ma·tism

rhine·stone

rhom·boid

rhom·bus

rhu·barb

rhyme

rhythm

rhyth·mic

rib

rib·ald

rib·bon

rice

rich

rich·er

rick

rick·ets

ric·o·chet

rid

rid·dle

ride

ridge

rid·i·cule

ri·dic·u·lous

rife

riff·raff

ri·fle

rift

rig

right

right·eous

right·ful

rig·id

ri·gid·i·ty

rig·ma·role

rig·or

rig·or·ous

rile

rim

rime

rind

ring

rink

✓ rinse

ri·ot

ri·ot·ous

rip

ri·par·i·an

ripe

rip·en

rip·ple

ri·poste

rip·saw

rise

risk

ris·qué

ris·sole

rite

rit·u·al

ri·val

riv·er

riv·er·side

riv·et

riv·u·let

roach

road

road·side

road·ster

road·way

roam	*ro*	rope	*rop*
roar	*ro*	ro·sa·ry	*rzy*
roast	*ro,*	rose	*rz*
rob	*rb*	rose·mar·y	*rzry*
rob·ber·y	*rby*	ro·sette	*rzt*
robe	*rob*	ros·in	*rzn*
rob·in	*rbn*	ros·ter	*rS*
ro·bot	*rbl*	ros·trum	*rS*
ro·bust	*rb,*	rot	*rt*
rock	*rc*	ro·ta·ry	*rly*
ro·co·co	*rcco*	ro·tate	*rla*
rod	*rd*	ro·ta·tion	*rly*
rode	*rd*	rote	*ro*
ro·dent	*rd–*	ro·tor	*ro*
ro·de·o	*rdo*	rot·ten	*rtn*
roent·gen	*r–n*	ro·to·gra·vure	*rlgvu*
rogue	*rog*	ro·tund	*rt—*
ro·guish	*rg8*	ro·tun·da	*rt—a*
roil	*ryl*	ro·tun·di·ty	*rt—)*
rois·ter	*ryS*	rough	*rf*
role	*rol*	rough·age	*rfs*
roll	*rol*	rough·en	*rfn*
rol·lick	*rlc*	rou·lade	*rld*
ro·mance	*r/*	rou·lette	*rll*
Ro·ma·ni·an	*rmen*	round	*ru—*
ro·man·tic	*r—c*	round·a·bout	*ru—ab*
ro·man·ti·cism	*r—sz*	roun·de·lay	*ru—la*
romp	*rp*	rouse	*ruz*
rood	*rd*	rout	*rul*
roof	*ruf*	route	*ru*
roof·less	*rfl'*	rou·tine	*rtn*
rook	*rc*	rove	*ro*
room	*r*	row	*ro*
room·mate	*rma*	row·boat	*robo*
roost	*ru,*	row·dy	*rude*
roost·er	*rS*	row·el	*ruel*
root	*ru*	roy·al	*ryl*

roy·al·ist	*ryl,*	ru·mi·na·tion	
roy·al·ty		rum·mage	
rub		✓ru·mor	
✓rub·ber		rump	
✓rub·ber·ize		rum·ple	
rub·bish		rum·pus	
rub·ble		run	
ru·bi·cund		run·a·bout	
ru·bric		run·a·way	
ru·by		rung	
rud·der		run·nel	
rud·dy		run·ner	
rude		runt	
ru·di·ment		run·way	
ru·di·men·ta·ry		ru·pee	
rue		rup·ture	
rue·ful		ru·ral	
ruff		ruse	
ruf·fi·an		rush	
ruf·fle		rus·set	
rug		Rus·sian	
ru·in		rust	
ru·in·ous		rus·tic	
rule		rus·ti·cate	
rul·er		rus·tle	
rum		rut	
rum·ble		ruth·less	
ru·mi·nant		rye	
ru·mi·nate			

Sab·bath	*sbl*	sad·ness	*sd'*
sab·bat·i·cal	*sblcl*	safe	*saf*
sa·ber	*sb*	safe·guard	*sfGd*
sa·ble	*sb*	safe·ly	*sfl*
sa·bot	*sbo*	saf·er	*sf*
sab·o·tage	*sblz*	✓safe·ty	*sf)*
sac	*sc*	saf·fron	*sfn*
sac·cha·rin	*sCn*	sag	*sq*
sac·er·do·tal	*ssdll*	sa·ga	*sga*
sa·chem	*sC*	sa·ga·cious	*sgx*
sa·chet	*ssa*	sa·gac·i·ty	*sgs)*
sack	*sc*	sage	*saj*
sack·cloth	*sccl*	sa·hib	*shb*
sac·ra·ment	*sC−*	said	*sd*
sac·ra·men·tal	*sC−l*	sail	*s*
sa·cred	*sCd*	sail·boat	*sbo*
sac·ri·fice	*sCfs*	sail·cloth	*scl*
sac·ri·fi·cial	*sCfx*	sail·or	*s/*
sac·ri·lege	*sClg*	saint	*sa−*
sac·ri·le·gious	*sClgx*	saint·li·ness	*sa−l'*
sac·ris·tan	*sCsn*	saint·ly	*s−l*
sac·ris·ty	*sCs)*	sake	*sc*
sac·ro·sanct	*sCsq*	sa·laam	*sl*
sa·crum	*sC*	sal·a·bil·i·ty	*sb)*
sad	*sd*	sal·a·ble	*sb*
sad·dle	*sdl*	sa·la·cious	*slx*
sad·dler	*sdl*	sal·ad	*sld*

212

sal·a·man·der		sanc·ti·mo·ni·ous	
sa·la·mi		sanc·tion	
✓sal·a·ry		sanc·ti·ty	
✓sale		sanc·tu·ar·y	
✓sales·man		sanc·tum	
sales·man·ship		sand	
sales·men		san·dal	
sales·room		san·dal·wood	
sales·wom·an		sand·pa·per	
sal·i·cyl·ic		sand·wich	
sa·li·ence		sane	
sa·li·ent		sang	
sa·line		san·gui·nar·y	
sa·li·va		san·guine	
sal·i·var·y		san·i·ta·ry	
sal·low		san·i·ta·tion	
salm·on		san·i·ty	
sa·lon		sank	
sa·loon		sans	
salt		sap	
sa·lu·bri·ous		sap·id	
sal·u·tar·y		sa·pi·ent	
sal·u·ta·tion		sa·pon·i·fy	
sa·lu·ta·to·ri·an		sap·phire	
sa·lute		sar·casm	
sal·vage		sar·cas·tic	
sal·va·tion		sar·co·ma	
salve		sar·coph·a·gi	
sal·ver		sar·choph·a·gus	
sal·vo		sar·dine	
✓same		sar·don·ic	
sam·i·sen		sar·to·ri·al	
sam·ite		sash	
✓sam·ple		sat	
san·a·to·ri·um		sa·tan·ic	
sanc·ti·fi·ca·tion		sat·ch·el	
sanc·ti·fy		sate	

sa·teen	*stn*	scald	*scld*
sat·el·lite	*stli*	scale	*scal*
sa·ti·ate	*sSa*	scal·lion	*scln*
sa·ti·e·ty	*sti)*	scal·lop	*sclp*
sat·in	*stn*	scalp	*sclp*
sat·ire	*sti*	scal·pel	*sclp*
sa·tir·i·cal	*stil*	scal·y	*scl*
sat·i·rize	*st3*	scamp	*scrp*
√ sat·is·fac·tion	*sal*	scam·per	*scrp*
sat·is·fac·to·ri·ly	*sal*	scan	*scn*
sat·is·fac·to·ry	*sal*	scan·dal	*sc — l*
sat·is·fy	*sal*	scan·dal·ize	*sc — lz*
sa·trap	*stP*	scan·dal·mon·ger	*sc—lrg*
sat·u·rate	*sCra*	scan·dal·ous	*sc — ls*
sat·u·ra·tion	*sCry*	Scan·di·na·vi·an	*sc— nven*
√ Sat·ur·day	*st*	scant	*sc-*
sat·ur·nine	*strn*	scant·i·ly	*sc - l*
sat·yr	*s*	scant·y	*sc - e*
sauce	*ss*	scape·goat	*scpgo*
sau·cer	*ss*	scap·u·la	*scpla*
saun·ter	*s*	scap·u·lar	*scpl*
sau·sage	*ssy*	scar	*scr*
sau·té	*sta*	scar·ab	*sCb*
sav·age	*svy*	√ scarce	*sCs*
sa·van·na	*svna*	scar·ci·ty	*sCs)*
sa·vant	*sv-*	scare	*sca*
save	*sv*	scarf	*sCf*
sav·ior	*sv*	scar·i·fi·ca·tion	*sCfcy*
sa·vor	*sv*	scar·i·fy	*sCf*
sa·vo·ry	*svy*	scar·la·ti·na	*sCllna*
saw	*sa*	scar·let	*sCll*
sax·o·phone	*sxfn*	scathe	*scal*
say	*sa*	√ scat·ter	*sc*
says	*s3*	scav·en·ger	*scvy*
scab	*scb*	sce·na·ri·o	*snyo*
scab·bard	*scBd*	√ scene	*sn*
scaf·fold	*scfol*	scen·er·y	*sny*

sce·nic	*snc*	✓score	*sco*
scent	*s-*	scorn	*sCn*
scep·ter	*sp*	scorn·ful	*sCnf*
scep·tic	*scpc*	scor·pi·on	*sCpen*
sched·ule	*scdl*	scotch	*scC*
scheme	*sce*	scoun·drel	*scu —rl*
schism	*sz*	scour	*scu*
schiz·o·phre·ni·a	*scztna*	scourge	*sCj*
schol·ar	*scl*	scout	*scut*
schol·ar·ly	*scdl*	scow	*scu*
schol·ar·ship	*scdS*	scowl	*scul*
scho·las·tic	*sclsc*	scrab·ble	*sCb*
school	*scl*	scram·ble	*sCrb*
school·book	*sclbc*	scrap	*sCp*
school·boy	*sclby*	scrape	*sCap*
school·girl	*sclgl*	scratch	*sCC*
school·house	*sclhus*	scrawl	*sCal*
school·mate	*sclra*	scrawny	*sCne*
school·room	*sclrn*	scream	*sCe*
school·teach·er	*scllC*	screech	*sCeC*
school·work	*sclrc*	screen	*sCn*
schoon·er	*scn*	screw	*sCu*
sci·at·ic	*silc*	scrib·ble	*sCb*
sci·at·i·ca	*silca*	scribe	*sCib*
sci·ence	*si/*	scrim·mage	*sCy*
sci·en·tif·ic	*si-fc*	scrimp	*sCrp*
sci·en·tist	*si-,*	scrip	*sCp*
scin·til·la	*s-la*	script	*sCp*
scin·til·late	*s-la*	scrip·ture	*sCpC*
sci·on	*sin*	scroll	*sCol*
scis·sors	*sz/*	scrub	*sCb*
scle·ro·sis	*sCss*	scruff	*sCf*
scoff	*scf*	scru·ple	*sCp*
scold	*scol*	scru·pu·lous	*sCpu*
scoop	*scup*	scru·ti·nize	*sClnz*
scope	*scop*	scru·ti·ny	*sClne*
scorch	*scC*	scu·ba	*scba*

scuf·fle	*scfl*	se·ces·sion	*ssj*
scul·ler·y	*scly*	✓ se·clude	*scd*
scul·lion	*scln*	✓ se·clu·sion	*scj*
sculp·tor	*sclp*	sec·ond	*sec*
sculp·ture	*sclpC*	sec·ond·ar·i·ly	*secyl*
scum	*sc*	sec·ond·ar·y	*secy*
scurf	*scf*	se·cre·cy	*sCse*
scur·ril·ous	*sClx*	se·cret	*sCl*
scur·ry	*scy*	sec·re·tar·i·al	*secl*
scur·vy	*sCve*	sec·re·tar·i·at	*secl*
scut·tle	*scll*	sec·re·tar·y	*sec*
scythe	*sil*	se·crete	*sCe*
sea	*se*	se·cre·tion	*sCj*
sea·coast	*seco,*	se·cre·tive	*sCv*
sea·far·er	*sefa*	sect	*sc*
sea·food	*sefd*	sec·tar·i·an	*scyn*
sea·go·ing	*seg*	✓ sec·tion	*scj*
seal	*sel*	sec·tion·al	*scjl*
seam	*se*	sec·tor	*sc*
sea·man	*sen—*	sec·u·lar	*scl*
seam·stress	*seS'*	✓ se·cure	*scu*
se·ance	*sa/*	✓ se·cur·i·ty	*scu)*
sea·plane	*sepn*	se·dan	*sdn*
sea·port	*sePl*	se·date	*sda*
sear	*se*	sed·a·tive	*sdv*
✓ search	*SC*	sed·en·tar·y	*sd—y*
sea·shore	*seSo*	sed·i·ment	*sd—*
sea·sick	*sesc*	se·di·tion	*sdj*
sea·son	*szn*	se·di·tious	*sdx*
sea·son·a·ble	*sznb*	se·duce	*sds*
sea·son·al	*sznl*	se·duc·er	*sds*
seat	*se*	se·duc·tion	*sdcj*
sea·way	*sewa*	se·duc·tive	*sdcv*
sea·wor·thy	*selte*	sed·u·lous	*sdlx*
se·ba·ceous	*sbv*	see	*se*
se·cant	*sc—*	seed	*sd*
se·cede	*ssd*	seed·ling	*sdlg*

seek	*sec*	self-pro·tec·tion	*s/ptcj*
✓seem	*se*	self-sac·ri·fice	*s/sCfs*
seem·ly	*sel*	sell	*sl*
seen	*sn*	sel·vage	*slvj*
seep	*sep*	se·man·tic	*sn-c*
seep·age	*spj*	sem·a·phore	*srf*
seer·suck·er	*ssc*	sem·blance	*srbl*
see·saw	*ssa*	se·mes·ter	*snS*
seethe	*sel*	sem·i·cir·cle	*snScl*
seg·ment	*sq-*	sem·i·co·lon	*srcln*
seg·re·gate	*sgga*	sem·i·con·scious	*srkx*
seg·re·ga·tion	*sggj*	sem·i·fi·nal	*srfl*
sei·gneur	*sny*	sem·i·month·ly	*srmol*
seis·mo·graph	*szgf*	sem·i·nar	*smr*
seiz·a·ble	*szb*	sem·i·nar·y	*smy*
seize	*sz*	sen·ate	*snl*
sei·zure	*sz*	sen·a·tor	*sn*
✓sel·dom	*sld*	sen·a·to·ri·al	*snlyl*
se·lect	*slc*	✓ send	*s—*
✓se·lec·tion	*slcj*	se·nes·cent	*sns-*
se·lec·tive	*slcv*	se·nile	*snl*
se·lect·man	*slc-*	se·nil·i·ty	*snl)*
se·le·ni·um	*(Se)slne*	sen·ior	*sr*
✓self	*s/*	sen·ior·i·ty	*sr)*
self·ad·dressed	*s/ad,*	✓sen·sa·tion	*s/j*
✓self·con·fi·dence	*s/kfd/*	sen·sa·tion·al	*s/jl*
self·con·scious	*s/kx*	✓ sense	*s/*
self·con·tained	*s/kln*	sense·less	*s/l'*
self·con·trol	*s/kl*	sen·si·bil·i·ty	*s/l)*
self·de·fense	*s/dfl*	sen·si·ble	*s/l*
self·es·teem	*s/ese*	sen·si·tive	*s/v*
self·gov·ern·ment	*s/gvl*	sen·si·tiv·i·ty	*s/v)*
self·im·por·tance	*s/ipl*	sen·si·tize	*s/lz*
self·in·ter·est	*s/n,*	sen·so·ry	*s/y*
self·ish	*s/8*	sen·su·al	*s/ul*
self·less	*s/l'*	sen·su·ous	*s/x*
self·pos·sessed	*s/pz,*	sent	*s-*

✓ sen·tence		ser·mon·ize	
sen·ten·tious		ser·pent	
sen·tient		ser·pen·tine	
sen·ti·ment		ser·rate	
sen·ti·men·tal		ser·ra·tion	
sen·ti·men·tal·i·ty		se·rum	
sen·ti·nel		serv·ant	
sen·try		✓ serve	
sep·a·ra·ble		serv·ice	
✓ sep·a·rate		serv·ice·a·ble	
sep·a·ra·tion		ser·vile	
sep·a·ra·tor		ser·vil·i·ty	
se·pi·a		ser·vi·tor	
sep·sis		ses·a·me	
Sep·tem·ber		✓ ses·sion	
sep·tet		set	
sep·tic		set·tee	
sep·tum		set·ter	
se·pul·chral		set·tle	
se·quel		set·tle·ment	
↓ se·quence		set·up	
↓ se·quen·tial		sev·en	
se·ques·ter		sev·en·teen	
se·ques·trate		sev·enth	
se·quin		sev·er	
ser·aph		✓ sev·er·al	
se·raph·ic		sev·er·ance	
ser·e·nade		✓ se·vere	
se·rene		se·ver·i·ty	
se·ren·i·ty		sew	
serf		sew·age	
ser·geant		sew·er	
se·ri·al		sex	
se·ries		sex·tant	
ser·if		sex·tet	
↓ se·ri·ous		sex·ton	
ser·mon		shab·bi·ness	

shab·by	*Sbe*	sheep	*Sep*
shack	*Sc*	sheer	*Se*
shack·le	*Scl*	sheet	*Se*
shade	*Sd*	shelf	*Slf*
shad·ow	*Sdo*	shell	*Sl*
shad·ow·y	*Sdoe*	shel·lac	*Slc*
shaft	*Sf*	shel·ter	*Sl*
shag·gy	*Sge*	shep·herd	*Spd*
shake	*Sc*	sher·bet	*Srbt*
shak·i·ly	*Scl*	sher·iff	*Srf*
shall	*S*	sher·ry	*Sy*
shal·low	*Slo*	shield	*Seld*
sham	*S*	shift	*Sf*
sham·ble	*Srb*	shift·less	*Sfl'*
shame	*Sa*	shil·ling	*(Sh) Slg*
shame·ful	*Saf*	shim·mer	*S*
shame·less	*Sal'*	shin	*Sn*
sham·poo	*Srpu*	shine	*Sin*
sham·rock	*Src*	shin·gle	*Sgl*
shank	*Sg*	ship	*S*
shan·ty	*S-e*	ship·ment	*S-*
shape	*Sap*	ship·per	*S*
shape·less	*Spl'*	ship·shape	*SSp*
share	*Sa*	ship·wreck	*Src*
share·hold·er	*Sahol*	ship·yard	*Slfd*
sharp	*Srp*	shirk	*Src*
sharp·en·er	*Srpn*	shirr	*S*
sharp·er	*Srp*	shirt	*Srl*
sharp·shoot·er	*SrpSu*	shiv·er	*Sv*
shave	*Sa*	shock	*Sc*
shawl	*Sal*	shod	*Sd*
she	*S*	shod·dy	*Sde*
sheaf	*Sef*	shoe	*Su*
shear	*Se*	shone	*Sn*
sheathe	*Sel*	shook	*Sc*
shed	*Sd*	shoot	*Su*
sheen	*Sn*	shop	*Sp*

shop·keep·er		shrive	
shop·lift·er		shriv·el	
shop·per		shroud	
shop·walk·er		shrub	
shop·worn		shrub·ber·y	
shore		shrug	
shorn		shrunk	
short		shrunk·en	
short·age		shud·der	
short·com·ing		shuf·fle	
short·en		shun	
short·hand		shunt	
short·ly		shut	
shot		shut·ter	
shot·gun		shut·tle	
should		shy	
shoul·der		sib·i·lant	
shout		sib·yl	
shove		sick	
shov·el		sick·en	
show		sick·le	
show·down		sick·li·ness	
show·er		sick·ness	
show·i·ly		side	
shown		side·band	
show·room		side·board	
show·y		side·long	
shrap·nel		side·track	
shred		side·walk	
shrew		side·ways	
shrewd		sid·le	
shriek		siege	
shrill		si·en·na	
shrimp		si·es·ta	
shrine		sieve	
shrink		sift	
shrink·age		sigh	

sight	*su*	✓sim·ple	*srp*
sight·less	*sil'*	sim·ple·ton	*srpln*
sign	*sin*	sim·plex	*srpx*
sig·nal	*sgnl*	sim·plic·i·ty	*srps)*
sig·na·to·ry	*sgnly*	sim·pli·fi·ca·tion	*srpfcy*
✓sig·na·ture	*sig*	✓sim·pli·fy	*srpf*
sign·er	*sin*	✓sim·ply	*srp*
sig·net	*sgnl*	sim·u·la·crum	*srlC*
✓sig·nif·i·cance	*sgnfc/*	sim·u·late	*srla*
✓sig·nif·i·cant	*sgnfc−*	sim·u·la·tion	*srly*
sig·ni·fy	*sgnf*	sim·u·la·tor	*srla*
sign·post	*sinpo,*	si·mul·ta·ne·ous	*srllnx*
si·lage	*sly*	sin	*sn*
✓si·lence	*sl/*	✓since	*s/*
si·lent	*sl−*	✓sin·cere	*s/e*
si·lex	*slx*	sin·cere·ly	*s/el*
sil·hou·ette	*slrl*	sin·cer·i·ty	*s/n)*
sil·i·ca	*slca*	si·ne·cure	*sncu*
sil·i·cate	*slca*	sin·ew	*snu*
sil·i·cone	*slcn*	sin·ful	*snf*
silk	*slc*	sing	*sq*
silk·en	*slcn*	singe	*sy*
silk·y	*slce*	sin·gle	*sgl*
sill	*sl*	sin·gle·ton	*sglln*
sil·ly	*sl*	sin·gly	*sgl*
si·lo	*slo*	sin·gu·lar	*sgl*
silt	*sll*	sin·is·ter	*snS*
sil·ver	*(aq) slv*	sink	*sq*
sil·ver·ware	*slvra*	sin·u·ous	*snx*
sil·ver·y	*slvy*	si·nus	*sinx*
✓sim·i·lar	*srl*	sip	*sp*
✓sim·i·lar·i·ty	*srl)*	si·phon	*sfn*
sim·i·le	*srl*	sir	*s*
si·mil·i·tude	*srlld*	sire	*su*
sim·mer	*sr*	si·ren	*Sn*
si·mo·nize	*smz*	sir·loin	*Slyn*
sim·per	*srp*	si·roc·co	*Sco*

sir·up	*Sp*	skulk	*sclc*
si·sal	*ssl*	skull	*scl*
✓ sis·ter	*sS*	skull·cap	*sclcp*
⟋ sis·ter-in-law	*sSnla*	skunk	*scq*
sit	*sl*	sky	*sci*
site	*si*	sky·light	*scli*
sit·u·ate	*scl*	sky·rock·et	*scircl*
✓ sit·u·a·tion	*sil*	sky·scrap·er	*sciscp*
six	*6*	sky·ward	*sci rd*
siz·a·ble	*szb*	slab	*sb*
size	*sz*	slack	*sc*
siz·zle	*szl*	slack·en	*scn*
skate	*sca*	slag	*sg*
skein	*scn*	slain	*sn*
skel·e·ton	*sclln*	slake	*sc*
skep·tic	*scpc*	slam	*sr*
skep·ti·cal	*scpcl*	slan·der	*s ⟋*
skep·ti·cism	*scpsz*	slan·der·ous	*s — rx*
sketch	*scC*	slang	*sg*
sketch·i·ly	*scCl*	slant	*s -*
sketch·y	*scCe*	slap	*sp*
skew·er	*scu*	slash	*s8*
ski	*sce*	slat	*sl*
skid	*scd*	slate	*sa*
skill	*scl*	slat·tern	*sᵗⁿ*
skill·ful	*sclf*	slaugh·ter	*s ⟋*
skim	*sc*	slave	*sa*
skimp	*scp*	slav·er·y	*say*
skimp·y	*scpe*	slay	*sa*
skin	*scn*	slea·zy	*sze*
skip	*scp*	sled	*sd*
skip·per	*scp*	sledge	*sj*
skir·mish	*scr8*	sleek	*sec*
skirt	*scl*	sleep	*sep*
skit	*scl*	sleep·er	*sp*
skit·tish	*scl8*	sleep·less	*spl'*
skive	*sci*	sleet	*se*

sleeve	*se*	slug·gard	*sgd*
sleigh	*sa*	sluice	*sus*
sleight	*si*	slum	*s*
slen·der	*s—*	slum·ber	*srb*
slept	*sp*	slump	*srp*
sleuth	*sul*	slung	*sg*
slew	*su*	slur	*s*
slice	*sis*	slush	*ss*
slick	*sc*	sly	*si*
slide	*sd*	smack	*src*
slight	*si*	√ small	*sra*
slim	*s*	small·er	*sra*
slime	*si*	small·est	*sra,*
sling	*sg*	√ smart	*srt*
slink	*sg*	smash	*srs*
slip	*sp*	smat·ter·ing	*sr_*
slip·per	*sp*	smear	*sre*
slip·per·y	*spy*	smell	*srl*
slit	*sl*	smelt	*srll*
slith·er	*sT*	smelt·er	*srl*
sliv·er	*sv*	smile	*srul*
slob·ber	*sb*	smirch	*srC*
slo·gan	*sgn*	smirk	*src*
slop	*sp*	smith	*srl*
slope	*sop*	smock	*src*
slot	*sl*	smog	*srg*
sloth	*sl*	smoke	*sroc*
sloth·ful	*slf*	smok·y	*srce*
slouch	*si-C*	smol·der	*srol*
slough	*sf*	smooth	*srul*
slov·en	*svn*	smor·gas·bord	*srgsBd*
slov·en·ly	*svnl*	smoth·er	*srt*
√ slow	*so*	smudge	*sr*
slow·er	*so*	smug	*srg*
slow·ly	*sol*	smug·gle	*srgl*
sludge	*sl*	smut·ty	*sr)*
slug	*sg*	snack	*snc*

snag	*snq*	so·ber	*sb*
snail	*snal*	so·bri·e·ty	*sßu)*
snake	*snc*	so·bri·quet	*sßca*
snap	*snp*	soc·cer	*sc*
snare	*sna*	so·cia·ble	*sSb*
snarl	*sNl*	✓so·cial	*sx*
snatch	*snC*	so·cial·ism	*sez*
sneak	*snec*	so·cial·ist	*se,*
sneer	*sne*	so·cial·ize	*sez*
sneeze	*snz*	so·cial·ly	*sx*
snick·er	*snc*	✓so·ci·e·ty	*ssu)*
snide	*snd*	so·ci·ol·o·gy	*sselje*
sniff	*snf*	sock	*sc*
snip	*snp*	sock·et	*scl*
sniv·el	*snvl*	sod	*sd*
snob	*snb*	so·da	*sda*
snob·ber·y	*snby*	so·dal·i·ty	*sdl)*
snob·bish	*snbß*	sod·den	*sdn*
snoop	*snup*	so·di·um	*(na) sde*
snooze	*snz*	so·fa	*sfa*
snore	*sno*	soft	*sf*
snor·kel	*sNcl*	sof·ten	*sfn*
snort	*sNl*	sog·gy	*sge*
snout	*snul*	soil	*syl*
snow	*sno*	soi·ree	*sura*
snow·y	*snoe*	so·journ	*sJn*
snub	*snb*	sol·ace	*sls*
snuff	*snf*	so·lar	*sl*
snuf·fle	*snfl*	so·lar·i·um	*sly*
snug	*snq*	sold	*sol*
so	*so*	sol·der	*sd*
soak	*soc*	sol·dier	*slj*
soap	*sop,*	sole	*sol*
soap·i·ness	*spe'*	sol·e·cism	*slsz*
soap·y	*spe*	sole·ly	*sol*
soar	*so*	sol·emn	*sl*
sob	*sb*	so·lem·ni·ty	*slm)*

sol·em·nize		so·nar	
so·le·noid		so·na·ta	
✓ so·lic·it		song	
so·lic·i·ta·tion		song·stress	
so·lic·i·tor		son·ic	
so·lic·it·ous		son-in-law	
so·lic·i·tude		son·net	
sol·id		so·no·rous	
sol·i·dar·i·ty		soon	
so·lid·i·fy		soot	
so·lid·i·ty		soothe	
so·lil·o·quize		sooth·say·er	
so·lil·o·quy		sop	
sol·i·taire		soph·ism	
sol·i·tar·y		so·phis·ti·cate	
sol·i·tude		so·phis·ti·ca·tion	
so·lo		soph·ist·ry	
sol·stice		soph·o·more	
sol·u·ble		so·po·rif·ic	
✓ so·lu·tion		so·pra·no	
solve		sor·cer·er	
solv·a·ble		sor·cer·y	
sol·ven·cy		sor·did	
sol·vent		sore	
som·ber		sor·ghum	
som·bre·ro		so·ror·i·ty	
some		sor·rel	
some·bod·y		✓ sor·row	
some·how		sor·row·ful	
some·one		✓ sor·ry	
som·er·sault		✓ sort	
some·thing		sor·tie	
some·time		sot	
some·what		sou·brette	
some·where		souf·flé	
som·no·lent		✓ sought	
son		soul	

soul·ful	*slf*	spas·mod·ic	*szrdc*
soul·less	*sll'*	spas·tic	*ssc*
sound	*sv—*	spat	*sl*
soup	*sup*	spate	*sa*
soup·con	*spsn*	spa·tial	*sx*
sour	*sv*	spat·ter	*s/*
source	*Ss*	spat·u·la	*sCla*
souse	*svs*	spawn	*sn*
south	*S*	speak	*sec*
south·east	*SE*	speak·er	*sc*
south·ern	*Srn*	spear	*se*
South·ern·er	*Srn*	spear·head	*sehd*
south·ward	*Slrd*	spe·cial	*sx*
sou·ve·nir	*svne*	spe·cial·ist	*sx,*
sov·er·eign	*slrn*	spe·cial·ize	*sxz*
sov·er·eign·ty	*slrn)*	spe·cial·ty	*sx)*
so·vi·et	*svel*	spe·cie	*sSe*
sow	*so*	spe·cif·ic	*ssfc*
soy	*sy*	spe·cif·i·cal·ly	*ssfcl*
spa	*Sa*	spe·ci·fi·ca·tion	*ssfcj*
space	*Sas*	spec·i·fy	*ssf*
spa·cious	*Sx*	spec·i·men	*ssm*
spade	*sd*	spe·cious	*sx*
spa·ghet·ti	*sq)*	speck	*sc*
span	*sn*	spec·ta·cle	*sccl*
span·drel	*s—rl*	spec·tac·u·lar	*sccl*
span·gle	*sgl*	spec·ta·tor	*sca*
Span·iard	*snlfd*	spec·ter	*sc/l*
span·iel	*snl*	spec·tral	*sc/l*
spank	*sq*	spec·tro·scope	*sc scp*
spar	*sr*	spec·trum	*sc*
spare	*sa*	spec·u·late	*scla*
spark	*Sc*	spec·u·la·tion	*sclj*
spar·kle	*Scl*	spec·u·lum	*scl*
spar·row	*So*	speech	*seC*
sparse	*Ss*	speech·less	*sCl'*
spasm	*sz*	speed	*sd*

speed·i·ly	*sdl*	spite·ful	
speed·om·e·ter	*sd*	spit·tle	
Speed·writ·ing	(Sl) *sdru*	spit·toon	
spell	*sl*	splash	
spend	*s——*	splat·ter	
spend·thrift	*s—— If*	splay	
spent	*s-*	spleen	
sperm		splen·did	
sphere		splen·dor	
spher·i·cal		sple·net·ic	
sphe·roid		splice	
sphinc·ter		splint	
sphinx		splin·ter	
spice		split	
spic·ule		splotch	
spic·y		splurge	
spi·der		spoil	
spig·ot		spoil·er	
spike		spoke	
spill		spo·ken	
spilt		spokes·man	
spin		spo·li·a·tion	
spin·ach		sponge	
spi·nal		spon·sor	
spin·dle		spon·ta·ne·i·ty	
spine		spon·ta·ne·ous	
spine·less		spoof	
spin·et		spook	
spin·ster		spool	
spi·ral		spoon	
spire		spoon·ful	
spir·it		spoor	
spir·it·less		spo·rad·ic	
spir·it·u·al		spore	
spir·it·u·ous		sport	
spit		sports·man	
spite		sports·man·ship	

spot	*sL*	squal·id	*sqld*
spot·less	*sLl'*	squall	*sqal*
spot·light	*sLli*	squal·or	*sql*
spouse	*sus*	squan·der	*sg —*
spout	*suL*	square	*sq*
sprang	*sq*	squash	*sqs*
sprain	*sn*	squat	*sqt*
sprawl	*sal*	squaw	*sqa*
spray	*sa*	squawk	*sqc*
spread	*sd*	squeak	*sqec*
spree	*se*	squeal	*sqel*
✓ spring	*sq*	squeam·ish	*sqrs*
spright·ly	*siL*	squee·gee	*sqse*
spring·i·ness	*sge'*	squeeze	*sqz*
spring·time	*sqli*	squelch	*sqlC*
sprin·kle	*sql*	squib	*sqb*
sprint	*s–*	squint	*sq–*
sprite	*sL*	squire	*squ*
sprock·et	*scl*	squirm	*sq*
sprout	*suL*	squir·rel	*sql*
spruce	*sus*	squirt	*sqt*
sprung	*sq*	stab	*sb*
spry	*sL*	✓ sta·bil·i·ty	*sb)*
spume	*su*	✓ sta·bi·lize	*sbz*
spun	*sn*	sta·bi·liz·er	*sbz*
spunk	*sq*	sta·ble	*sb'*
spur	*s*	stac·ca·to	*sclo*
spu·ri·ous	*suy*	stack	*sc*
spurn	*sn*	sta·di·um	*sden*
spurt	*sL*	staff	*sf*
sput·nik	*slnc*	stag	*sq*
sput·ter	*s*	stage	*saj*
spu·tum	*sL*	stag·ger	*sg*
spy	*sL*	stag·nant	*sgn–*
squab·ble	*sqb*	stag·nate	*sgna*
squad	*sqd*	stag·na·tion	*sgnj*
squad·ron	*sqDn*	staid	*sd*

stain	*ɔn*	star·ling	*Slg*
stain·less	*ɔnl'*	star·lit	*Sll*
stair	*ɔa*	✓start	*Sl*
stair·case	*ɔacɔ*	start·er	*S/*
stair·way	*ɔaʋa*	star·tle	*Sll*
stake	*ɔc*	star·va·tion	*Svƴ*
sta·lac·tite	*ɔlcɪ*	starve	*Sv*
sta·lag·mite	*ɔlgɪ*	✓state	*ɔa*
stale	*ɔal*	state·hood	*ɔahd*
stale·mate	*ɔlɾa*	state·ly	*ɔal*
stalk	*ɔc*	✓state·ment	*ɔa—*
stall	*ɔal*	state·room	*ɔaɾ*
stal·lion	*ɔln*	states·man	*ɔaɔ—*
stal·wart	*ɔlʋl*	stat·ic	*ɔlc*
sta·men	*ɔɔn*	✓sta·tion	*ɔƴ*
stam·i·na	*ɔɔna*	sta·tion·ar·y	*ɔƴƴ*
stam·mer	*ɔʋ*	sta·tion·er	*ɔƴ*
✓stamp	*ɔ⁓p*	sta·tion·er·y	*ɔƴƴ*
stam·pede	*ɔ⁓pd*	sta·tis·ti·cal	*ɔlɔcl*
stamp·er	*ɔ⁓p*	stat·is·ti·cian	*ɔlɔƴ*
stance	*ɔnɔ*	sta·tis·tics	*ɔlɔcɔ*
stanch	*ɔC*	stat·u·ar·y	*ɔCƴ*
stan·chion	*ɔCn*	stat·ue	*ɔCu*
✓stand	*ɔ___*	stat·u·esque	*ɔCɔc*
✓stand·ard	*ɔ___ rd*	stat·u·ette	*ɔCʋl*
stand·ard·ize	*ɔ___ rdz*	stat·ure	*ɔC*
stand·by	*ɔ___ b*	sta·tus	*ɔlx*
stand·point	*ɔ___ pƴ—*	sta·tus quo	*ɔlx go*
stand·still	*ɔ___ sl*	stat·ute	*ɔCu*
stan·za	*ɔnza*	stat·u·to·ry	*ɔClƴ*
sta·ple	*ɔp*	staunch	*ɔC*
✓star	*S*	stave	*ɔa*
starch	*SC*	✓stay	*ɔa*
stare	*ɔa*	stead	*ɔd*
stark	*Sc*	stead·fast	*ɔdf*
star·let	*Sll*	stead·i·ly	*ɔdl*
star·light	*Slɪ*	✓stead·y	*ɔde*

steak	*ıc*	ste·ve·dore	*ıvdo*
steal	*ıel*	stew	*ıu*
stealth	*ıll*	stew·ard	*ılld*
steam	*ıe*	stew·ard·ess	*ılld'*
steam·boat	*ıebo*	stick	*ıc*
steam·er	*ıe*	stick·ler	*ıcl*
steam·ship	*ıe8*	stick·i·ness	*ıce'*
steed	*ıd*	stiff	*ıf*
√ steel	*ıel*	sti·fle	*ıfl*
steep	*ıep*	stig·ma	*ıgra*
stee·ple	*ıp*	stig·ma·tize	*ıgrlz*
steer	*ıe*	stile	*ıil*
steer·age	*ıej*	sti·let·to	*ıllo*
stel·lar	*ıl*	still	*ıl*
stem	*ı*	stilt	*ıll*
stench	*ıC*	stim·u·lant	*ırl–*
sten·cil	*ınıl*	stim·u·late	*ırla*
ste·nog·ra·pher	*ınɑff*	stim·u·la·tion	*ırlj*
sten·o·graph·ic	*ınɑfc*	stim·u·li	*ırli*
ste·nog·ra·phy	*ınɑffe*	stim·u·lus	*ırlx*
sten·to·ri·an	*ıyın*	sting	*ıq*
√ step	*ıp*	stin·gi·ness	*ıje'*
step·child	*ıpch*	stin·gy	*ıje*
step·fa·ther	*ıpf*	stink	*ıq*
step·lad·der	*ıpld*	stint	*ı*
step·moth·er	*ıpı*	sti·pend	*ıp–*
ster·e·o	*ıo*	stip·ple	*ıp*
ster·e·o·phon·ic	*ıefnc*	stip·u·late	*ıpla*
ster·e·o·type	*ıelp*	stip·u·la·tion	*ıplj*
ster·ile	*ıl*	stir	*ı*
ste·ril·i·ty	*ıl)*	stir·rup	*ıp*
ster·il·ize	*ılz*	stitch	*ıC*
ster·ling	*ılq*	stock	*ıc*
stern	*ın*	stock·ade	*ıcd*
ster·num	*ın*	stock·bro·ker	*ıcBc*
ster·to·rous	*ı*	stock·hold·er	*ıchol*
steth·o·scope	*ıtscp*	stodg·y	*ıje*

sto·ic	*zoc*	strap	*Sp*
stoke	*zoc*	stra·ta	*Sla*
stole	*zol*	strat·a·gem	*Sy*
stol·id	*zld*	stra·te·gic	*Syc*
stom·ach	*znc*	strat·e·gist	*Sy,*
stone	*zn*	strat·e·gy	*Sye*
ston·i·ly	*znl*	strat·i·fy	*Sf*
stood	*zd*	stra·to·sphere	*Sisfe*
stooge	*zuj*	stra·tum	*Sr*
stool	*zul*	straw	*Sa*
stoop	*zup*	straw·ber·ry	*Sby*
✓ stop	*zo*	stray	*Sa*
stop·gap	*zogp*	streak	*Sec*
stop·per	*zo*	stream	*Se*
✓ stor·age	*Sy*	stream·line	*Seli*
store	*S*	✓ street	*sl*
store·house	*Shro*	✓ strength	*Sgl*
store·room	*Srn*	strength·en	*Sgln*
storm	*Sr*	stren·u·ous	*Snx*
sto·ry	*Se*	strep·to·coc·cus	*Spccx*
stout	*zul*	strep·to·my·cin	*Sprsn*
stove	*zo*	stress	*S,*
stow	*zo*	stretch	*SC*
stow·age	*zoy*	strew	*Su*
stow·a·way	*zoawa*	stri·a·tion	*Sy*
stra·bis·mus	*Sbzx*	strick·en	*Scn*
strad·dle	*Sdl*	strict	*Sc*
strag·gle	*Sgl*	stric·ture	*ScC*
straight	*Sa*	stride	*Sd*
strain	*Sn*	stri·dent	*Sd–*
strait	*Sa*	strife	*Sf*
strand	*S—*	strike	*Sic*
✓ strange	*Sy*	string	*Sq*
stran·ger	*Sy*	strin·gent	*Sy–*
strange·ly	*Sgl*	strip	*Sp*
stran·gle	*Sgl*	stripe	*Sip*
stran·gu·late	*Sgla*	strive	*Sc*

stro·bo·scope	*Sbscp*	✓ stu·pid	*2pd*
strode	*Sd*	stu·pid·i·ty	*2pd)*
stroke	*Soc*	stu·por	*2p*
stroll	*Sol*	stur·dy	*Sde*
✓ strong	*Sg*	stur·geon	*Syn*
strong·er	*Sg*	stut·ter	*2*
strong·hold	*Sghol*	sty	*2c*
strong·ly	*Sgl*	style	*2el*
strop	*Sp*	styl·ish	*2l8*
strove	*So*	sty·lus	*2lx*
struck	*Sc*	sty·mie	*2e*
struc·tur·al	*ScCrl*	styp·tic	*2pc*
struc·ture	*ScC*	suave	*sur*
strug·gle	*Sgl*	sua·vi·ty	*sur)*
strum	*Sm*	sub·al·tern	*slTn*
strung	*Sg*	sub·ca·ble	*scb*
strut	*St*	✓ sub·com·mit·tee	*sk*
strych·nine	*Scnun*	sub·con·scious	*skx*
stub	*2b*	sub·con·trac·tor	*sKc*
stub·ble	*2b*	sub·cu·ta·ne·ous	*sclnx*
stub·born	*2Bn*	sub·di·vide	*sdvd*
stuc·co	*2co*	sub·due	*sdu*
stuck	*2c*	sub·ed·i·tor	*sed*
stud	*2d*	sub·head	*shd*
stu·dent	*2d–*	✓ sub·ject	*sj*
stu·di·o	*2do*	sub·jec·tive	*sjv*
stu·di·ous	*2dx*	sub·ju·gate	*sjga*
stud·y	*2de*	sub·junc·tive	*sjgv*
stuff	*2f*	sub·lease	*sls*
stuff·i·ness	*2fe'*	sub·li·mate	*slra*
stul·ti·fy	*2llf*	sub·li·ma·tion	*sly*
stum·ble	*2b*	sub·lime	*sli*
stump	*2p*	sub·lim·i·nal	*slml*
stun	*2n*	sub·ma·rine	*sm*
stunt	*2*	sub·merge	*sy*
stu·pe·fy	*2pf*	sub·mer·sion	*sy*
stu·pen·dous	*2p——x*	sub·mis·sive	*srsv*

sub·mit		sub·urb	
sub·nor·mal		sub·ur·ban	
sub·or·di·nate		sub·ver·sion	
sub·or·di·na·tion		sub·ver·sive	
sub·orn		sub·vert	
sub·poe·na		sub·way	
sub·rou·tine		✓suc·ceed	
sub·scribe		✓suc·cess	
sub·scrib·er		suc·cess·ful	
sub·scrip·tion		suc·cess·ful·ly	
sub·se·quent		suc·ces·sion	
sub·se·quent·ly		suc·ces·sive	
sub·ser·vi·ent		suc·ces·sor	
sub·side		suc·cinct	
sub·sid·ence		suc·cor	
sub·sid·i·ar·y		suc·cu·lent	
sub·si·dize		suc·cumb	
sub·si·dy		such	
sub·sist		suck	
sub·sis·tence		su·crose	
sub·stance		suc·tion	
✓ sub·stan·dard		sud·den	
sub·stan·tial		sue	
sub·stan·tial·ly		suede	
sub·stan·ti·ate		su·et	
sub·stan·tive		suf·fer	
sub·sti·tute		suf·fer·ance	
sub·sti·tu·tion		suf·fice	
sub·ter·fuge		suf·fi·cien·cy	
sub·ter·ra·ne·an		suf·fi·cient	
sub·tle		suf·fix	
sub·tle·ty		suf·fo·cate	
✓ sub·tract		suf·fo·ca·tion	
sub·trac·tion		suf·frage	
sub·tra·hend		suf·fra·gette	
sub·treas·ur·y		suf·fuse	
sub·trop·i·cal		suf·fu·sion	

sug·ar	*Sg*	Sun·day	*sn*
✓sug·gest	*sj,*	sun·di·al	*sndil*
✓sug·ges·tion	*sjsj*	sun·down	*sndn*
sug·ges·tive	*sjsv*	sun·der	*s—*
su·i·cid·al	*susdl*	sun·dry	*s—re*
su·i·cide	*susd*	sun·glass	*sng'*
suit	*su*	sunk	*sg*
suit·a·ble	*sub*	sunk·en	*sgn*
suit·a·bly	*sub*	sun·light	*snli*
suit·case	*sucs*	sun·rise	*snrz*
suite	*sve*	sun·set	*snsl*
suit·or	*su*	sun·shine	*snSn*
sul·fa	*slfa*	sun·stroke	*snSc*
sulk	*slc*	sup	*sp*
sulk·i·ness	*slce'*	su·per	*sp*
sul·len	*sln*	su·per·an·nu·ate	*sᵖna*
sul·ly	*sl*	✓su·perb	*ssb*
sul·phate	*slfa*	su·per·car·go	*sᵖCg*
sul·phide	*slfd*	su·per·cil·i·ous	*sᵖslr*
sul·phite	*slfi*	su·per·fi·cial	*sᵖfx*
sul·phur	*(5) slf*	su·per·flu·i·ty	*ssfu)*
sul·tan	*slln*	su·per·flu·ous	*sᵖfx*
sul·tan·a	*sllna*	su·per·hu·man	*sᵖhr—*
sul·try	*slᵗe*	su·per·im·pose	*sᵖipz*
sum	*s*	su·per·in·tend	*ssnl—*
sum·ma·ri·ly	*s·ll*	su·per·in·tend·ent	*supl*
sum·ma·rize	*s·rz*	✓su·pe·ri·or	*spy*
✓sum·ma·ry	*s·ry*	su·pe·ri·or·i·ty	*spy)*
✓sum·ma·tion	*s·ry*	su·per·la·tive	*sᵖlv*
sum·mer	*s·v*	su·per·man	*sᵖr—*
sum·mit	*s·vl*	su·per·nal	*sᵖnl*
sum·mon	*s·m*	su·per·nat·u·ral	*sᵖnCrl*
sump·tu·ous	*s·vCx*	su·per·nu·mer·ar·y	*sᵖnry*
sun	*sn*	su·per·sede	*ssd*
sun·beam	*snbe*	su·per·son·ic	*sᵖsnc*
sun·burn	*snBn*	su·per·sti·tion	*ssj*
sun·burst	*snB,*	su·per·sti·tious	*ssx*

su·per·struc·ture		sur·feit	
su·per·vise		surge	
su·per·vi·sion		sur·geon	
su·per·vi·sor		sur·ger·y	
su·pine		sur·gi·cal	
sup·per		sur·ly	
sup·plant		sur·mise	
sup·ple		sur·mount	
sup·ple·ment		sur·name	
sup·ple·men·tal		sur·pass	
sup·ple·men·ta·ry		sur·plice	
sup·pli·ance		sur·plus	
sup·pliant		sur·prise	
sup·pli·cant		sur·rend·er	
sup·pli·cate		sur·rep·ti·tious	
sup·pli·ca·tion		sur·ro·gate	
sup·pli·er		sur·round	
sup·ply		sur·tax	
sup·port		sur·veil·lance	
sup·port·er		sur·vey	
sup·pose		sur·vey·or	
sup·po·si·tion		sur·vive	
sup·pos·i·to·ry		sur·vi·vor	
sup·press		sus·cep·ti·ble	
sup·pres·sion		sus·pect	
sup·press·or		sus·pend	
sup·pu·rate		sus·pense	
su·prem·a·cy		sus·pen·sion	
su·preme		sus·pi·cion	
su·preme·ly		sus·pi·cious	
sur·cease		sus·tain	
sur·charge		sus·te·nance	
sure		sut·ler	
sure·ly		su·ture	
sure·ty		svelte	
surf		swab	
sur·face		swad·dle	

swag		swoop	
swag·ger		sword	
swal·low		swore	
swam		sworn	
swamp		syb·a·rite	
swan		syc·a·more	
swank		syc·o·phant	
swap		syl·lab·i·cate	
swarm		syl·la·ble	
swarth·y		syl·la·bus	
swas·ti·ka		sylph	
swat		syl·van	
sway		✓sym·bol	
swear		sym·bol·ic	
sweat		sym·bol·ize	
Swede		sym·met·ri·cal	
sweep		sym·me·**try**	
sweet		sym·pa·thet·ic	
swell		sym·pa·thize	
swel·ter		sym·pa·thy	
swept		sym·phon·ic	
swerve		sym·pho·ny	
swift		sym·po·si·um	
swift·ly		symp·tom	
swim		syn·a·gogue	
swin·dle		syn·chro·nize	
swin·dler		syn·chro·niz·er	
swine		syn·chro·nous	
swing		syn·co·pate	
swirl		syn·co·pa·tion	
swipe		syn·co·pe	
swish		syn·di·cate	
Swiss		syn·er·gism	
switch		syn·od	
swiv·el		syn·o·nym	
swol·len		syn·on·y·mous	
swoon		syn·op·ses	

syn·op·sis	*snpss*	syr·up	*Sp*
syn·the·size	*snlsz*	✓sys·tem	*ss*
syn·thet·ic	*snttc*	sys·tem·at·ic	*ssrlc*
sy·phon	*sfn*	sys·tem·a·tize	*ssrlz*
sy·ringe	*Sy*	sys·to·le	*ssl*

tab	*lb*	tab·loid	*lbyd*
tab·er·na·cle	*lbncl*	ta·boo	*lbu*
✓ta·ble	*lb*	ta·bor	*lb*
tab·leau	*lbo*	tab·o·ret	*lbl*
tab·leaux	*lbz*	tab·u·lar	*lbl*
ta·ble·cloth	*lbcl*	tab·u·late	*lbla*
ta·ble d'hôte	*lb do*	tab·u·la·tor	*lbla*
ta·ble·spoon	*lbsn*	ta·chom·e·ter	*lcr*
✓tab·let	*lbl*	tac·it	*lsl*
ta·ble·ware	*lbra*	tac·i·turn	*lsrn*

tack		tang	
tack·le		tan·gent	
tact		tan·ge·rine	
tact·ful		tan·gi·ble	
tac·ti·cal		tan·gle	
tac·ti·cian		tank	
tac·tic		tan·kard	
tac·tile		tan·ner·y	
tact·less		tan·nic	
tad·pole		tan·ta·lize	
taf·fe·ta		tan·ta·mount	
taff·rail		tan·trum	
tag		tap	
tail		tape	
tail·light		ta·per	
tai·lor		tap·es·try	
taint		tar	
take		tar·dy	
tak·en		tare	
take·off		tar·get	
talc		tar·iff	
tale		tar·la·tan	
tal·ent		tar·nish	
tal·is·man		tar·pau·lin	
talk		tar·pon	
talk·a·tive		tar·ry	
tall		tart	
tall·er		tar·tan	
tal·low		tar·tar	
tal·ly		task	
tal·on		tas·sel	
tam·bou·rine		✓ taste	
tame		taste·less	
tamp		tast·y	
tam·per		tat·ter	
tam·pon		tat·ter·de·mal·ion	
tan		tat·tle	

tat·too		tee·ter	
taught		teeth	
taunt		tee·to·tal·er	
tav·ern		tele·cast	
taw·dry		tel·e·gram	
taw·ny		tel·e·graph	
tax		te·leg·ra·pher	
tax·a·tion		te·lem·e·try	
tax·i		te·lep·a·thy	
tax·i·cab		tel·e·phone	
tax·i·der·my		tel·e·phon·ic	
tax·pay·er		tel·e·pho·to	
tea		tel·e·scope	
teach		tel·e·type	
teach·er		tel·evise	
team		tel·e·vi·sion	
team·mate		tell	
team·ster		tell·er	
team·work		tem·blor	
tea·pot		te·mer·i·ty	
tear		tem·per	
tear sheet		tem·per·a·ment	
tea·room		tem·per·ance	
tease		tem·per·ate	
tea·spoon·ful		tem·per·a·ture	
tea·time		tem·pest	
tech·ni·cal		tem·pes·tu·ous	
tech·ni·cal·i·ty		tem·plate	
tech·ni·cian		tem·ple	
tech·nique		tem·po	
tech·noc·ra·cy		tem·po·ral	
tech·nol·o·gy		tem·po·rar·i·ly	
te·di·ous		tem·po·rar·y	
te·di·um		tem·po·rize	
tee		tempt	
teem		temp·ta·tion	
tee·pee		tempt·ress	

ten	10	ter·race	
ten·a·ble		ter·ra-cot·ta	
te·na·cious		ter·ra fir·ma	
te·nac·i·ty		ter·rain	
ten·an·cy		ter·ra·pin	
ten·ant		ter·res·tri·al	
✓tend		ter·ri·ble	
✓tend·en·cy		ter·ri·er	
tend·er		ter·rif·ic	
ten·der·loin		ter·ri·fy	
ten·don		ter·ri·to·ry	
ten·dril		ter·ror	
ten·e·ment		ter·ror·ist	
ten·et		ter·ror·ize	
ten·nis		terse	
ten·on		ter·ti·ar·y	
ten·or		tes·sel·late	
✓tense		✓test	
ten·sile		tes·ta·ment	
ten·sion		tes·ta·tor	
tent		test·er	
ten·ta·cle		tes·ti·fy	
ten·ta·tive		tes·ti·mo·ni·al	
ten·ter·hook		tes·ti·mo·ny	
tenth		tet·a·nus	
ten·u·ous		tête-à-tête	
ten·ure		teth·er	
tep·id		text	
term		text·book	
ter·ma·gant		tex·tile	
ter·mi·nal		tex·ture	
ter·mi·nate		Thai	
ter·mi·na·tion		than	
ter·mi·ni		✓thank	
ter·mi·nol·o·gy		thank·ful	
ter·mi·nus		thank·less	
ter·mite		thanks·giv·ing	

that	*la*	therm·i·on·ic	
thatch		ther·mo·dy·nam·ic	
that's		ther·mom·e·ter	
thaw	*la*	ther·mo·nu·cle·ar	
the	*.*	ther·mo·stat	
the·a·ter		the·sau·rus	
the·at·ri·cal		these	
theft		the·sis	
their		thes·pi·an	
the·ism		they	
them		they're	
theme		thick	
them·selves		thick·et	
then		thief	
thence·forth		thieves	
the·oc·ra·cy		thigh	
the·od·o·lite		thim·ble	
the·o·log·i·cal		thin	
the·ol·o·gy		thing	
the·o·rem		think	
the·o·ret·i·cal		third	
the·o·rize		thirst	
the·o·ry		this	
the·os·o·phy		thirst·y	
ther·a·peu·tic		this·tle	
ther·a·pist		thith·er	
ther·a·py		thing	
there		tho·rac·ic	
there·af·ter		tho·rax	
there·by		tho·ri·um	
there·fore		thorn	
there·in		thor·ough	
there·of		thor·ough·fare	
there's		thor·ough·ly	
there·up·on		those	
ther·mal		though	
ther·mite		thought	

Word	Outline	Word	Outline
✓thought·ful	*Lof*	thun·der·show·er	*l— rSw*
✓thou·sand	*Jd*	thun·der·struck	*l— rSc*
thrall·dom	*Zld*	✓Thurs·day	*Lh*
thrash	*ZS*	✓thus	*Ls*
thread	*Zd*	thwart	*tL*
thread·bare	*Zdba*	thyme	*Le*
threat	*Zu*	thy·mus	*Lx*
three	*3*	thy·roid	*Lyd*
three·fold	*3 fol*	ti·ar·a	*Va*
three·score	*3 sco*	Ti·bet·an	*Lbln*
thresh	*ZS*	tib·i·a	*Lba*
thresh·old	*ZSol*	tic	*lc*
threw	*Zu*	tick	*lc*
thrift	*Zf*	tick·et	*lcl*
thrift·less	*Zfl'*	tick·le	*lcl*
thrill	*Zl*	tick·ler	*lcl*
thrive	*Zu*	tid·al	*ldl*
throat	*Zo*	tid·bit	*ldbl*
throb	*Zb*	tide	*ld*
throm·bo·sis	*Zrbss*	ti·di·ly	*ldl*
throne	*Zn*	tie	*Lu*
throng	*Zg*	tier	*Le*
throt·tle	*Zll*	tiff	*lf*
✓through	*Zu*	ti·ger	*lg*
✓through·out	*Zuo*	tight	*Lu*
throw	*Zo*	tile	*lil*
thrown	*Zn*	till	*ll*
thrust	*Z,*	tilt	*lll*
thud	*ld*	tim·bale	*lrb*
thug	*lg*	tim·ber	*lrb*
thumb	*Ln*	tim·bre	*lrb*
thump	*Lrp*	time	*Le*
thun·der	*l—*	time·less	*lil'*
thun·der·bolt	*l— rbll*	time·ly	*lil*
thun·der·cloud	*l— rcvd*	time·piece	*lips*
thun·der·head	*l— rhd*	time·ta·ble	*lilb*
thun·der·ous	*l— rx*	tim·id	*lrd*

ti·mid·i·ty		toad	
tim·or·ous		toast	
tim·o·thy		toast·er	
tin		toast·mas·ter	
tinc·ture		to·bac·co	
tin·der		to·bac·co·nist	
tine		to·bog·gan	
tinge		toc·sin	
tin·gle		√ to·day	
tink·er		tod·dle	
tinkle		tod·dy	
tin·sel		toe	
tin·smith		tof·fee	
tint		to·ga	
tin·type		√ to·geth·er	
tin·ware		tog·gle	
ti·ny		toil	
tip		toi·let	
tip·ple		toi·lette	
tip·ster		to·ken	
tip·toe		told	
tip·top		tol·er·ance	
ti·rade		tol·er·ant	
tire		tol·er·ate	
tire·some		toll	
tis·sue		tom·a·hawk	
ti·tan		to·ma·to	
ti·tan·ic		tomb	
tithe		tome	
tit·il·late		√ to·mor·row	
tit·i·vate		ton	
ti·tle		ton·al	
tit·ter		to·nal·i·ty	
ti·trate		tone	
ti·tra·tion		tongs	
tit·u·lar		tongue	
to		ton·ic	

to·night		tor·pid	
ton·nage		tor·por	
ton·neau		torque	
ton·sil		tor·rent	
ton·sil·li·tis		tor·ren·tial	
ton·so·ri·al		tor·rid	
ton·sure		tor·sion	
too		tor·so	
took		tor·til·la	
tool		tor·toise	
toot		tor·tu·ous	
tooth·ache		tor·ture	
tooth·pick		toss	
tooth·some		tot	
top		to·tal	
to·paz		to·tal·i·tar·i·an	
top·coat		to·tem	
top·er		tot·ter	
top·flight		touch	
top·ic		√tough	
top·i·cal		tou·pee	
top·knot		tour	
top·most		tour·ist	
to·pog·ra·pher		tour·ma·line	
to·pog·ra·phy		tour·na·ment	
top·ple		tour·ney	
top·sail		tour·ni·quet	
top·side		tou·sle	
top·soil		tout	
top·sy-tur·vy		tow	
torch		√ to·ward	
tor·e·a·dor		tow·el	
tor·ment		tow·er	
tor·men·tor		town	
torn		town·ship	
tor·na·do		towns·man	
tor·pe·do		towns·peo·ple	

tox·e·mi·a		tran·quil	
tox·ic		tran·quil·iz·er	
tox·i·col·o·gy		✓ trans·act	
tox·in		✓ trans·ac·tion	
toy		trans·at·lan·tic	
trace		tran·scend	
trac·er		tran·scribe	
tra·che·a		tran·script	
tra·che·ot·o·my		tran·scrip·tion	
tra·cho·ma		tran·sept	
track		✓ trans·fer	
track·less		trans·fig·ure	
tract		trans·fix	
trac·ta·ble		trans·form	
trac·tile		trans·form·er	
trac·tion		trans·fuse	
trac·tor		trans·gress	
trade		trans·gres·sion	
✓ trade·mark		trans·gres·sor	
trades·man		tran·sient	
tra·di·tion		tran·sis·tor	
tra·duce		trans·it	
traf·fic		tran·si·tion	
tra·ge·di·an		tran·si·to·ry	
trag·e·dy		trans·late	
trag·ic		trans·la·tor	
trail		trans·lit·er·ate	
train		trans·lu·cent	
trait		trans·mi·grate	
trai·tor		trans·mis·sion	
trai·tor·ous		trans·mit	
tra·jec·to·ry		trans·mit·ter	
tram		trans·mu·ta·tion	
tram·mel		trans·mute	
tramp		tran·som	
tram·ple		trans·pa·rent	
trance		tran·spire	

trans·plant		trek	
tran·spon·der		trel·lis	
√ trans·port		trem·ble	
√ trans·por·ta·tion		tre·men·dous	
trans·pose		tre·men·dous·ly	
trans·po·si·tion		trem·o·lo	
trans·ship		trem·or	
trans·verse		trem·u·lous	
trap		trench	
tra·peze		trench·ant	
trap·per		trench·er·man	
trash		trend	
trau·ma		tre·pan	
tra·vail		tre·phine	
trav·el		trep·i·da·tion	
trav·el·er		√ tres·pass	
tra·verse		tres·pass·er	
trav·es·ty		tress	
trawl		tres·tle	
tray		tri·ad	
treach·er·ous		tri·al	
treach·er·y		tri·an·gle	
trea·cle		tri·an·gu·lar	
tread		trib·al	
trea·dle		tribe	
tread·mill		trib·u·la·tion	
trea·son		tri·bu·nal	
trea·sure		tri·bune	
trea·sur·er		trib·u·tar·y	
trea·sur·y		trib·ute	
treat		trick	
trea·tise		trick·er·y	
treat·ment		trick·le	
trea·ty		trick·ster	
treb·le		tri·col·or	
tree		tri·cy·cle	
tre·foil		tri·dent	

tri·en·ni·al		trope	
tri·fle		tro·phy	
tri·fo·cal		trop·ic	
trig		tro·po·pause	
trig·ger		tro·po·sphere	
trig·o·nom·e·try		trot	
trill		troth	
tril·lion		trou·ba·dour	
tril·o·gy		✓ trou·ble	
trim		trou·ble·some	
trin·i·ty		trough	
trin·ket		trounce	
tri·o		troupe	
tri·ode		trou·sers	
trip		trous·seau	
tri·par·tite		trow·el	
tripe		troy	
✓ tri·ple		tru·an·cy	
tri·plet		tru·ant	
tri·plex		truce	
trip·li·cate		truck	
tri·pod		truck·le	
trip·tych		truc·u·lent	
tri·reme		trudge	
tri·sect		true	
trite		truf·fle	
tri·umph		tru·ism	
tri·um·vi·rate		trump	
triv·et		trump·er·y	
triv·i·al		trum·pet	
tro·che		trun·cate	
trod		trun·cheon	
trog·lo·dyte		trun·dle	
troll		trunk	
trol·ley		truss	
trom·bone		✓ trust	
troop		trus·tee	

trus·tee·ship		tur·bine	
trust·wor·thy		tur·bo·jet	
trust·y		tur·bo·prop	
✓ truth		tur·bu·lence	
truth·ful		tur·bot	
try		tur·bu·lent	
tryst		turf	
tru·ly		tur·gid	
tub		tur·key	
tu·ba		tur·moil	
tube		✓ turn	
tu·ber		tur·nip	
tu·ber·cu·lar		turn·out	
tu·ber·cu·lo·sis		turn·o·ver	
tu·bu·lar		turn·pike	
tuck		turn·stile	
✓ Tues·day		turn·ta·ble	
tuft		tur·pen·tine	
tug		tur·pi·tude	
✓ tu·i·tion		tur·quoise	
tu·lip		tur·ret	
tulle		tur·tle	
tum·ble		tusk	
tum·bler		tus·sle	
tum·brel		tus·sock	
tum·id		tu·te·lage	
tu·mor		tu·tor	
tu·mult		tux·e·do	
tu·mul·tu·ous		twad·dle	
tun		twang	
tune		tweak	
tung·sten	(W)	tweed	
tu·nic		tweet·er	
Tu·ni·sian		tweez·ers	
tun·nel		✓ twice	
tur·ban		twi·light	
tur·bid		twin	

twine	
twinge	
twin·kle	
twirl	
twist	
twitch	
two	2
ty·coon	
tym·pa·num	
type	
type·cast	
type·script	
type·set·ter	
type·write	

type·writ·er	
ty·phoid	
ty·phoon	
ty·phus	
typ·i·cal	
typ·i·fy	
typ·ist	
ty·pog·ra·pher	
ty·pog·ra·phy	
ty·ran·ni·cal	
tyr·an·ny	
ty·rant	
ty·ro	

u·biq·ui·tous	
ud·der	
ug·ly	
u·ku·le·le	
ul·cer	

ul·cer·ous	
ul·na	
ul·ster	
ul·te·ri·or	
ul·ti·mate	

ul·ti·ma·tum		un·con·scious	
ul·tra		un·couth	
ul·tra·ma·rine		un·cov·er	
ul·tra·son·ic		unc·tu·ous	
ul·tra·vi·o·let		un·de·ni·a·ble	
ul·u·la·tion		✓un·der	
um·ber		un·der·brush	
um·bil·i·cal		un·der·clothes	
um·brage		un·der·cur·rent	
um·brel·la		un·der·glaze	
um·pire		un·der·go	
✓un·a·ble		un·der·hand·ed	
un·a·bridged		un·der·line	
un·ac·count·a·ble		un·der·mine	
un·ac·cus·tomed		✓un·der·neath	
un·af·fect·ed		un·der·rate	
un·A·mer·i·can		un·der·score	
u·na·nim·i·ty		un·der·shirt	
u·nan·i·mous		✓un·der·stand	
un·as·sum·ing		un·der·stood	
un·a·void·a·ble		un·der·stud·y	
un·a·ware		un·der·take	
un·bal·anced		un·der·tak·er	
un·be·com·ing		un·der·tone	
un·bend		un·der·val·ue	
un·bi·ased		un·der·wa·ter	
un·bid·den		un·der·way	
un·bound·ed		un·der·wear	
un·but·ton		un·der·weight	
un·can·ny		un·der·world	
un·cer·tain		un·der·write	
un·char·i·ta·ble		un·doubt·ed·ly	
un·civ·i·lized		un·du·la·tion	
un·cle		un·du·ly	
un·clean		un·earth·ly	
✓un·com·fort·a·ble		un·eas·y	
un·con·di·tion·al		un·em·ploy·ment	

un·e·qual

un·e·quiv·o·cal

un·err·ing

un·ex·pect·ed

un·fair

un·fa·mil·iar

un·fa·vor·a·ble

un·for·tu·nate

un·for·tu·nate·ly

un·furl

un·gain·ly

un·guent

un·hap·py

u·ni·cam·er·al

u·ni·fi·ca·tion

u·ni·form

u·ni·fy

u·ni·lat·er·al

un·im·proved

un·in·ter·est·ed

un·ion

u·nique

u·ni·son

u·nit

u·nite

u·ni·ver·sal

u·ni·verse

u·ni·ver·si·ty

un·kempt

un·law·ful

un·less

un·like·ly

un·lim·it·ed

un·man·ly

un·nat·u·ral

un·nec·es·sar·y

un·ob·tru·sive

un·oc·cu·pied

un·paid

un·par·al·leled

un·pleasant

un·prec·e·dent·ed

un·prej·u·diced

un·pre·med·i·tat·ed

un·pre·ten·tious

un·prin·ci·pled

un·qual·i·fied

un·ques·tion·a·ble

un·rav·el

un·re·al

un·rea·son·a·ble

un·re·gen·er·ate

un·re·mit·ting

un·sat·is·fac·to·ry

un·sa·vor·y

un·scru·pu·lous

un·seem·ly

un·skilled

un·so·cia·ble

un·so·phis·ti·cat·ed

un·speak·a·ble

un·strung

un·ti·dy

un·tie

un·til

un·time·ly

un·told

un·to·ward

un·truth·ful

un·u·su·al

un·var·nished

un·want·ed

un·war·y

un·wield·y

un·wise	*un3*	urge	*uy*
un·wont·ed	*un=*	ur·gent	*uy-*
un·wor·thy	*ul*	u·ric	*uc*
un·writ·ten	*urln*	urn	*un*
✓up	*p*	us	*us*
up·braid	*pBd*	us·a·ble	*uzb*
up·heav·al	*phel*	us·age	*usy*
up·hold	*phol*	use	*us (uz)*
up·hol·ster·er	*phlS*	use·ful	*usf*
up·hol·ster·y	*phlSe*	use·ful·ness	*usf'*
up·keep	*pcp*	use·less	*usl'*
up·lift	*plf*	ush·er	*uS*
up·on	*pn*	✓u·su·al	*x*
up·per	*p*	✓u·su·al·ly	*x*
up·per·most	*pro,*	u·su·fruct	*uzfc*
up·range	*pry*	u·su·rer	*uz*
up·right	*pru*	u·su·ri·ous	*uzyx*
up·ris·ing	*prz*	u·surp	*usp*
up·roar·i·ous	*pryx*	u·surp·er	*uSp*
up·root	*pru*	u·su·ry	*uzy*
up·set	*psl*	u·ten·sil	*ul/l*
up·shot	*pSl*	u·ter·ine	*urn*
up·stairs	*psas*	u·til·i·tar·i·an	*ulllyn*
up·start	*pSl*	u·ti·lize	*ullz*
up·ward	*plrd*	ut·most	*ulro,*
u·ra·ni·um	*(u)urne*	u·to·pi·a	*ulpa*
ur·ban	*ubn*	ut·ter	*u*
ur·bane	*ubn*	ux·o·ri·ous	*xyx*
ur·chin	*uCn*		

va·can·cy	✓	*vc /*	
va·cant		*vc -*	
va·cate		*vca*	
va·ca·tion	✓	*vcy*	
vac·ci·nate		*vcsna*	
vac·ci·na·tion		*vcsny*	
vac·cine		*vcsn*	
vac·il·late		*vsla*	
va·cu·i·ty		*vcu)*	
vac·u·ous		*vcx*	
vac·u·um		*vc⌒*	
vag·a·bond		*vgb —*	
va·gar·y		*vgy*	
va·gran·cy		*vg /*	
va·grant		*vg -*	
vague	✓	*vaq*	
vain		*vn*	
val·ance		*vl /*	
vale		*val*	
val·e·dic·to·ri·an		*vldcyn*	
val·en·tine		*vl - in*	
val·et		*vll*	
val·iant		*vl -*	
val·id		*vld*	
val·i·date		*vlda*	
va·lid·i·ty		*vld)*	
va·lise		*vls*	

val·ley	*vl*	
val·or	*vl*	
val·or·ous	*vlx*	
val·u·a·ble	*vlueb*	
val·u·a·tion	*vluy*	
val·ue	*vlue*	
valve	*vlv*	
val·vu·lar	*vlvl*	
vamp	*v rp*	
vam·pire	*v rpu*	
van	*vn*	
van·dal·ism	*v — lz*	
vane	*vn*	
van·guard	*vngd*	
va·nil·la	*vnla*	
van·ish	*vns*	
van·i·ty	*vn)*	
van·quish	*vgs*	
van·tage	*v -1*	
vap·id	*vpd*	
va·por	*vp*	
va·por·i·za·tion	*vszy*	
va·por·iz·er	*vsz*	
var·i·a·ble ✓	*vyb*	
var·i·ance	*vy /*	
var·i·a·tion	*vyy —*	
var·i·col·ored	*vcl*	

var·i·e·gate	*vyga*	Ve·ne·tian	*vny*
va·ri·e·ty	*vri*	ven·geance	*vyl*
var·i·ous	*vys*	venge·ful	*vyf*
var·nish	*Vns*	ve·ni·al	*vnel*
var·y	*vy*	ven·i·son	*vnsn*
vas·cu·lar	*vscl*	ven·om	*vn*
vase	*vas*	ve·nous	*vnx*
vas·e·line	*vsln*	vent	*v–*
vas·sal	*vsl*	ven·ti·late	*v– la*
vast	*v,*	ven·ti·la·tor	*v– la*
vaude·ville	*vdvl*	ven·tral	*v– rl*
vault	*vll*	ven·tri·cle	*v– rcl*
vec·tor	*vc*	ven·tril·o·quist	*v– rlq,*
veer	*ve*	ven·ture	*vC*
veg·e·ta·ble	*vglb*	ven·ture·some	*vCrs*
veg·e·tar·i·an	*vglyn*	ven·tur·ous	*vCx*
veg·e·tate	*vgla*	ven·ue	*vnu*
veg·e·ta·tion	*vgly*	ve·ra·cious	*vX*
ve·he·mence	*ve /*	ve·rac·i·ty	*vs)*
ve·he·ment	*ve–*	ve·ran·da	*V– a*
ve·hi·cle	*vecl*	verb	*vb*
ve·hic·u·lar	*vhcl*	ver·bal	*vbl*
veil	*val*	ver·ba·tim	*vbt*
vein	*vn*	ver·be·na	*vbna*
vel·lum	*vl*	ver·bi·age	*vby*
ve·loc·i·pede	*vlspd*	ver·bose	*vbs*
ve·loc·i·ty	*vls)*	ver·bo·ten	*vbtn*
ve·lour	*vlu*	ver·dant	*vd–*
vel·vet	*vlvt*	ver·dict	*vdc*
vel·vet·een	*vlvtn*	ver·di·gris	*vdGs*
ve·nal	*vnl*	ver·dure	*vj*
vend	*v–*	verge	*vj*
ven·det·ta	*v– la*	ver·i·fi·ca·tion	*vfcj*
ven·dor	*v–*	ver·i·fy	*vf*
ve·neer	*vne*	ver·i·si·mil·i·tude	*vsrlld*
ven·er·a·ble	*vNb*	ver·i·ta·ble	*vlb*
ven·er·ate	*vNa*	ver·i·ty	*V)*

ver·mi·cel·li		vex	
ver·mi·form		vex·a·tion	
ver·mi·fuge		via	
ver·mil·ion		vi·a·ble	
ver·min		vi·a·duct	
ver·nac·u·lar		vi·al	
ver·nal		vi·and	
ver·ni·er		vi·brant	
ver·sa·tile		vi·brate	
ver·sa·til·i·ty		vi·bra·tion	
verse		vic·ar	
versed		vi·car·i·ous	
ver·si·fy		vice	
ver·sion		vice-pres·i·dent	
ver·sus		vice-re·gal	
ver·te·bra		vice·roy	
ver·te·brae		vi·ce ver·sa	
ver·te·brate		vi·cin·i·ty	
ver·tex		vi·cious	
ver·ti·cal		vi·cis·si·tude	
ver·tig·i·nous		vic·tim	
ver·ti·go		vic·tim·ize	
verve		vic·tor	
ver·y		vic·to·ri·a	
ves·i·cle		vic·to·ry	
ves·per		vict·ual	
ves·sel		vid·e·o	
vest		vie	
ves·tal		Vi·et·nam·ese	
ves·ti·bule		view	
ves·tige		vig·il	
ves·tig·i·al		vig·i·lant	
vest·ment		vig·i·lan·te	
ves·try		vi·gnette	
vet·er·an		vig·or	
vet·er·in·ar·y		vig·or·ous	
ve·to		vile	

Word	Shorthand	Word	Shorthand
vil·i·fy		vis·cos·i·ty	
vil·la		vis·count	
vil·lage		vis·cous	
vil·lain		vise	
vil·lain·ous		✓vis·i·bil·i·ty	
vin·ai·grette		✓vis·i·ble	
✓vin·di·cate		✓vi·sion	
vin·di·ca·tion		vi·sion·ar·y	
vin·dic·tive		vis·it	
vine		vis·i·tor	
vin·e·gar		vis·or	
vin·tage		vis·ta	
vint·ner		vis·u·al	
vi·nyl		vis·u·al·ize	
vi·ol		vi·tal	
vi·o·la		vi·tal·i·ty	
vi·o·late		vi·ta·min	
vi·o·lent		vi·ti·ate	
vi·o·let		vit·re·ous	
vi·o·lin		vit·ri·fy	
vi·per		vit·ri·ol	
vi·ra·go		vi·tu·per·a·tion	
vir·gin		vi·tu·per·a·tive	
vir·ile		vi·va·cious	
vir·tu·al		vi·vac·i·ty	
vir·tue		viv·id	
vir·tu·os·i·ty		viv·i·sec·tion	
vir·tu·o·so		vix·en	
vir·tu·ous		vi·zier	
vir·u·lent		vo·cab·u·lar·y	
vi·rus		vo·cal	
vi·sa		vo·cal·ist	
vis·age		vo·cal·ize	
vis·à·vis		vo·ca·tion	
vis·cer·a		voc·a·tive	
vis·cid		vo·cif·er·ous	
vis·cose		vod·ka	

vogue		vom·it	
voice		vo·ra·cious	
voiced		vo·rac·i·ty	
voice·less		vor·tex	
void		vo·ta·ry	
vol·a·tile		vote	
vol·ca·no		vo·tive	
vo·li·tion		vouch	
vol·ley		vouch·er	
volt		vouch·safe	
volt·age		vow	
vol·u·ble		vow·el	
vol·ume		voy·age	
vo·lu·mi·nous		vul·can·ize	
vol·un·tar·i·ly		vul·gar	
vol·un·tar·y		vul·gar·i·ty	
vol·un·teer		vul·ner·a·ble	
vol·up·tu·ar·y		vul·ture	
vo·lup·tu·ous			

wad	⌣d	wal·rus	⌣lrx
wade	⌣d	wam·pum	⌣xps
wa·fer	⌣f	wan	⌣n
waf·fle	⌣fl	wand	⌣ɔ__
waft	⌣f	wan·der	⌣ɔ__/
wag	⌣g	wane	⌣n
wage	⌣ay	wan·gle	⌣gl
wa·ger	⌣y	want	⌣ɔ_
wag·on	⌣gn	wan·ton	⌣ɔ_n
waif	⌣af	war	⌣o
wail	⌣al	war·ble	⌣ob
wain	⌣n	ward	⌣od
wain·scot	⌣nscl	ward·en	⌣odn
waist	⌣a,	ward·robe	⌣odrb
wait	⌣a	ware	⌣a
wait·er	⌣a,	ware·house	⌣hs
wait·ress	⌣ɔ_,	war·fare	⌣ofa
waive	⌣a	war·head	⌣ohd
waiv·er	⌣a/	war·i·ly	⌣l
wake	⌣c	war·like	⌣olc
walk	⌣c	warm	⌣l
walk·ie-talk·ie	⌣clce	warmth	⌣l
wall	⌣al	warn	⌣n
wal·let	⌣ll	warp	⌣p
wal·low	⌣lo	war·rant	⌣ɔ_
wall·pa·per	⌣lpp	war·ran·tor	⌣ɔ_/
wal·nut	⌣lnl	war·ran·ty	⌣ɔ_e

war·ren		way	
war·ri·or		way·lay	
war·ship		way·bill	
war·time		way·side	
wart		way·ward	
war·y		we	
was		weak	
wash		weak·ling	
wash·a·ble		wealth	
wash·bowl		weap·on	
wash·cloth		wear	
wash·er		wear·a·ble	
was·n't		wea·ri·ness	
wasp		wea·ri·some	
was·sail		wea·ry	
waste		wea·sel	
waste·bas·ket		weath·er	
waste·pa·per		weath·er·proof	
wast·rel		weave	
watch		weav·er	
watch·ful		web	
watch·mak·er		wed	
watch·man		wedge	
wa·ter		wed·lock	
wa·ter·fall		Wed·nes·day	
wa·ter·fowl		week	
wa·ter·log		week·day	
wa·ter·mel·on		week·end	
wa·ter·proof		week·ly	
wa·ter·tight		weep	
wa·ter·way		wee·vil	
wa·ter·y		weigh	
watt		weight	
wave		weight·y	
wa·ver		weird	
wax		wel·come	
wax·en		weld	

wel·fare		whey	
well		which	
well-bred		which·ev·er	
wel·ter		whiff	
wend		while	
went		whim	
wept		whim·per	
were		whim·si·cal	
west		whine	
west·ern		whip	
West·ern·er		whip·lash	
west·ward		whip·pet	
wet		whirl	
whale		whirl·pool	
wharf		whirl·wind	
wharves		whisk	
what		whisk·er	
what·ev·er		whis·ky	
what·so·ev·er		whis·per	
wheat		whist	
whee·dle		whis·tle	
wheel		white	
wheel·bar·row		whith·er	
when		whit·tle	
whence		who	
when·ev·er		who·dun·it	
when·so·ev·er		who·ev·er	
where		whole	
where·a·bouts		whole·sale	
where·as		whole·sal·er	
where·by		whole·some	
wher·ev·er		whol·ly	
where·fore		whom	
where·in		whom·ev·er	
where·of		whoop	
wheth·er		whop·per	
whet·stone		whose	

who·so·ev·er	win·ter
why	win·ter·time
wick	wipe
wick·ed	wire
wick·er	wire·less
wick·et	wis·dom
wide	wise
wid·er	wise·a·cre
wide·spread	wish
wid·ow	wisp
wield	wist·ful
wife	wit
wig	witch·er·y
wig·gle	with
wild	with·draw
wil·der·ness	with·er
wild·fire	with·hold
will	with·in
will·ful	with·out
wilt	with·stand
wi·ly	wit·ness
win	wit·ti·cism
wince	wit·ty
wind	wives
wind·break	wiz·ened
wind·fall	woe
wind·lass	woe·be·gone
wind·mill	woke
win·dow	wolf
win·dow·pane	wolves
wind·pipe	wom·an
wind·shield	wom·an·hood
wine	wom·an·kind
wing	wom·an·like
wink	womb
win·now	wom·en
win·some	wom·en's

won		worth·less	
won·der		worth·while	
won·der·ful		wor·thy	
won·der·ment		would	
won·drous		would·n't	
won't		wound	
wood		wove	
wood·cut		wow	
wood·en		wraith	
wood·pile		wran·gle	
woods·man		wrap	
wood·work		wrap·per	
woof·er		wrath	
wool		wreath	
word		wreck	
wore		wrench	
work		wres·tle	
work·book		wres·tler	
work·day		wretch·ed	
work·er		wrig·gle	
work·man		wring	
work·man·like		wring·er	
work·man·ship		wrin·kle	
work·out		wrist	
work·room		writ	
world		write	
world·wide		writ·er	
worm		write·up	
worm·hole		writhe	
worn		writ·ten	
wor·ry		wrong	
worse		wrote	
wor·ship		wrought	
wor·sted		wrung	
worth		wry	

xe·non *(Ke)* zɱ
X ray *xra*

xy·lo·graph *zegf*
xy·lo·phone *zlfɱ*

yacht *yl*
yak *yc*
yam *y—*
yank *yg*
Yan·kee *yge*

yard *yd*
yard·age *ydy*
yard·stick *ydsc*
yarn *yn*
yar·row *yo*

yaw	*ya*	yoke	*yoc*
yawl	*yal*	yo·kel	*ycl*
yawn	*yn*	yolk	*yoc*
yea	*ya*	yon·der	*y—*
✓ year	*y*	yore	*yo*
year·book	*ybc*	you	*u*
year·ling	*ylg*	✓ young	*yg*
year·ly	*yl*	young·er	*yg*
yearn	*yn*	✓ you'll	*ul*
yeast	*ye,*	young·ster	*ygs*
yell	*yl*	your	*u*
yel·low	*ylo*	✓your·self	*us/*
yeo·man	*y—*	your·selves	*us//*
✓ yes	*ys*	youth	*yul*
✓ yes·ter·day	*ysd*	youth·ful	*ylf*
yet	*yl*	yowl	*yul*
yew	*u*	yule	*yul*
✓ yield	*yeld*		

za·ny	*zne*	zip·per	*zp*
zeal	*zel*	zir·con	*zk*
zeal·ous	*zls*	zir·co·ni·um (zr)	*zke*
ze·bra	*zBa*	zith·er	*zT*
ze·nith	*znl*	zo·di·ac	*zdec*
zeph·yr	*zf*	zo·di·a·cal	*zdicl*
zep·pe·lin	*zpn*	zone	*zn*
✓ ze·ro	*zo*	zoo	*zu*
✓ zest	*z,*	zoom	*zu*
zig·zag	*zgzg*	zo·o·log·i·cal	*zolgcl*
✓ zinc (zn)	*zg*	zo·ol·o·gy	*zolge*
Zi·on	*zn*	zwie·back	*swbc*
Zi·on·ism	*znz*	zy·mase	*zrs*
zip	*zp*	zy·mot·ic	*zrlc*

UNITED STATES

Alabama (Ala.) *ab̄ra*
Alaska (Alas.) *alsca*
Arizona (Ariz.) *azna*
Arkansas (Ark.) *acsa*
California (Calif.) *clfna*
Colorado (Colo.) *cldo*
Connecticut (Conn.) *kccl*
Delaware (Del.) *dlra*
Florida (Fla.) *Fda*
Georgia (Ga.) *Jja*
Hawaii *hve*
Idaho *idho*
Illinois (Ill.) *iny*
Indiana (Ind.) *ndena*
Iowa *iwa*
Kansas (Kans.) *czs*
Kentucky (Ky.) *c-ce*
Louisiana (La.) *lzena*
Maine *m*
Maryland (Md.) *rl—*
Massachusetts (Mass.) *rsCsls*
Michigan (Mich.) *Sgn*
Minnesota (Minn.) *msla*
Mississippi (Miss.) *rsspe*
Missouri (Mo.) *rzy*
Montana (Mont.) *r-na*
Nebraska (Nebr.) *nBsca*
Nevada (Nev.) *nvda*
New Hampshire (N. H.) *nu hrS*
New Jersey (N. J.) *nu Jze*
New Mexico (N. M.) *nu rexco*
New York (N. Y.) *nu Yc*
North Carolina (N. C.) *N Clina*
North Dakota (N. D.) *N dcla*
Ohio *oho*

Oklahoma (Okla.)	*ochra*
Oregon (Oreg.)	*ogn*
Pennsylvania (Pa.)	*p/ lvna*
Rhode Island (R. I.)	*rd*
South Carolina (S. C.)	*S Clina*
South Dakota (S. D.)	*S dcla*
Tennessee (Tenn.)	*Lnse*
Texas (Tex.)	*Les*
Utah	*ula*
Vermont (Vt.)	*V*
Virginia (Va.)	*Vgna*
Washington (Wash.)	*Sgln*
West Virginia (W. Va.)	*Vgna*
Wisconsin (Wis.)	*skan*
Wyoming (Wyo.)	*veng*

Cities

Akron	*aCn*
Albany	*albne*
Albuquerque	*abCce*
Amarillo	*rlo*
Annapolis	*apls*
Atlanta	*all-a*
Augusta	*agsa*
Austin	*asn*
Baltimore	*bllro*
Baton Rouge	*bln ruz*
Birmingham	*Brgh*
Bismarck	*bz rc*
Boise	*byze*
Boston	*bsn*
Bridgeport	*Zysl*
Buffalo	*bflo*
Cambridge	*kB*
Camden	*crdn*
Carson City	*Csn s)*

Charleston	*Crlsn*
Chattanooga	*Clnga*
Cheyenne	*Sen*
Chicago	*Scg*
Cincinnati	*snsn)*
Cleveland	*—cvl—*
Columbia	*clrba*
Columbus	*clrbx*
Concord	*kCd*
Dallas	*dls*
Dayton	*dln*
Denver	*dnv*
Des Moines	*de ryn*
Detroit	*dryt*
Dover	*dv*
El Paso	*ε pso*
Erie	*Ee*
Evansville	*evnzvl*
Flint	*f-*
Fort Wayne	*ft un*
Fort Worth	*ft Ct*
Frankfort	*fgfl*
Gary	*gy*
Grand Rapids	*g— rpds*
Greensboro	*gnzBo*
Harrisburg	*HsBg*
Hartford	*HtFd*
Helena	*hlna*
Honolulu	*hnllu*
Houston	*hsn*
Indianapolis	*ndenpls*
Jacksonville	*jcnsvl*
Jefferson City	*fsn s)*
Jersey City	*Jze s)*
Juneau	*Jno*
Kansas City	*czo s)*
Lansing	*l/q*

Little Rock	*ll rc*
Long Beach	*lg bel*
Los Angeles	*ls agls*
Louisville	*luvl*
Lincoln	*lgn*
Madison	*rdsn*
Memphis	*mfs*
Miami	*mre*
Milwaukee	*rlrce*
Minneapolis	*mepls*
Montgomery	*n-gry*
Montpelier	*n-pl*
Nashville	*nSvl*
New Haven	*nu hvn*
New Orleans	*nu olnz*
New York	*nu Yc*
Newark	*nllc*
Norfolk	*nfc*
Oakland	*ocl—*
Oklahoma City	*och ra s)*
Olympia	*o-pa*
Omaha	*orha*
Paterson	*p-sn*
Pierre	*pa*
Philadelphia	*fldlfa*
Phoenix	*fnx*
Pittsburgh	*plsBg*
Portland	*pll—*
Providence	*pvd/*
Raleigh	*rl*
Richmond	*rC-—*
Rochester	*rCS*
Sacramento	*sC-o*
Salem	*sl*
Santa Fe	*s-a fa*
Savannah	*svna*
St. Louis	*sa- lus*

St. Paul	*sa-pal*
St. Petersburg	*sa-p βg*
Salt Lake City	*sll lc s)*
San Antonio	*sn alno*
San Diego	*sn deg*
San Francisco	*sn 7nssco*
San Jose	*sn hza*
Seattle	*sell*
Shreveport	*Susl*
South Bend	*S b —*
Spokane	*sc*
Springfield	*Sgfld*
Syracuse	*Scz*
Tacoma	*lc^a*
Tallahassee	*llhse*
Toledo	*lldo*
Trenton	*Z-m*
Tucson	*Lsn*
Tulsa	*Ulsa*
Washington	*Sgln*
Wichita	*Cla*
Worcester	*S*
Yonkers	*yg*
Youngstown	*ygzlm*

CANADA

Provinces and Territories

Alberta	*(shorthand)*
British Columbia	*(shorthand)*
Manitoba	*(shorthand)*
New Brunswick	*(shorthand)*
Newfoundland	*(shorthand)*
Northwest Territory	*(shorthand)*
Nova Scotia	*(shorthand)*
Ontario	*(shorthand)*
Prince Edward Island	*(shorthand)*
Quebec	*(shorthand)*
Saskatchewan	*(shorthand)*
Yukon Territory	*(shorthand)*

Cities

Alma	*(shorthand)*
Amherst	*(shorthand)*
Arvida	*(shorthand)*
Barrie	*(shorthand)*
Belleville	*(shorthand)*
Brampton	*(shorthand)*
Brandon	*(shorthand)*
Brantford	*(shorthand)*
Brockville	*(shorthand)*
Calgary	*(shorthand)*
Cap-de-la-Madeleine	*(shorthand)*
Charlottetown	*(shorthand)*
Chicoutimi	*(shorthand)*
Cornwall	*(shorthand)*
Cote-St.-Michel	*(shorthand)*
Dartmouth	*(shorthand)*
Drummondville	*(shorthand)*
Edmonton	*(shorthand)*

Edmundston	*ed ⟋ — sn*
Fairville	*Fvl*
Flin Flon	*Fn Fn*
Forest Hill	*f, hl*
Ft. William	*fl vl*
Ft. William-Pt. Arthur	*fl vl pl a⊤*
Fredericton	*7Dcn*
Galt	*gll*
Glace Bay	*— gas ba*
Granby	*gnbe*
Guelph	*gulf*
Halifax	*hlfx*
Hamilton	*hrlln*
Hull	*hl*
Jacques-Cartier	*zcCla*
Jasper-Place	*jSpl*
Joliette	*zlel*
Jonquiere	*zce*
Kenogami	*cngre*
Kenora	*cMa*
Kingston	*cgsn*
Kirkland Lake	*Ccl — lc*
Kitchener	*cAn*
Lachine	*lAn*
LaSalle	*lsl*
La Tuque	*la luc*
Lauzon	*lzn*
Laval-des-Rapides	*lvldrpd*
Leaside	*lsd*
Lethbridge	*llBj*
Lindsay	*l — ze*
London	*l — n*
Long Branch	*lg bC*
Magog	*ngg*
Medicine Hat	*dsn hl*
Mimico	*nco*
Moncton	*gn*

Montreal

Moose Jaw

Nanaimo

New Toronto

New Westminster

Niagara Falls

North Bay

North Vancouver

Orillia

Oshawa

Ottawa

Owen Sound

Pembroke

Penticton

Peterborough

Pointe-aux-Trembles

Pointe-Claire

Portage la Prairie

Port Alberni

Port Arthur

Port Colborne

Prince Albert

Prince George

Prince Rupert

Quebec

Red Deer

Regina

Rimouski

Riverside

St. Boniface

St. Catharines

St. Hyacinthe

St. James

St. Jean

St. Jerome

St. John's

St. Lambert

St. Laurent	*sᴅn*
St. Michel	*s ᴠSl*
St. Thomas	*sa – lᴠs*
Ste. Foy	*sa – fy*
Sarnia	*Sna*
Saskatoon	*ssᴄln*
Sault Sainte Marie	*su sa – ᴠe*
Shawinigan Falls	*Sᴠngn fals*
Sherbrooke	*SrBc*
Sillery	*sly*
Sorel	*Sl*
Stratford	*SᴜAd*
Sudbury	*sdby*
Swift Current	*sᴠf C–*
Sydney	*sdne*
Thetford Mines	*ttAd ᴠns*
Timmins	*ᴠmz*
Toronto	*J–o*
Trail	*Zal*
Trenton	*Z–n*
Trois-Rivieres	*Zᴠᴠy*
Truro	*Jo*
Valleyfield	*ᴠlfld*
Vancouver	*ᴠncᴠ*
Verdun	*ᴠdn*
Victoria	*vcya*
Victoriaville	*vcyᴠl*
Ville-Jaques-Cartier	*vlzcCla*
Waterloo	*J lu*
Welland	*ᴠl —*
Whitehorse	*ᴠᴠHo*
Windsor	*ᴠnz*
Winnipeg	*ᴠnpg*
Woodstock	*ᴠdsc*

NOTES

NOTES